Acclaim for

When Mom and Dad Need Help

"This is a much needed book that is well written for the consumer. The telephone surveys, as well as the tour and interview checklists, are excellent guidelines and tools."
— **Sister Roseann E. Kasayka Ph.D., MT-BC, DA**

"For those caring for aging parents and loved ones, this book is a must read. With the multiple choices and complexities associated with senior health care options, it is imperative that caregivers become educated consumers. This book is a comprehensive resource that will give you the education and information you need to be the best advocate for your loved one."
— **Lisa Fluhart, LNHA, Licensed Nursing Home Administrator**

"This is an excellent "how to" reference book on options for caring for a parent. I especially appreciated the suggested language on how to have those difficult conversations."
— **Elizabeth Ford Pitorak MSN, CNS, FPCN**

"This book provides excellent step-by-step instructions that can be followed down multiple pathways, which is exactly what is needed."
— **Carol Faytol, RN**

A Step-by-Step Guide to Senior Housing and Care

WHEN Mom and Dad NEED HELP

Help Your Family Achieve the
Quality of Life You All Deserve

Michael C. Campbell

Iffenwen
Publishing
Company

IFFENWEN PUBLISHING COMPANY
PO Box 168
Painesville, OH 44077-0168
www.iffenwen.com

Cover design by Mendocino Graphics
Front cover photograph © Creatas/Creatas/PictureQuest
Book design by Cypress House

PUBLISHER'S CATALOGING-IN-PUBLICATION DATA

Campbell, Michael C.
  When Mom and Dad need help : a step-by-step guide to senior housing and care : help your family achieve the quality of life you all deserve / Michael C. Campbell. -- 1st ed. -- Painesville, OH : Iffenwen Pub. Co., c2010.
    p. ; cm.
    ISBN: 978-0-9742984-0-5
    Includes index.
    1. Aging parents--Care--United States--Handbooks, manuals, etc. 2. Aging parents--Family relationships--United States. 3. Adult children of aging parents--United States--Handbooks, manuals, etc. 4. Parent and adult child--United States. 5. Finance, Personal--United States. I. Title. II. Guide to senior housing and care.
    HQ1063.6 .C36 2009   2009935560
362.6/0973--dc22 0912

Printed in the USA
2 4 6 8 9 7 5 3 1
FIRST EDITION

Photo Permissions

PAGE	ILLUSTRATION ID	COPYRIGHT
1	0930817	©iStockphoto.com/
3	2861614	©iStockphoto.com/
5	8806676	©iStockphoto.com/
5	9026636	©iStockphoto.com/
5	7763018	©iStockphoto.com/
7	1018067	©iStockphoto.com/
9	8666495	©iStockphoto.com/
10	5994502	©iStockphoto.com/
11, 15, 25, 33, 41, 56, 76, 84, 151, 153	6972313	©iStockphoto.com/
12, 16, 26, 34, 44, 61, 76, 86	0793483	©iStockphoto.com/
14	1741856	©iStockphoto.com/
16, 26, 35, 45, 62, 76, 86	5668573	©iStockphoto.com/
17, 27, 36, 50, 63, 77, 88, 95	2069939	©iStockphoto.com/
18	0940971	©iStockphoto.com/
31	9769760	©iStockphoto.com/
38	7770249	©iStockphoto.com/
43	0622142	©iStockphoto.com/
53	9186837	©iStockphoto.com/
65	7060199	©iStockphoto.com/
67	3178724	©iStockphoto.com/
68	0392462	©iStockphoto.com/
91	7278449	©iStockphoto.com/
97	1312070	©iStockphoto.com/
103	8819243	©iStockphoto.com/
108	7927672	©iStockphoto.com/
110	7391385	©iStockphoto.com/
111	8971179	©iStockphoto.com/
112	5721884	©iStockphoto.com/
115	0661630	©iStockphoto.com/
121	6875088	©iStockphoto.com/
135	4913150	©iStockphoto.com/
136	4351995	©iStockphoto.com/
141, 165, 180, 201, 214	5926418	©iStockphoto.com/
144	7817764	©iStockphoto.com/
145	3039957	©iStockphoto.com/
147	3914718	©iStockphoto.com/
149	7232597	©iStockphoto.com/
155	8332817	©iStockphoto.com/
168	4531045	©iStockphoto.com/
173	6728966	©iStockphoto.com/
179	8351451	©iStockphoto.com/
186	1540915	©iStockphoto.com/
195	1985275	©iStockphoto.com/
199	7096909	©iStockphoto.com/

PAGE	ILLUSTRATION ID	COPYRIGHT
202	0666964	©iStockphoto.com/
204	8775683	©iStockphoto.com/
222	0188882	©iStockphoto.com/
223	3576104	©iStockphoto.com/
223	8006005	©iStockphoto.com/
224	7590326	©iStockphoto.com/
224	7233524	©iStockphoto.com/
226	7286355	©iStockphoto.com/
228, 250	2585189	©iStockphoto.com/
230	9548068	©iStockphoto.com/
232	7145192	©iStockphoto.com/
232	0744336	©iStockphoto.com/
233	6321594	©iStockphoto.com/
233	4679742	©iStockphoto.com/
233	0612612	©iStockphoto.com/
233	1920418	©iStockphoto.com/
233	7936476	©iStockphoto.com/
234	3801099	©iStockphoto.com/
234	8819265	©iStockphoto.com/
235	3253892	©iStockphoto.com/
235	3449642	©iStockphoto.com/
235	5641180	©iStockphoto.com/
236	7890358	©iStockphoto.com/
238	7860067	©iStockphoto.com/
247	0147540	©iStockphoto.com/
249	8191431	©iStockphoto.com/
251	6836876	©iStockphoto.com/
251	1132686	©iStockphoto.com/
252	1017603	©iStockphoto.com/
253	1627940	©iStockphoto.com/
254	4056949	©iStockphoto.com/
257	8691297	©iStockphoto.com/
263	3658507	©iStockphoto.com/
274	3390628	©iStockphoto.com/
275	1997013	©iStockphoto.com/
275	3807969	©iStockphoto.com/
279	9427803	©iStockphoto.com/
281	5818930	©iStockphoto.com/
281	0603292	©iStockphoto.com/
282	5717780	©iStockphoto.com/
283	2647751	©iStockphoto.com/
285	2727623	©iStockphoto.com/
293	8194407	©iStockphoto.com/
311	4934135	©iStockphoto.com/
313	0828287	©iStockphoto.com/
317	8947909	©iStockphoto.com/

Dedication

To my mother ∞ Doris Campbell-White

To this day, I still remember the moment I asked my mother about "the meaning of life."

"Why are we here?" I asked.

"What is the purpose of our existence?"

The year was 1974 and I was nine years old. I was an inquisitive young lad! I can still remember every detail of our exchange like it was yesterday. She was looking out the kitchen window at our old house at 36200 Chardon Road as the afternoon sun made its way into the west side of the old farmhouse. I clearly remember this because of the way the sun was shining on her face as she spoke. She looked like an angel sent from the heavens above. My mother never looked more beautiful.

What impressed me most was how she answered this end-all, be-all question without hesitation or thought. She said, "Our purpose in this life is to make the world a better place because we are in it. To love and cherish our family so that once we've left this earth, we've raised our children well enough to pass along our values and beliefs to another generation to come."

What a great philosophy on life! Parents take note here. Be very aware of the impact you can make in just one brief, valuable moment in time. One brief moment in time with your children can make an impression that can last a lifetime. I challenge all of you to pass on my mother's message to your children as I have to mine.

"Make the world a better place because you are in it."

Thus far in my lifetime, I'm not quite sure I've lived up to my end of the bargain on this. Well, it's time for me to make up some ground right here, right now. In my mind, if I can help ease the fear, pain, and anxiety of just one family by releasing this book, that'll be enough for me.

Mom, this book is dedicated to you. Thank you from the bottom of my heart for all of your love, guidance, and support. I love you dearly, and promise to pass on your message to my children and your grandchildren each and every day!

Your loving son,
Mike

Acknowledgments

I wish to thank several individuals who helped me, in some way, shape or form with the preparation and production of this book. I would like to thank Karen Cox, Lynn Crnko, Carol Faytol, Lisa Fluhart, Lisa Gables, Sister Roseann Kasayka, William Keane, Michael Moore, Elizabeth Ford Pitorak, Kathy Tekely, Greg Storer and Bill Yost for their contributions. I'd also like to thank my wife Diane for her steadfast love, help, and support throughout this whole process. I would also like to acknowledge a pair of mentors who taught me a great deal about the senior housing and care industry over the years: Mr. Steve Hays and Mr. Scot Park.

I sincerely thank all of these talented and dedicated professionals. I hope they understand how grateful I am because without them, this book would not exist, and without it, we could not help thousands of American families' breathe a little easier during a most difficult and stressful time. I've always wanted to be involved in a profession that really made a difference in people's lives, a profession that helped serve the greater good of humanity. I can think of no better way to do this than to help people find quality senior housing and care for their aging loved ones. I hope you're all proud of the part you played in making this book possible.

Contents

*When
Mom and Dad
Need Help*

Chapter One

The Difficult Decision

O ne of the most difficult and emotionally trying decisions that adult children in America face today is how they're going to care for their aging parents once they're unable to care for themselves. The realization that parents need care is usually precipitated by some traumatic event that leaves the adult child very little time to make some very important decisions. In most cases, the children are left to make these gut-wrenching, life-changing decisions on their own without much information available to them.

Considering the economic turmoil America is already facing these days, the aging of America is going to be one of the biggest economic and social concerns this country will face over the next twenty years. With the 78 million members of the "Baby Boomer" generation (the largest population group in the history of the United States) beginning to retire in 2010, it's estimated that one in five Americans will be sixty-five years of age or older by 2020. How are we going to care for all these people? And how in the world are we going to pay for it? More and more families across America are dealing with these difficult decisions every day. How we prepare for this unprecedented change today will determine the quality of life we all enjoy tomorrow.

Most adult children are unaware of the various senior housing and care options available in the market. Many still believe they have only two options: have their parents move in with them; or move their parents into the dreaded nursing home. Fortunately, there are several other options, which I will discuss in detail.

Researchers are now saying that each of us has a 90 percent chance of someday caring for our parents, grandparents, or other loved ones. Of all the research I've read, I believe this statistic is the most revealing of all. With the release of this book, I believe I can help provide you and your family with clear and practical ways to deal with the issues and problems that arise when your parents or other loved ones are unable to care for themselves. My hope is to help make everyone's life a little bit easier during these difficult and stressful times. I've found that most of the anxiety is created by the fear of the unknown. This book eliminates the unknown by educating its readers. I believe that knowing what to expect is half the battle. This book will provide you with an easy-to-follow road map to help you find the housing and care option that is the perfect fit for your aging parents.

Chapter Two

Common Signs or Indicators That Your Parents May Need Help

When Will You Know When Your Parents Need Help?

One thing is certain: your parents won't be the ones who tell you they need help! Aging seniors have a strong desire to remain independent and in control of their own lives for as long as possible. In their place, wouldn't you feel the same way?

The last thing they want is to become a burden to their children or loved ones. Typically, the aging senior will experience a traumatic event or "wake-up call" precipitating the realization that they need assistance. For example, they may suffer a stroke or a serious injury due to a fall; or their cognitive situation may result in a danger to themselves or others, like leaving an article of clothing sitting on a stovetop burner.

Because you, the adult child, are unable to anticipate your parents' need for assistance until this traumatic event takes place, the emotional distress and the work/life crisis can hit you like a runaway train, making it very painful and difficult to make educated decisions you can become comfortable with. One way to avoid this is to start monitoring your parents' physical and mental abilities today, and research your care options should your parents begin to show signs of needing assistance.

So, what are some of the common indicators that your parents may need some form of assistance or care? Here are some of the telltale signs.

Your parents have difficulty with or are incapable of performing routine activities of daily living (ADLs) such as:

- Bathing
- Dressing and grooming
- Toileting
- Transferring or moving from place to place (e.g., moving from the bed to a chair)
- Walking
- Eating

Changes in their physical appearance may indicate they need assistance:

- Noticeable weight loss (difficulty cooking, eating, shopping for food, etc.)
- Sloppy appearance/poor hygiene (difficulty bathing, dressing, and grooming)
- Black-and-blue marks on the body could indicate they've fallen and might be having trouble walking or moving from place to place
- Noticeable burns on the skin could indicate they've experienced problems cooking

Certain physical clues around your parents' home may be a red flag:

- The yard has not been maintained as it normally has (difficulty completing regular tasks)
- The house interior has not been maintained as it normally has (difficulty completing regular tasks)
- Automobile dents and scratches could indicate impaired driving ability
- Carpet stains, perhaps caused by dropping and spilling things

- Urine odor in house (signs of incontinence)
- Pots and pans with noticeable burn marks could indicate they forgot about food on the stove and left it burning
- Unopened mail/unpaid bills may indicate difficulty completing regular tasks
- Unfilled prescriptions (difficulty completing regular tasks)
- Low food supply (difficulty completing regular tasks)

You may observe some unusual behavior by your parent:

- Lack of drive or motivation
- Failure to return your phone calls
- Verbally or physically abusive

You may notice some of the warning signs that your parent might be developing some form of dementia or cognitive impairment:

- Consistent memory lapses
- Confusion
- Loss of reasoning skills
- Difficulty performing familiar tasks
- Frequently misplaces things
- Frequently gets lost walking or driving
- Repetitive speech

- Unable to complete a sentence
- Rapid mood swings or changes in behavior
- Changes in personality
- Wears the same clothes over and over
- Cannot recall names of familiar people or objects, or
- Loss of initiative

If you believe your parents are experiencing one or more of the above indicators, then the next step is to talk with them about their care needs in such a way that they themselves identify the problem and come up with the solutions.

It's very important that your parents are the ones making the decision to seek help and decide which option best meets their care and assistance needs. Tough decisions such as selling their home and moving elsewhere should be their own and not yours or their doctor's or some other interested party's. Put yourself in their shoes. The decision to move out of their home where they've created a very comfortable, secure environment for themselves over the years is a very traumatic change and must be handled with extreme care and sensitivity. How do we broach the subject of senior housing and care with our parents? I've outlined ways to do this in Chapter 4: *Have "The Talk" with Your Parents Today!*

Chapter Three

What Types of Housing and Care Options are Available?

Contrary to popular belief, several different types of senior housing and care options are available to help provide your parents with quality care and, more important, the quality of life they so richly deserve. The $1,000,000 question is: Which type of senior housing and care is best suited to meet your parent's needs?

Other important questions:

- ► How much will each one of these senior housing and/or care options cost?

- ► How much will Medicare or Medicaid cover?

- ► What about long-term care insurance? Is it worth it for my parents to buy a long-term care policy? If so, which type, and how much of the cost of my parents' care will it cover?

This chapter will touch on each of the senior housing and care options available. Each is discussed in detail, including the types of services provided, with the advantages and disadvantages of each listed. The chapter also focuses on approximately how much each option costs and whether any government or public programs will help cover the cost of care in each setting. Chapter 9 will help answer any questions you might have on long-term care insurance.

Option One

Your Parents Move In With You

This is usually the first option that runs through a person's mind when a parent needs care or can no longer live alone. Because you've purchased this book, you've probably already gone through an extensive evaluation of this first option on your own. Just in case some of these items slipped your mind, you'll need to consider the following.

For most, the love and admiration you feel for your parents, and your sense of responsibility to them, will naturally lead you to the conclusion that having your parents move in with you is the only option. Many of you will end up telling yourselves that you're not going to be the cold-hearted jerk who makes his or her parents move into some "old folks'" home to die! This is a completely natural reaction; after all, your parents took care of you for many years. They fed you, bathed and clothed you, and nursed you through many illnesses. Isn't it reasonable to expect that you should give back the care and love they've given you? For some of you, the circumstances may be perfect and the decision to have your parents move in with you may seem like an easy one to make. But before you jump to conclusions, both you and your parents will need to consider several factors before making a joint decision as to whether this really is the best option. What may seem like the perfect solution today may not be the best option over the long haul.

First, as the adult child, you must ask yourself the following questions:

- Is this decision based on guilt, obligation, or a sense of entitlement?
- How will this living arrangement affect my lifestyle?
- How will this living arrangement affect my relationship with my parents? My spouse? My children?
- Have there been any past conflicts? If so, have they been resolved?
- What will the living arrangements be?
- Will there be enough room for everyone in the household to preserve each family member's privacy?
- How much care or assistance does my parent need?
- Can the care and assistance that Mom or Dad needs realistically be satisfied in my home?
- Can I provide both the quality of care and the quality of life my parents deserve?
- What will happen if more care is needed?
- Is my family both financially and emotionally stable enough to handle this caregiving situation?
- Do any other family members currently need a great deal of time and attention?
- Are my family members ready to share in the responsibility?

If, after completing your self-evaluation, you still feel this is the best option, then it's your responsibility to sit down with each member of the family, including your parents, and ask them how they feel about this potential living arrangement. Ask each family member many of the same questions outlined above. They should be questioned separately at first so they can answer honestly about any concerns they might have, without any outside influence. Then a group discussion should take place among all the family members involved to talk about what action should be taken next.

As you can see, the circumstances would have to be nearly perfect for your parents to move in with you. First of all, they would have to want to move in with you; and you and your family would have to be in total agreement and comfortable with the new living arrangement. Additionally, your parents would have to be somewhat independent for you to personally care for them in your home. Obviously, home health care nurses or aides can be hired to make daily visits, and adult daycare services are readily available; this, however, can become very costly as their care needs increase.

Advantages of Having Your Parents Move in With You

Your parents have a great deal to offer in terms of their experience in dealing with many of the everyday problems that you, your spouse, and your children face. When I was a teenager, my grandfather came to live with us after my grandmother had passed away. Though I did not realize it until many years after Granddad had passed, his contribution to our family was very beneficial to me both as a person and a father today. He told stories about my family history and what times were like when he was growing up. He offered me real advice about my problems, which I could often accept more graciously from him than if I had received it from my parents. My granddad taught me a great deal during the years he lived with us. The most important lesson was how to act like a gentleman. In short, there is much to say about multigenerational living.

Disadvantages of Having Your Parents Move in With You

Living with a parent can become especially painful and stressful when the level of care he or she needs reaches a point where you can no longer provide care in your home. Moving your parents once (i.e., into your home) is traumatic enough. When they're forced to move again, into an assisted living community or a nursing home, for example, it'll be twice as hard for all involved.

It's important to understand the significant difference between a parent-child relationship and a patient-caregiver relationship. You may have always had a caring, loving relationship with your mother. It may have been one in which you were not only mother and daughter or son but you were also best friends. The transition from child to child-caregiver will be a very difficult one. Let's say your mother is in the early stages of Alzheimer's when she moves into your home. Usually, people in the early stages of this disease are very functional; they need very little assistance physically, but their cognitive skills are lacking. As the disease progresses to its later stages, your parent will eventually lose all memory of who you are as well as the identities of the rest of the family. Caring for a loved one whom you've known all your life as a loving, caring, intelligent, and vibrant person who virtually turns into a complete stranger right before your very eyes can be emotionally devastating. As the disease worsens, the person will typically develop erratic mood swings and temper tantrums. Also, keep in mind that your home is not designed to care for a person suffering Alzheimer's disease. They are wanderers and are easily confused by their surroundings, which can frustrate them and make them panic. The benefits of moving your parents into a building specifically designed to reduce a resident's confusion are immense. These benefits are discussed later.

After investigating all the senior housing and care options outlined in this book, I think most people will find that having your parent at home with you is not the best option. Your parent will likely not receive the quality care they could receive in a state-of-the-art senior housing and care community. Chances are, the quality of all your lives would be much better if the care for your mom or dad were handled elsewhere. It's imperative you explore all the senior housing and care options before jumping to the guilt-free, knee-jerk reaction that Mom or Dad is coming to live with you. Take the time to complete the five-step process for selecting the best housing and care option outlined in Chapter 6 and I think you'll find there are some very kind, caring professionals out there who can do their jobs quite well.

Option Two

Adult Day Services

If your spouse, your parents, and the rest of your family collectively decide that having Mom or Dad move in with you is the best option available, an adult day program is an excellent care option to consider. Adult day programs provide services to seniors and adults with disabilities who need specific levels of supervision and/or modest levels of assistance. These services are typically provided at adult day centers by community-based agencies, to help preserve and maximize an aging adult's dignity and independence. Senior housing and care communities such as CCRCs, assisted living communities, and Alzheimer's/dementia care communities may offer adult day services as well. In an effort to meet the needs of all aging adults in their market areas, it's becoming more prevalent for senior housing and care communities to offer adult day programs on their community campuses.

Adult day programs provide aging adults with opportunities for regular social interaction, relationship building, recreation, and learning.

One of the primary goals of adult day services is to maintain a senior's skills and capacity for independent living. Many seniors are isolated at home before participating in an adult day program. Once in the program, they can receive the necessary supervision and medical care, as well as the opportunity to interact with other people and partake in a wide array of supervised activities.

Many adult day programs offer a variety of activities designed to promote physical and intellectual stimulation, social involvement, and creative release. Services offered by adult day programs typically include assistance with activities of daily living, meals (continental breakfast and hot lunch), scheduled trips and transportation, educational programs, exercise programs, intergenerational programs (with young children), rehabilitation opportunities such as physical or speech therapy, medication management, incontinence care, and, in many instances, Alzheimer's/dementia care.

Advantages of Adult Day Services

- ▶ Opportunities for your parents to interact with their peers and remain socially active with many stimulating activities;

- ▶ Your parents will feel better about themselves knowing they won't be a twenty-four-hour burden to their children;

- ▶ Allows the adult children to keep working and lead active and productive lives;

- ▶ Provides the adult child caregiver much-deserved time away from the pressures of caring for an elderly family member, which can become physically and mentally exhausting.

Disadvantages of Adult Day Services

▸ If your parents require round-the-clock supervision, the burden of caring for them will remain your responsibility in the evenings and weekends;

▸ Certain group environments could be harmful to your parents' morale. For example, a program might mix seniors without cognitive impairments with those who have Alzheimer's or other forms of dementia. Most programs, however, offer activity programming designed to deal with this issue.

When choosing an adult day program, it's extremely important to first identify what your parents' needs really are. Are they social needs? Are they physical needs? Are they cognitive needs? Based on this assessment, you and your parents can choose which adult day program best meets their needs.

How Much Do Adult Day Services Cost?

The cost of adult day services depends on the number of services included in the daily fee, the length of time spent at the center each day, and in which market the adult day program is located. Adult day programs may charge by the hour, half-day, full day, or by the week. Many have a minimum and maximum charge per day as well. I've found that rates generally range from $40–$80 per full day, with an average around $65 per full day. Of the adult day programs I've encountered, about half provide transportation to and from the program free of charge. Additional charges for transportation typically range from $8–$15 per day for round-trip transportation, while others charge by the mile (e.g., 50¢ per mile).

Make sure to ask the administrator of the program if there are any other services that require additional fees. These types of questions are included in the "Checklist to Conduct a Telephone Survey of an Adult

Day Program," which is on the CD that came with this book. The survey is designed to gather all the information you'll need to help your parents make an informed decision. Refer to Chapter 6, Step 3 to understand why each question in the survey is so important to their final evaluation and decision.

Who'll Pay the Bills?

Unfortunately, Medicare does not cover adult day services. If your parents have a long-term care insurance policy, they may, depending on the policy, be eligible to receive a daily benefit for adult day services. Make sure to review the policy with your parents' attorney, CPA, or eldercare consultant to help determine whether adult day services are covered.

More often than not, if your parents have the means to do so, they'll pay for these services with their own funds. If, over time, your parents deplete their assets to certain lower levels, they may qualify for one of the state-administered assistance programs, such as Medicaid, for lower-income individuals. Qualifications for such programs vary from state to state. Contact your local Area Agency on Aging or your State Department of Health and Human Services for financial-aid information.

Option Three

Home Care Services

As Judy Garland said in the 1939 classic The Wizard of Oz, "There's no place like home." It's where we find warmth, security, and the comfort of familiar surroundings. This is precisely why people prefer to remain in their own homes when facing the challenges of aging or illness. Independence is important to everyone, including your parents. Because seniors prefer to live in their own homes for as long as possible, home care may be a viable option for your parents.

Home care can help your parents live independently in their own homes and communities by providing them a wide array of supportive and health care services. The amount of care can be tailored to include as much as your parents and their personal physician feel is necessary.

What are the Different Types of Home Care Services?

Home care services can encompass a wide range, from periodic visits by a homemaker to help your parents with shopping, light housekeeping, or preparing meals, to skilled nursing services provided by a registered nurse. Based on their initial care assessment, your parents' customized care plan may include any combination of the following:

Homemaker / Companion Services – These include home-based supervision and monitoring activities, which assist seniors in maintaining a safe environment when they can no longer do so alone. Homemaker and companion services typically include:

- Meal planning and preparation
- Washing dishes
- Monitoring diet
- Preparing grocery list
- Light housekeeping
- Changing linens
- Doing laundry
- Taking out the garbage
- Assisting with care of houseplants
- Assisting with pet care
- Supervising and coordinating home maintenance and lawn care
- Assisting with errands
- Shopping
- Sorting and/or reading mail
- Reading books, newspapers, or other
- Writing letters
- Mailing bills and letters
- Taking phone calls
- Answering the door
- Supervising and maintaining medication schedules
- Arranging appointments
- Appointment reminders
- Escorting to doctor's appointments, church services, entertainment, and other activities or functions
- Light assistance with walking, bathing, and grooming, as well as
- Providing friendly conversation and companionship

As the name suggests, homemaker and companion workers provide homemaker and companion services. While no formal training is required of homemakers and companions, most agencies require they have at least some experience assisting aging adults. Some home care agencies require their homemakers and companions to complete a specific number of hours of formal training prior to taking their first assignment, and to complete a specific minimum amount of continuing education each year.

Custodial / Personal Care Services – These include assistance with activities of daily living which comprise some or all of the following:

- ▸ Assistance with transferring (e.g., getting in and out of bed)
- ▸ Assistance with bathing
- ▸ Assistance with walking
- ▸ Assistance with dressing
- ▸ Assistance with eating, and
- ▸ Assistance with toileting

Custodial or personal care services are provided by certified home health aides, home care aides, personal care aides, or certified nursing assistants. Most states require that people who provide custodial or personal care services complete at least some formal training, as stipulated in each state's regulations, prior to providing these types of services.

Skilled Nursing Care Services – Skilled nursing services in the home can include, but are not limited to:

- ▸ Monitoring and administering of medications (e.g., injections)
- ▸ Intravenous therapy
- ▸ Catheter care
- ▸ Ventilator care
- ▸ Wound care (e.g., changing of dressings), and
- ▸ Pain management

Skilled care services are performed by licensed professionals such as registered nurses (RNs) and licensed practical nurses (LPNs). RNs are required to have two or more years of specialized education and must be licensed to practice nursing in the state in which they are providing such care. LPNs are required to have one year of specialized education and must be licensed to provide care under the supervision of an RN. Your parents' condition and required course of treatment will determine whether an RN or an LPN will provide their care.

Rehabilitation and Therapy Services – These services, generally needed by people who have suffered a debilitating injury, surgery, or stroke, include:

- ▸ **Physical therapy** – A physical therapist helps a person recover from an injury, surgery, or stroke by teaching exercises designed to restore and maintain their strength, range of motion, coordination, and balance. The physical therapist's goal is to help each individual reach his or her maximum level of independence in the most efficient and cost-effective manner.

- ▸ **Speech therapy** – Following a neurological event such as a stroke, patients may have deficits in their ability to understand and use language. Speech therapists are specially trained to help individuals regain their oral motor function and ability to communicate. People who have suffered a debilitating injury, surgery, or stroke can also experience difficulty swallowing. Speech therapists are also trained to help these individuals restore their ability to swallow.

▸ **Occupational therapy** – Trained occupational therapists use rehabilitative and adaptive techniques designed to help patients become more independent in performing activities of daily living. The occupational therapist assesses a patient's capabilities and limitations in the home environment and recommends changes or adaptations that promote independent living.

All states require a license to practice therapy. To obtain a license, applicants must have at least a bachelor's degree in their respective fields, and most states require therapists to complete a minimum amount of continuing education each year to maintain their licenses.

Other Home Care Services –

▸ **Medical social services** – Licensed medical social workers address social, environmental, and emotional problems that may impede an individual's medical condition or rate of recovery or interfere with the patient's ability or willingness to follow the treatment plan. Licensed medical social workers also improve the coping skills of the family or caregiver.

▸ **Nutrition services** – A nutritionist assists and counsels individuals and families by compiling a special or restricted diet based on the patient's needs.

▸ **Live-in or twenty-four-hour care** – Many home care providers offer live-in or twenty-four-hour companion, custodial, or skilled nursing services, providing round-the-clock supervision for your parent.

Who Provides Home Care Services?

+ **Home health care agencies** – As the name suggests, home health care agencies provide health care services including skilled nursing care. Some provide the full gamut of home care services, including personal care, homemaker, and companion services. Most, however, limit their services to just skilled nursing and one or two other specialties such as rehabilitation and therapy services. Because these agencies provide health care services, most states require them to be licensed; most are Medicare-certified as well, which means they must meet the minimum federal requirements for quality patient care. Home health care agencies are responsible for recruiting and supervising all personnel, which may include physicians, nurses, home care aides, homemaker and companion workers, therapists, dietitians, and social workers. Because the nurses and other home care workers are employees of the agency, they assume full liability for all the care they provide.

+ **Private-duty nursing agencies** – Like home health care agencies, private-duty agencies can also offer a full range of home care services including skilled nursing care, personal care, homemaker, and companion services. The primary difference between the two types of providers is that home health care agencies are Medicare-certified, while private-duty agencies are not. Because they are Medicare-certified, the services provided by home health care agencies must be provided intermittently over short periods of time, while private-duty nursing agencies usually provide home care services over longer periods of time. Like home health care agencies, they recruit and supervise their own personnel, and the responsibility for the patients' care rests with each agency. Unlike home health care agencies, most states do not require private-duty agencies to be licensed or meet regulatory requirements.

+ **Homemaker and home care aide agencies** – Homemaker and home care aide agencies employ homemaker and companion workers as well as home care aides to provide customers with homemaker, companion, and personal care services. Like home health care agencies and private-duty nursing agencies, most homemaker and home care aide agencies are responsible for recruiting and supervising their employees, and assume full liability for all care provided to their customers. Some states require homemaker and home care aide agencies to be licensed and meet certain minimum operating standards established by the state.

* **Independent home care providers** – Independent home care providers are caregivers of all disciplines including nurses, therapists, home health aides, and homemaker and companion workers hired directly by the people that need care or assistance. Independent providers are not employed by another organization; therefore, the responsibility for recruiting, hiring, and supervising the provider rests squarely on the shoulders of the person in need of care—your parents. They, with the help of family members and friends, will need to perform a certain amount of due diligence during the interview process, including checking references and performing background checks. If your parents choose to hire an independent provider, they become an employer, which means additional paperwork and responsibilities. With the help of their attorney, CPA, or financial advisor, your parents will need to comply with all state and federal labor, health, and safety regulations, which includes employee withholdings for payroll and social security taxes.

* **Registries** – Registries are essentially employment agencies that match independent providers with customers such as your parents. Based on your parents' care and assistance needs, the registries will provide you and them with a list of potential providers, including their résumés. The registries, like employment agencies or headhunters, will collect a finder's fee from your parents for placing the provider. Typically, it's your parents' responsibility (with your help, of course) to interview potential candidates, check their references, and perform background checks. To provide their customers

better service, some registries conduct background checks on their providers as well as offering an avenue for clients to file complaints about the independent providers they've placed.

Many home care providers offer free in-home assessment of your parents' care and assistance needs. If the provider does charge a fee, the cost of this assessment will range anywhere from $75–$300. Typically, the provider will send a registered nurse (RN) to meet with you and your parents to evaluate their home environment, health status, and other factors. Based on this meeting, the RN will develop a "care plan" tailor-made to meet the specific needs of your parent. When the home care provider develops such a care plan, make sure the provider includes the involvement of your parent, his or her personal physician, yourself, and other interested family members. Everyone's involvement will make the process much easier for your parent to accept.

Selecting a home care provider should be handled with the same level of due diligence and care that one would go through in selecting a personal physician, lawyer, accountant, or other professional. Your parents should choose a provider that helps relieve them of their emotional and health burdens and doesn't add to their worries with unsatisfactory or costly care. To help you achieve this goal, the CD that came with this book includes telephone survey checklists to help you prescreen the home care providers you're considering. Refer to Step 3 of Chapter 6, which discusses the various factors you and your parents will need to consider when conducting telephone surveys of home care providers.

Advantages of Home Care Services

▸ **Services are provided at "Home Sweet Home"** – As mentioned previously, the familiar surroundings of your parents' home make it much easier for them to cope with the challenges of aging or illness;

▸ **Services are paid for as needed** – our parents purchase services only as they need them;

▸ **Remain independent longer and age in place** – Because your parents remain at home, they retain their sense of independence, dignity, and security.

Disadvantages of Home Care Services

▸ **Affordability** – If not covered by a third party payer (e.g., Medicare, Medicaid, or long-term care insurance), home care services can become very expensive.

▸ **Off-site services are limited** – There is a limit to the amount of medical services that can be provided off-site. For the most part, only intermediate-type care is covered by long-term care insurance, and Medicare will cover home care services only for a limited period of time following an acute (short-term) condition or illness.

▸ **Lack of opportunities for parents to socialize with peers** – Recent research suggests that seniors with active social lives and exposure to constant social interaction will have a slower mental decline than those without. The study also says that seniors with active social lives may gain greater self-esteem, which may lead them to take better care of themselves. Food for thought.

How Much Does Home Care Cost?

The cost of home care services varies greatly depending on the type and number of services provided. Typically, the home health provider will charge an hourly rate, which will depend on whether your parents need a registered nurse (RN), licensed practical nurse (LPN), a certified nurse's aide (CNA), or a homemaker or companion worker. Based on my experience in visiting and talking with home care providers nationwide, rates typically range from as low as

$15 per hour for a homemaker to as high as $75 per hour for the services of an RN. Nights, weekends, and holidays are generally a few dollars more per hour.

Be careful when asking about hourly rates, because some home care providers have a minimum charge per visit. For example, one agency in the Midwest advertises an hourly rate based on whether the person requiring care needs an RN ($42/hr.), LPN ($34/hr.), CNA ($19/hr.), or homemaker ($18/hr.). Let's say your Mom needs a CNA to come to her home for an hour a day to help her get in and out of the tub every morning. Even though the CNA's hourly rate is only $19, and Mom needs only an hour of assistance per day, this particular agency charges a minimum rate of $40 per visit by a CNA. Make sure you keep this in mind when talking to home care providers.

The cost of live-in or twenty-four-hour care will vary significantly depending on the hours needed, the level of care (ranging from companion to skilled nursing care), and the region where your parents reside. Live-in or twenty-four-hour rates can range anywhere from $100–$300 per day, with an average rate of around $200 per day. These rates could be offset by a provision for room and board should your parents hire an independent home care provider. The various factors you and your parents will need to consider before bringing a live-in caregiver into your home is discussed in detail in Chapter 6, Step 3, under "Telephone Surveys of Independent Home Care Providers."

Who'll Pay the Bills?

Private-Pay (your parents)

As you can see in the rates above, home care services can become very expensive as your parents' needs become more complicated and labor intensive. What are your options for payment? Unfortunately, home health care services will, for the most part, be paid for out of your parent's own private funds. Some other third-party payer options are listed below.

Medicare

The Medicare program will pay for a very limited amount of home health care. Medicare is very restrictive when it comes to the amount and length of services provided. Medicare HMOs are even more restrictive. In short, Medicare does not cover long-term home health care needs. Your parents' care needs must be "acute" or short term for Medicare to cover them. For example, your parents must be recovering from an acute illness or skilled condition (e.g., surgery) for the cost of care to be covered by Medicare.

If your parents are recovering from an acute illness or skilled condition, Medicare will cover the cost of home health care services such as visits by a RN or LPN (approximately one hour per day), and home health aides (approximately one to two hours per day), to Medicare beneficiaries who are considered homebound. "Homebound" means that your parents cannot leave home without "considerable taxing effort." If they're used to leaving their home regularly, they wouldn't be considered 'homebound" and would not qualify for reimbursement under the Medicare program.

Medicare also requires your parents' physician to certify or prescribe the home health care services, and a Medicare-certified home health agency must provide these services. The federal government regulates certified home health agencies to ensure that they meet specific cost and quality care standards.

Home health care services covered by Medicare are not unlimited. The home health care services they receive must be intermittent (i.e., part-time) care. If the care required is more than intermittent, then your parents will have to pay for their home health care out of their own pockets. For example, let's say your mom was discharged from the hospital following a minor surgery. Depending on the type of surgery and your mom's diagnosis, she may be allowed a nurse and a home health aide to visit her daily during the first week she's recovering at home. During the second week she may be allowed a nurse to visit twice, and a home health aide to visit once daily. The third week she may be allowed a nurse to visit once and a home health aide to visit twice, and so on until Mom is discharged and has recovered from the acute illness or skilled condition.

In summary, the Medicare home health care benefit is beneficial to those who need home care to recover from an acute (short-term) illness or skilled condition. It is not intended to be an ongoing unlimited benefit. Medicare never covers long-term care needs such as assistance with activities of daily living. This is the main reason why long-term care insurance is so vital today and in the future.

It's worth mentioning here that if your parents need hospice care, the Medicare program will cover it. Hospice care is care provided to individuals who are terminally ill and have a life expectancy of six months or less if the disease takes its normal course. For more information on hospice care, refer to Option 9 of this book, which covers the subject in detail.

Medicaid

Medicaid programs are medical assistance programs primarily benefiting lower income, elderly and disabled individuals. Both the federal and state governments jointly fund the Medicaid programs. The administration and operation of the Medicaid programs, however, are handled only at the state level; therefore, the eligibility requirements and the coverage of certain home care services varies from state to state. Contact your local Area Agency on Aging, your State Medicaid Agency or the Department of Health and Human Services for more information on how your parents can qualify for financial assistance under this program.

Older Americans Act of 1965

Your parents may be eligible to receive benefits to pay for a portion of their home care benefits under the Older Americans Act (OAA) of 1965. The OAA provides federal funds for state and local social service programs that enable frail and disabled elderly individuals to remain independent in their communities. This includes home care services for individuals who are sixty years of age and older with the greatest social and financial need. Your parents may be able to qualify for this program. More recently, individuals who can afford to pay for some of these services can still qualify as long as they contribute in proportion to their income. You might still be able to benefit from this program even if you do not meet the financial need qualification. Contact your local Area Agency on Aging for more information on the program nearest you.

Long-Term Care Insurance

Most long-term care insurance policies include coverage for in-home services. Review your parent's policy carefully with your attorney or eldercare consultant to make sure the desired home care services are covered under the policy. Please refer to Chapter 9, which discusses the different types of long-term care coverage and policies available in the market today.

Commercial Health Insurance

Your parents' regular commercial health insurance coverage may cover home care services. Benefits for home care services for long-term care needs vary from policy to policy. Review your parent's coverage with your attorney or eldercare consultant to determine if your parents' home care needs are covered.

Option Four

Independent Living Communities

An independent living community is a viable senior housing option for the more active senior who can still function independently. Being able to function independently means being able to perform the routine activities of daily living, which includes bathing, dressing and grooming, toileting, transferring (moving from place to place), walking, and eating. In general, your parents must be able to manage their home and personal needs on their own.

Independent living communities might be an option for your parent if he or she has just lost their spouse and wants to reside near his or her children and grandchildren but moving in with them is not an option. This type of community might also be attractive to those seniors that do not want to be burdened with the responsibility (or are physically unable) of maintaining their residence and allows them more time for travel or other interests.

Independent living communities offer living spaces in a range of styles and configurations. They are often apartment units, but many communities do offer separate cottages, townhouses, or ranch-style cluster homes for rent on a monthly basis.

An independent living community not only provides your parents with housing, it also provides them with numerous hospitality-type supportive services.

In exchange for a monthly fee, along with the right to live in one of the community's independent living apartments, the resident typically receives the following basic bundle of services:

- ▶ One meal per day in a central dining area (additional meals can be purchased for an additional charge per month)
- ▶ Weekly housekeeping, laundry and linen services (laundry and linen services typically have a small additional charge)
- ▶ Twenty-four-hour security
- ▶ Scheduled transportation
- ▶ Maintenance services
- ▶ Emergency call system, wireless or with emergency pull cords located in apartments
- ▶ Activities programs, and
- ▶ Utilities (typically excludes telephone and cable)

No care or assistance is provided in this type of setting. This means that as long as your parents can function independently and have the means to pay the rent each month, they'll continue to reside at the community. Once they're unable to function independently or pay the rent, they will, in most cases, be asked to move out of the community. Most independent living communities allow home care services to be provided in their apartments, cottages, or townhouses, and some even have home health agencies located on site. When conducting telephone surveys of independent living communities in your parents' area, be sure to ask what happens when your parents can no longer function independently. Ask for specifics regarding the protocol when this situation occurs. This question is outlined in the checklist for conducting telephone surveys of independent living communities, which is provided on the CD. Refer to Step 3 of Chapter 6, which discusses the various factors that you and your parents should consider when conducting the telephone surveys of independent living communities.

Advantages of an Independent Living Community

▶ **Meals served in central dining area** – You may be concerned about your parents cooking and/or eating habits; good nutrition is vital to your parents' good health.

▶ **Housekeeping and laundry services** – No longer will you have to worry about your parents trying to keep up with these burdensome tasks.

▶ **Twenty-four-hour security** – You might be concerned about your parents' neighborhood deteriorating.

▶ **Scheduled transportation to/from shopping, church services, doctors' appointments** – You might be concerned about your parents driving capabilities.

▶ **Maintenance services** – Home maintenance will no longer be your parents' responsibility. For example, for something as simple as changing a light bulb, all they need to do is pick up the phone and call the maintenance director, who will have someone come replace it.

▶ **Twenty-four-hour emergency care available with emergency call system in the apartments** – This provides you with peace of mind, knowing your parents have help available should a medical emergency occur; nursing care may also be available right on the community's campus.

- **Apartment, cottage, or townhouse design** – The living spaces are specifically designed to accommodate a senior's needs. Design features typically include grab bars in the bathroom and tub areas, as well as kitchen counters and cupboards that are strategically placed at a lower height to make them more accessible. Raised toilet seats are also a popular design feature, making it easier for residents to get on and off the toilet.

- **Opportunity for social interaction with their peers** – Living alone at home can sometimes lead to isolation and loneliness; living in a housing complex and sharing life with peers can help combat loneliness. The more people they meet socially and form friendships with, the better they will feel about themselves and their lives.

Disadvantages of an Independent Living Community

- **The issue of aging in place** – If the independent living community is a stand-alone community with no other levels of care available on its campus (such as assisted living, Alzheimer's/dementia care, or skilled nursing care), then the emotional distress of eventually moving your parents again will become an issue. Often, the second move can be the most traumatic because your parents may be forced to leave a community where they've developed many new friendships in their peer group. As the years pass, seniors continually lose their friends and loved ones, while facing the uncertainty of their own inevitable passing. To combat this, seniors seek the comfort of familiar surroundings. Also, as seniors develop cognitive impairment, they become more easily confused and aggravated when exposed to unfamiliar surroundings.

How Much Will it Cost to Live in an Independent Living Community?

The monthly rental fees for independent living accommodations vary greatly depending on the size of the living unit, the number of services included in the rent, and the market in which the community is located. Independent living communities are owned by both for-profit and not-for-profit entities. Some are government subsidized and provide their tenants with assistance in paying the rent.

Monthly rental fees for moderate to upper-income seniors typically range anywhere from $1,000 to $4,500 per month depending on the size of the apartment, cottage, or townhouse, the number of services included, and the housing market where the community is located. Some communities financially qualify applicants before allowing them admittance. Can your parents afford to live in an independent living community? The general guidelines most independent living communities follow require the prospective residents to have an annual income at least one and one-half times the annualized monthly rental. Therefore, if the monthly rental fee were $1,500, your parents should have an annual income of $27,000 per year ($1,500 × 12 months = $18,000 × 1.5 = $27,000). Were the monthly rental fee $2,500, then your parents should have an annual income of $45,000.

The affordability of an independent living community is likely to be a concern for your parents. At first glance, the monthly rental fees may appear excessive, but they're often quite reasonable once you compare them to your parents' current cost of living at home.

To overcome the initial "sticker shock," use Appendix A (included on the CD that came with your book) to add up all your parents' monthly costs to live at home. These may include some or all of the following:

- Mortgage/rent payment
- Association fees
- Maintenance fees charged by Association
- Routine costs of maintaining property
- Property taxes
- Homeowners/renter's insurance
- Electricity, gas, water and sewer
- Groceries, and
- Other expenses

After tallying up what it actually costs your parents to live at home, you may find the independent living community more affordable than you initially thought.

Who'll Pay the Bills?

Private Pay (your parents)

Most of the rent payments made to traditional independent living communities that provide the hospitality-type supportive services described above are paid for out of the resident's own private funds. A limited number of public and government programs are available to help seniors with low to moderate incomes pay for this type of housing; however, the supportive services at these government–subsidized communities are usually extremely limited.

Public Housing and Government-Subsidized Housing Options

If your parents' income and assets are minimal, you can explore qualifying for government-subsidized senior housing.

> **There are three major types of federally funded housing programs offered by the U.S. Department of Housing and Urban Development ("HUD"):**
>
> **(1) Public Housing**
> **(2) Section 8 Housing**
> **(3) Section 202 Supportive Housing for the Elderly**

Public housing is available in most areas of the country, and prospective residents who qualify financially are required to pay no more than 30 percent of their household income for rent. Section 8 housing pays the difference above 30 percent by providing rent vouchers. The Section 202 Housing Program provides for housing to low-income seniors and usually includes limited supportive services such as meals and scheduled transportation. If you're fairly certain your parents qualify for low-income housing, during your telephone survey be sure to ask the admissions director if such accommodations are available in their community.

The demand for senior housing is strongest at the lower income levels. Low-income seniors are more likely to move to federally funded senior housing because they're less likely to have the financial resources to pay for services that will enable them to keep living in their homes as they age. Since such housing programs are in high demand, there are usually extensive waiting lists at these types of communities. Plan ahead and contact the public senior housing complexes in your parents' desired area of residence, and, with your parents' permission, put their names on the waiting list.

Option Five

Assisted Living Communities

During the past decade, one of the fastest-growing segments in the senior housing industry has been assisted living. Assisted living communities can provide your parents a combination of housing, a variety of hospitality and supportive services, and assistance with activities of daily living, as they need them. An assisted living community is tailored to meet the needs of aging parents who require a degree of assistance that prevents them from living alone, but don't need the twenty-four-hour nursing care provided in a nursing home.

Most assisted living communities developed over the past ten to fifteen years were specifically designed to convey a residential or home-like feel. All residents have their own apartments, with locking doors, which they can furnish with their personal belongings from home. Assisted living apartments typically range from 200–500 square feet, averaging around 300. The apartments typically include a full-sized bathroom consisting of a shower stall, sink, and toilet. Most apartments don't have full kitchens, but most have small kitchenettes, which typically include a small refrigerator, sink, and microwave. The monthly fees most assisted living communities charge include three meals per day served in a central dining area, so a full kitchen isn't really necessary. If the thought of your parents' cooking and/or nutrition is troubling you, this type of setting will help ease your worried mind.

Like an independent living community, an assisted living community can offer your parents a variety of hospitality and supportive services for a monthly fee. In addition, an assisted living community also provides help with activities of daily living, as your parents need them.

Services provided at a typical assisted living community include:

► Three meals served daily in a central dining area
► Weekly housekeeping
► Weekly linen service
► Maintenance and grounds services
► Twenty-four-hour security
► Scheduled transportation to and from certain appointments
► Utilities (except telephone and cable TV)
► Emergency call system, wireless or with pull cords in apartments
► Activities programs
► Medication reminders
► Assistance with activities of daily living as needed, and
► A certified nurse's aide on call twenty-four-hours a day on site

To capture the residential feel, many recently developed assisted living communities have used Victorian mansion-type architecture with attractive, home-like wraparound porches; many communities use single-story ranch-style structures as well. In most, nearly 50 percent of the building's square footage and living space is allocated to common areas, where residents can gather and socialize if they wish. Design features vary from community to community. Some have gift shops, convenience stores, beauty and barbershops, bank branches, and ice-cream parlors; some even have swimming pools, which are used primarily for physical therapy.

The popularity of assisted living communities has grown out of the realization that there needs to be a more humane, dignified, and less medically intense approach to caring for people in the later stages of life. The demand grew out of the need for a form of housing somewhere between no care at all and the high levels of care offered at nursing homes. Market studies have shown that there is substantial demand for long-term care services that offer less intense and less expensive care in a residential setting. I'm sure most of you have visited a nursing home at one time or another. I think we can all agree that most nursing homes are no fun to visit, let alone fun places to live. The residential home-like feel, comfort, and warmly lit atmosphere of an assisted living community is unquestionably the more appealing option to an adult facing the difficult question "What do we do with Mom or Dad?"

Even though assisted living communities have been around since the mid-1980s, they're still in the process of defining themselves. They come in many shapes, forms, and sizes; they have different architectural features, different living arrangements (private or semi-private accommodations), and offer different and varying levels of assistance to their residents.

During my career as a consultant to the senior housing industry, I visited over 500 assisted living communities nationwide. I found that many market themselves as assisted living communities when, in fact, they are not. For example, while performing fieldwork on a study for a client contemplating the development of an assisted living community, I visited a community identified as a potential competitor. It was listed in the Yellow Pages under "Assisted Living," and had a quarter-page ad with big bold lettering that read, "The Area's Premier Assisted Living Community." When I visited, they told me they could not provide any assistance with activities of daily living other than helping residents in and out of the bathtub. When I asked why they called themselves an assisted living community when they don't provide assistance with activities of daily living, they replied, "Well, we do cook their meals and provide housekeeping and linen services."

"Back home," I replied, "we call this an independent living community with supportive living services." The point here is caveat emptor—"buyer beware." The CD includes checklists to help you survey and tour the assisted living communities in your parents' desired area of residence. Make sure you get all the questions on the checklists answered, so you and your parents can make an educated decision about which assisted living community best fits their needs.

Nationwide, assisted living facilities have many different names, depending on where you're located. They may be called assisted living, enriched housing, sheltered housing, board and care homes, rest homes, residential care facilities, or personal care facilities. If a facility is called something other than an "assisted living community," it usually means it's a smaller facility housing fewer than twenty residents. For example, "board and care homes" are usually converted homes that claim to offer assisted living, but usually lack the qualified and trained staff needed to care for seniors who need assistance with activities of daily living.

Assisted living communities are licensed by state governments; each state has its own rules and regulations regarding staffing, the amount of care and assistance to be provided, and establishes specific standards for quality of care.

Advantages of an Assisted Living Community

All the advantages identified in the independent living housing section apply here as well because both options offer similar supportive and hospitality services. There are many additional advantages to add to your evaluation of assisted living housing for your parents, as outlined below:

- **Three meals served daily in central dining area** – You might be concerned about your parents' cooking and/or eating habits; good nutrition is vital to their good health.

- **Housekeeping and laundry services** – You'll no longer have to worry about your parents trying to keep up with these burdensome tasks.

- **Maintenance services** – Home maintenance will no longer be your parents' responsibility. For something as simple as replacing a light bulb, for example, your parents need only phone the maintenance director, who'll have someone come and do it.

- **Twenty-four-hour security** – You might be concerned about your parents' neighborhood deteriorating.

- **Scheduled transportation to/from shopping, church services, doctors' appointments** – You might be concerned about your parents' driving capabilities.

- **Available twenty-four-hour emergency care and emergency call system** – This provides you peace of mind, knowing help is available should a medical emergency occur; nursing care may also be available right on the community's campus.

- **Apartment design** – The apartments are specifically designed to accommodate a senior's needs. Features typically include grab bars in the bathroom and tub areas, as well as kitchen counters and cupboards that are strategically placed at a lower height to make them more accessible. Raised toilet seats are also a popular feature, making it easier for residents to get on and off the toilet.

- **Opportunity for social interaction with peers** – Living alone at home can sometimes lead to isolation and loneliness; living in a housing complex and sharing life with peers can help your parents' combat loneliness. The more people they meet socially and form friendships with, the better they'll feel about themselves and their lives.

▶ **Assistance with activities of daily living (ADLs)** – You'll rest easier knowing your parents will receive assistance with a variety of ADLs as they need it. Such ADLs may include bathing, dressing, grooming, transferring, toileting, and eating.

▶ **Reminders and/or assistance with medications** – You might be concerned about your parents under- or over-medicating. A registered nurse at one of the larger operators of assisted living communities in the country told me the average senior age  seventy-five or older requires about eight medications per day. I'm required to take just one pill per day and I find even that difficult to remember! Most state regulations governing assisted living care do not allow the professional staff to directly administer medications. In most states, the professional staff may only supervise the senior taking the medication.

▶ **Maximize your parents' dignity, independence, and privacy** – Your parents will be concerned about being "institutionalized" and losing control of their lives. They'll already feel badly enough about being unable to live without assistance; therefore, placing them in an impersonal, institutional atmosphere could be mentally devastating. That's why having the option to live in a residential, home-like setting in a private apartment, with locking doors, where they'll be able to bring their personal belongings and receive assistance on an as needed basis is certainly the desired choice. The assisted living environment is designed to respond to the residents' individual needs and improve the overall quality of their lives.

▶ **Lower cost of care** – The amount of help a resident receives at an assisted living community is customized to each individual's needs. Typically, upon admitting them to the community, the medical director will assess your parents, and thereafter reassess quarterly to determine whether they'll need more or less care. The monthly fee will be adjusted up or down based on the need for more or less care; this allows your parents to avoid paying for more care than they actually need.

Disadvantages of an Assisted Living Community

- ▶ **Affordability** – Assisted living housing and supportive services are primarily paid for with the resident's private funds. Third-party government reimbursement (i.e., Medicare and Medicaid) for assisted living housing and care has only proceeded at the state level through the use of Medicaid Waiver programs. Public awareness that assisted living needs to become more accessible to seniors with low to moderate income levels has increased the number of states creating Medicaid reimbursement programs. Currently, however, nearly all the money needed to live in an assisted living community is paid out of the resident's private funds, and, in most cases, the adult children provide supplemental financial assistance. Many long-term care insurance policies provide benefits for assisted living services. Please refer to Chapter 9, which discusses the advantages and disadvantages of obtaining long-term care insurance, so you can make an informed decision as to whether such insurance is right for both you and your aging parents.

- ▶ **The issue of aging in place** – If the assisted living community is a stand-alone community and doesn't offer the higher levels of care on campus (such as Alzheimer's/dementia care or skilled nursing care), then the emotional distress of eventually moving your parents again will be an issue. Often, the second move can be the most traumatic, because your parents may be forced to leave a community where they developed many new friendships among their peers.

As the years pass, seniors are continually losing their friends and loved ones, while also facing the uncertainty of their own inevitable passing. To combat this, seniors seek the comfort of familiar surroundings. This is important to remember because, as seniors develop cognitive impairments, they become more easily confused and aggravated when exposed to unfamiliar surroundings. Many assisted living communities are designed to care for your parents until they are nearly bedridden and need the twenty-four-hour care and assistance provided by a nursing home; however, statistics have shown that approximately 70 to 80 percent of assisted living residents will need to move to another setting to obtain a higher level of supervision, care, or assistance.

▸ **Sometimes difficult for an "active" spouse to accept** – If one of your parents is relatively active and doesn't need assistance, but is unable to act as the caregiver for his or her spouse, it's often difficult for the active spouse to accept an assisted living environment.

How Much Will it Cost to Live in an Assisted Living Community?

The cost of living in an assisted living community can vary greatly, depending on the unit size, whether your parents choose private or semi-private accommodations, the market where the community is located, and the amount of assistance your parents need. Be careful when comparing the daily or monthly rates for different assisted living communities. Don't dismiss a community right away if they quote you a monthly fee that seems outrageously high. Conversely, don't automatically assume a community that quotes you a really low monthly fee is the "place to be." Be careful: some communities will quote a single monthly fee that includes all their services, while others will segment their charges (i.e., only quote you the basic monthly fee, which may or may not include any assistance with activities of daily living).

Most assisted living communities with competent management teams will charge a basic monthly rate for the following group of bundled services:

- ▸ Three meals served daily in a central dining area
- ▸ Weekly housekeeping
- ▸ Weekly linen service
- ▸ Maintenance and grounds services
- ▸ Twenty-four-hour security
- ▸ Scheduled transportation to and from certain appointments
- ▸ Utilities (except telephone and cable TV)
- ▸ Emergency call system, wireless or with pull cords in apartments
- ▸ Activities program
- ▸ Medication reminders
- ▸ Assistance with one activity of daily living (usually assistance with bathing), and
- ▸ A certified nurse's aide on call twenty-four-hours a day on site

Based on the nationwide information I've accumulated, the monthly fees, which include the basic bundle of services outlined above (in 2008 dollars), can range from as little as $1,100 to as much as $6,000. This equates to approximately $36–$200 per day. I think you'll find most communities' fees range from about $70–$150 per day, with an average of around $100 per day.

As your parents' needs for care and assistance increase, each community will have a system to capture the additional cost of caring for them and will charge additional fees. Typically, your parents' care plan will be assessed quarterly by the community's medical director. When a decision is made to adjust your parents' customized care plan and increase or decrease their care and rates, the medical director will usually involve your parents, their personal physician, and even the adult children if your parents desire.

Generally, assisted living communities will have different levels of fees based on the different levels of care or assistance your parents receive. I've provided some examples below to show how "cost creep" can occur if you're not mindful of these additional costs as your parents' care needs increase.

One community, in the Midwest, offers a monthly fee that includes all the basic services outlined above, for fees ranging from approximately $1,850–$3,500, depending on the size of the apartment and whether the prospective resident desires private or semi-private accommodations. This amounts to approximately $61–$115 per day. Keep in mind that the basic fee includes assistance with only one activity of daily living (ADL).

As your parents' needs for care and assistance increase, each community will have a system to capture the additional cost of caring for them, and will charge additional fees. The community mentioned above, for example, has three additional levels of fees should a parent require additional assistance as follows:

- **If your parent needs assistance with two to three ADLs, the community will charge an additional $550 per month (or $18 per day).**

- **If your parent needs assistance with four to five ADLs, the community will charge an additional $850 per month (or $28 per day).**

- **If your parent needs assistance with six or more ADLs, the community will charge an additional $1,150 per month (or $38 per day).**

As you can see, the monthly fees will increase significantly as your parents' care needs increase. If your parents needed assistance with six or more ADLs at this assisted living community, they'd be required to pay anywhere from $2,981–$4,623, depending on the size of the unit and whether they've chosen private or semi-private accommodations. This amounts to approximately $98–$152 per day.

Some assisted living communities charge for assistance based on each occurrence. For example, one community I visited charges $6 for each meal fed to your parent by one of their staff. Help with bathing or showering was $10 per occurrence; help with dressing was $5 per day; and assistance with toileting was $15 per day. If an assisted living community allows a resident who is incontinent (i.e., unable to control bladder and bowels), they'll typically charge a substantial fee to help cover the cost of labor (assistance) and supplies (adult diapers). Most assisted living communities require their residents to be continent to allow them admittance, but there are some exceptions.

Most state laws regulating assisted living communities do not allow them to directly administer a resident's medication; residents must take their medications themselves. Most communities do offer a medication reminder and supervision service, which helps ensure your parents are not over- or under-medicating. Periodically throughout the day, the staff will hand the residents their medications and supervise them as they take it. Some states do allow medication administration; consequently, to capture this cost, the facility will charge an additional fee for the service. The typical rate for this type of service is about $10–$15 per day.

Once you've figured out how much each community will "truly" cost per month, it's time to figure out which communities your parents can afford. Most assisted living communities will financially qualify their applicants before allowing admittance into their community. General guidelines used by most assisted living communities require prospective residents have an annual income at least equal to the annualized monthly rental fee (a 1.0 multiplier). Using the assisted living community outlined above, if the monthly rental fee was $2,981 per month, your parents would need an annual income of $35,772 per year ($2,981 × 12 months = $35,772 × 1.0 multiplier = $35,772). Were the monthly rental fee $4,623, your parents would need an annual income of $55,476.

You might ask, "How can an assisted living community financially qualify someone based on income that covers only the cost of their monthly rental fee?" Some communities qualify prospective residents using multipliers as high as 1.25 times the annualized monthly rental fee, to allow the residents some cushion and some extra spending money for various additional living expenses. Most facilities use a 1.0 multiplier because of several factors. First, most residents who need assisted living services aren't as active as, say, seniors residing in independent living apartments, and therefore won't have as many discretionary living expenses. Most, if not all, living expenses will be covered by the community, including all meals, room, utilities, and maintenance, etc. Additionally, most aging seniors have other resources available to help pay for these additional living expenses, such as the equity they've accumulated in their homes, financial support from family, and private long-term care insurance.

The marketing director at each community will treat each individual case differently, based on each prospective resident's annual income and net worth. Make sure your parents are prepared to share their financial information with the admissions personnel at each community they visit. Many people feel uncomfortable revealing their financial status to complete strangers. I can understand: you feel as if your privacy is being violated; however, it's a necessary step in this business. Like buying a house or car, you must prove you're financially qualified to make the purchase before the sale is final. Make sure to refer to Chapter 8, which outlines the specific list of items you'll need to be familiar with when it comes to your parents' affairs—including their financial position.

As was the case with independent living apartments, affordability is an issue. The monthly rental fees may, at first glance, appear exorbitant, but they may be quite reasonable once you've performed a comparison of your parents' current costs of living at home to the monthly rental fee. Use the worksheet in Appendix A to help your parents decide whether it makes sense, from a financial standpoint, to move into an assisted living community.

Who'll Pay the Bills?

Assisted living services are not covered by Medicare; if, however, your parents' income and assets are minimal, and depending on which state they live in, they may qualify for admission through the state's Medicaid Waiver program. To find out if your parents live in a state with a Medicaid Waiver program for assisted living services, call your local Area Agency on Aging, the State Department of Health and Human Services, or the State Medicaid Agency as most states have a separate agency to administer these programs. Also, the telephone survey on the CD is designed to find out whether the assisted living community accepts residents who qualify for the Medicaid program, or if they have any other programs for seniors with lower fixed incomes.

Some private long-term care insurance policies provide a daily benefit for services that occur in an assisted living community. If your parents have a long-term care insurance policy, make sure to review it with your parent's attorney or eldercare consultant to determine if assisted living services are covered. Refer to Chapter 9 to get a better idea of what policies are available, what services are covered, and how much they cost.

Based on the available payment options noted above, unless your parents have a private long-term care insurance policy to help them pay for a portion of their daily fee, your parents are probably going to pay for their assisted living services out of their own private funds. What happens if your parents run out of money to pay the rent?

Most communities will financially qualify your parents before allowing them to move in; there have, however, been instances in which people have lived at a community for an extended period of time and, as a result, have depleted their assets to a level where they can no longer afford the rent. What happens then? Will the administration help your parents apply for Medicaid? What happens if the state where your parents reside doesn't have a Medicaid Waiver program for assisted living housing? Will they be forced to move out? These are the types of questions you'll want to ask the marketing director before signing the residency agreement with the community. Make them give specific answers. Most residency agreements specify when a community has the right to terminate a person's residency, including lack of funds.

Each resident of an assisted living community is required to execute a residency agreement prior to occupying an assisted living apartment. What exactly is a residency agreement? A residency agreement is a legal, binding contract between your parents and a community. It outlines the various terms of the contract including the payment of monthly fees, the services provided, refund provisions (if any), and when the community has the right to terminate your parent's agreement. The residency agreement should provide specific examples as to when the community has the right to force a resident to move out. For example, the agreement should be clear as to how much care the community can provide and, upon reaching specific higher levels of care, when the resident must move out. It should also outline what action the community will take if your parents can no longer pay the required monthly fees. Will your parents be required to move out? It's imperative that you and your parents review this agreement carefully with your parent's attorney or eldercare consultant before signing anything. These agreements are fairly standard, however, it's always better to be safe than sorry.

Some communities, especially not-for-profit communities or communities with not-for-profit sponsors, will have resident benevolent funds established to help residents that are no longer able to pay their monthly fees. These benevolent funds are typically funded by charitable contributions made by the more affluent existing residents, resident family members, former resident estates, as well as supporting members and trustees of the not-for-profit organization or sponsor. The funds allow residents that are no longer capable of paying the required fees, to continue to live at the community for as long as they desire. The "Checklist to Conduct a Telephone Survey of an Assisted Living Community," included on the CD, asks whether such a fund exists at each community, so this will be answered during your prescreening process.

Your Parents Will Have to Qualify Physically, Too

In addition to financially qualifying for admission to an assisted living community, your parents will also have to qualify physically. Before being allowed admittance, your parent will typically have to undergo a health evaluation by both an independent medical professional and the medical director employed at the assisted living community. As long as your parents are not bedridden or incontinent, they should qualify for admission to most assisted living communities. It really depends on the assisted living community and the amount of care they're capable of providing there. The initial health evaluation or care assessment will also allow the community to determine what level of assistance your parent's need, which will also determine the size of the initial monthly fee.

Option Six

Alzheimer's / Dementia Care Communities

Alzheimer's disease is a progressive, degenerative disease that attacks the brain, resulting in impaired memory, thinking, and behavior. It is one of several forms of dementia, which is defined as a disorder characterized by the loss of thinking skills severe enough to interfere with a person's daily functioning and quality of life. All forms of dementia involve brain degeneration, the death of neurons (cells) in the brain. Alzheimer's disease currently affects more than 4 million Americans. There are three stages of Alzheimer's disease:

► **First or early stage** – an individual starts to experience mild memory loss and confusion.

► **Second or middle stage** – memory loss and confusion worsen, and the individual begins to need assistance with some activities of daily living. A person in the second stage of Alzheimer's can become easily agitated, begin to wander, and have difficulty with language and speech.

▶ **Third or last stage** – the disease severely affects the individual's brain activity, requiring a high level of supervision and assistance with all activities of daily living; also, the individual's language and speech skills fall off dramatically.

The older a person gets, the greater the probability he or she will develop Alzheimer's disease or other forms of dementia. Based on statistics compiled by the Alzheimer's Disease and Related Disorders Association, Inc., nearly 20 percent of all people age seventy-five or older suffer some form of dementia; that increases to nearly 50 percent when people are eighty and older. From these statistics, one can conclude that people suffering the various forms of dementia can be found in all the senior housing and care categories described in this book.

Over the past several years, developers of both assisted living and Continuing Care Retirement Communities have been adding separate, dedicated wings for residents with Alzheimer's or other forms of dementia. Assisted living developers have also been busy developing stand-alone Alzheimer's/dementia care communities specifically designed and dedicated to caring for residents afflicted with this terrible disease.

As an adult child trying to care for a parent in the middle stage of Alzheimer's disease, you might find yourself in a situation in which your dad can walk and transfer from place to place and is in fine physical shape, but, because of cognitive impairment, needs varying degrees of help with activities of daily living. Because of his cognitive difficulties, a dedicated Alzheimer's/dementia care community or wing is probably the best housing and care option to meet his special needs.

The size of Alzheimer's/dementia care apartments are generally smaller than the apartments you'll find in an assisted living community. Assisted living apartments average 300 square feet, while Alzheimer's/dementia care apartments average 200. While visiting dedicated Alzheimer's communities and wings nationwide, I've occasionally expressed my concern about the small size of the apartments. These communities' executive directors have all explained to me that persons in the middle to late stages of Alzheimer's don't need or care to have a lot of living space; they spend most of their time in the common areas and, due to their need for constant supervision, spend relatively little time in their apartments. On a positive note, according to the directors, most Alzheimer's patients, once accustomed to their new accommodations, are considered among the happiest, most content residents in the community.

These dedicated communities or wings usually have all the same hospitality and support services you'll find in an assisted living community (listed again for convenient reference), and offers additional services and design features (discussed below) to help provide the best care environment possible for those with Alzheimer's.

In exchange for a monthly fee, a typical dedicated Alzheimer's/dementia care community or wing provides the following basic bundle of services:

- Three meals served daily in a central dining area
- Weekly housekeeping
- Weekly linen service
- Maintenance and grounds services
- Twenty-four-hour security
- Scheduled transportation to/from certain appointments
- Utilities (except telephone and cable television)
- Emergency call system, wireless or with pull cords in apartments
- Wireless wander prevention system
- Social and activities programs, most geared toward memory enhancement
- Medication reminders
- Assistance with activities of daily living, as your parents need them, and
- A certified nurse's aide on call twenty-four-hours a day on site

Advantages of a Dedicated Alzheimer's/Dementia Care Community or Wing

▶ **Three meals served daily in central dining area** – You may be concerned about your parents' cooking and/or eating habits; good nutrition is vital to their good health.

▶ **Housekeeping and laundry services** – You'll no longer have to worry about your parents trying to keep up with these burdensome tasks.

▶ **Maintenance services** – Home maintenance will no longer be your parents' responsibility. For something as simple as replacing a light bulb, for example, your parents need only phone the maintenance director, who'll have someone come and do it.

▶ **Twenty-four-hour security** – You might be concerned about your parents' neighborhood deteriorating.

▶ **Scheduled transportation to/from shopping, church services, doctors' appointments** – You might be concerned about your parents driving capabilities;

▶ **Twenty-four-hour emergency care available with emergency call system** – This provides you peace of mind, knowing help is available should a medical emergency occur; nursing care may be available right on the community's campus.

▶ **Opportunity for social interaction with peers** – Living alone at home can sometimes lead to isolation and loneliness; living in a housing complex and sharing life with peers can help your parents' combat loneliness. The more people they meet socially and form friendships with, the better they'll feel about themselves and their lives.

▶ **Assistance with one or more activities of daily living (ADLs)** – You'll rest easier knowing your parents will receive assistance with a variety of ADLs as they need them. Such ADLs may include bathing, dressing, grooming, transferring, toileting, and eating.

▶ **Reminders and/or assistance with medications** – You might be concerned about your parents under- or over-medicating. A registered nurse at one of the nation's larger operators of assisted living communities told me the average senior age 75 or older requires eight medications per day. I'm required to take just one pill per day and I find even that difficult to remember! Most state regulations governing assisted living care also govern the stand-alone Alzheimer's/dementia care communities, and do not allow their professional staff to directly administer medications. In most states, the professional staff may only supervise the senior taking the medication.

▶ **Minimize the need to relocate** – Many stand-alone Alzheimer's/dementia care communities are designed to care for your parents until they are nearly bedridden and need the twenty-four-hour assistance provided by a nursing home. People with Alzheimer's disease or other forms of dementia are primarily in need of care and assistance due to their memory impairments, not their physical limitations; Alzheimer's/dementia care residents are therefore not as likely to relocate to another setting.

▶ **Maximize your parents' dignity, independence, and privacy** – Your parents will be concerned about being "institutionalized" and losing control of their lives. They already feel badly enough about being unable to live without assistance, so placing them in an impersonal institutional atmosphere could be mentally devastating. That's why having the option to live in a residential, home-like setting in a private apartment, with locking doors, where they can bring their personal belongings and receive assistance on an as needed basis is certainly the desired choice. An Alzheimer's/dementia care community, like an assisted living environment, is designed to respond to residents' individual needs and improve the overall quality of their lives.

▶ **Lower cost of care** – The amount of help a resident receives at a dedicated Alzheimer's/dementia care community or wing, as with an assisted living community, is tailored to each individual's needs. Typically, the medical director will assess your parents upon their admission to the community, and will thereafter reassess them quarterly to determine whether they need more or less care. The monthly fee will be adjusted up or down based on the need for more or less care; this allows your parents to avoid paying for more care than they actually need.

▶ **Specially trained professional staff** – Dedicated Alzheimer's/dementia care wings or stand-alone communities offer professional staff that truly understand Alzheimer's disease and are skilled in handling the behavior associated with Alzheimer's and other forms of dementia. The highly trained staff will give your parents the respect and dignity they deserve.

▶ **Special activity programs** – Many dedicated Alzheimer's/dementia care communities have terrific memory enhancement programs designed to help slow the progress of this degenerative disease.

▶ **Wireless wander prevention systems** – People with Alzheimer's disease or other forms of dementia are prone to wandering. The Alzheimer's Association estimates it will happen to nearly 60 percent of patients. Keeping track of their residents is an ongoing safety and security issue for all Alzheimer's/dementia care communities. Many state-of-the-art communities now have remote wireless monitoring devices, worn by the resident, which will sound an alarm to alert caregivers when a resident has left a supervised area of the building.

▶ **Apartment design** – The apartments are specifically designed to accommodate a senior's needs. Design features typically include grab bars in the bathroom and tub areas, as well as kitchen counters and cupboards that are strategically placed at a lower height to make them more accessible. Raised toilet seats are also a popular feature, making it easier for residents to get on and off the toilet.

▶ **Memory-impaired design features** – In addition to the traditional design features that most senior housing and care communities have, dedicated Alzheimer's/dementia care wings and stand-alone communities have specific architectural features designed to help memory-impaired individuals cope with everyday activities. Be sure to look for these when helping your parents search for suitable care and housing. Specific design features include:

✓ **Continuous/circular hallways** with specific patterns, colors, and distinct visual cues, so residents can easily identify where they are at all times, which prevents them from getting easily confused or frustrated. Continuous hallways are designed so that following a hallway to its end will result in the resident returning to where he or she started. Oftentimes, these hallways are designed in a circular form. If a community doesn't have continuous hallways, residents are susceptible to wandering into a hallway that dead-ends or has no exit. People with Alzheimer's disease or other forms of dementia can find this confusing and become very agitated and uncomfortable with their surroundings.

✓ **Enclosed outdoor patios** are popular, allowing residents to enjoy the outdoors without concern about their wandering off the grounds and harming themselves or others. Outdoor patios are fenced in, have continuous walkways throughout, and are usually landscaped with flowers and other shrubbery. All landscaping should include nontoxic materials.

✓ **Buildings are designed to provide even lighting** in all areas, to further reduce confusion for residents. Shadows in a hallway can confuse a person with Alzheimer's disease. They may mistake the shadow for a large hole in the hallway and may become agitated or panicked.

✓ **Common areas are prevalent**, encouraging social interaction among residents.

✓ **Memory enhancement boxes** – In recent years, many Alzheimer's/dementia care communities have incorporated "memory boxes" to stimulate their residents' minds and memories. These memory boxes, usually located just outside the residents' apartment doors, commonly include photos of family members, of the residents themselves as children, and anything that rekindles fond memories. Many researchers believe that daily exposure to memory boxes helps slow the progress of dementia. The boxes also afford the professional staff insight into a resident's past, and a platform to communicate with the resident about each item in the box. This makes the resident's history an important part of the community, and, in doing so, brings the resident and the professional staff closer together.

✓ **Line-of-sight bathrooms** – Recent studies have determined that people with Alzheimer's disease and other forms of dementia become incontinent simply because they cannot find the bathroom. In response to this research, many architects are now designing senior housing communities with line-of-sight bathrooms. These are bathrooms without doors, so the residents can easily locate them. You might ask, "Wouldn't it be embarrassing or humiliating to have to use a bathroom with no door?" Well, in the case of residents with Alzheimer's disease or other forms of dementia, it's much more humiliating to be incontinent. The goal of this design feature is to delay incontinence, consequently delaying the move to a higher level of care. Line-of-sight bathrooms enable residents to live as independently as possible in a residential setting for as long as possible.

✓ **Line-of-sight refrigerators and closets** – Much like line-of-sight bathrooms, some Alzheimer's/dementia care communities or wings have incorporated line-of-sight refrigerators and closets in resident apartments. Clear glass doors allow the residents to easily see the contents of the refrigerator and closets without opening the door.

Disadvantages of a Dedicated Alzheimer's/Dementia Care Community or Wing

► **Affordability** – Like assisted living, Alzheimer's/dementia care housing and supportive care services are primarily paid for with the resident's private funds. Third-party government reimbursement (i.e., Medicaid) for Alzheimer's/dementia care is typically lumped in with assisted living services, which has only proceeded at the state level through Medicaid Waiver programs. Over the past several years, it's become increasingly apparent that assisted living and Alzheimer's/dementia care services desperately need to become more accessible to people with low-to-moderate income levels. This has resulted in an increased number of states creating Medicaid-reimbursement programs for assisted living and Alzheimer's/dementia care. Still, most people pay for such care out of their own private funds and, in most cases, with an adult child providing supplemental financial assistance. Like assisted living, most long-term care insurance policies provide benefits for Alzheimer's/dementia care services. Refer to Chapter 9, which discusses the advantages and disadvantages of obtaining long-term care insurance, so you can make an informed decision as to whether such insurance is right for both you and your parents.

► **The issue of aging in place** – If the Alzheimer's/dementia care community is a stand-alone community with no other levels of care available on campus (such as a skilled nursing care unit), then the emotional distress of moving your parents again will be an issue you'll need to consider. Moving a person with Alzheimer's disease or other forms of dementia can be especially traumatic and could cause them to regress, losing whatever progress they've made.

► **Very difficult for an active spouse to accept** – The environment of an Alzheimer's/dementia care community can be hard to accept for the spouse who is not suffering with Alzheimer's disease. Each person's situation is unique, so each case must be evaluated and treated differently. In some instances, where the community has multiple levels of care and living arrangements (i.e., independent living or assisted living apartments with a dedicated Alzheimer's wing), the couple may be able to occupy the same apartment. Under this arrangement, a couple could reside together in an independent living apartment, and, each morning, the community staff would walk the resident who has Alzheimer's to the dedicated wing where he or she can participate in daily group and memory enhancement activities. The person suffering from Alzheimer's will be calmer having their spouse living with them, while the independent spouse can enjoy their spouse without the worry or burden of caring for them.

How Much Does it Cost to Live in a Dedicated Alzheimer's/Dementia Care Community or Wing?

The cost of living in a dedicated Alzheimer's/dementia care apartment will generally be slightly higher than the rates charged for an assisted living apartment, due to the additional supervision required for a memory-impaired resident. Because people with Alzheimer's or other forms of dementia require assistance with several activities of daily living, the rates will naturally be near the high end of the assisted living range due to the need for increased care and assistance.

The cost of living in an Alzheimer's/dementia care residence varies greatly, depending on unit size, whether your parents have chosen private or semi-private accommodations, the market where the community is located, and the level of care and assistance needed. Based on the nationwide information I've accumulated on Alzheimer's/dementia care accommodations, the range of monthly fees, which include the basic bundle of services outlined above (in 2008 dollars), can range from as little as $2,715 to as much as $7,450. This equates to approximately

$89–$245 per day, with an average of about $150 per day (or $4,563 per month).

Who'll Pay the Bills?

Alzheimer's/dementia care communities provide assistance with activities of daily living for individuals with cognitive impairments, so payment for these services will essentially fall under the same category as assisted living services. As you and your parents are going to have to travel down the same road here, refer to the assisted living section of "Who's Going to Pay the Bills?"

Other Things to Consider

As soon as you suspect your parents might be experiencing some mild memory loss and confusion, it'll be important to encourage them to see their personal physician. Be open and honest with your parents about your concerns. Their own involvement in the decision to seek help and find solutions is vital to the process. You might even consider calling your parents' personal physician directly to voice your concerns. Ask the physician whether it's possible to refer your parents to a specialist involved in diagnosing and treating Alzheimer's disease and other forms of dementia.

If it's determined your parents are in the early to middle stages of Alzheimer's disease, then you and they should immediately begin to go through the evaluation of available housing options in your parents' desired area of residence. Caring for a parent with Alzheimer's in your home can be one of the most traumatic, mentally and physically exhausting experiences of your life. It's important to be aware of the effects this could have on your own mental and physical health.

Nurses and aides across the country who are experienced in caring for seniors with Alzheimer's and other forms of dementia have all emphasized that, if your parent is experiencing the early or middle stages of Alzheimer's or another dementia, it's in everybody's best interest to consider choosing a community with a dedicated Alzheimer's/dementia care wing, or a community entirely dedicated to seniors suffering any form of dementia. The reason is twofold: first, a dedicated community or wing has the architectural design and professionally trained staff necessary to provide your parents the best overall environment to live in; secondly, an additional move later to another housing and care option could be devastating to their emotional well-being.

People who have Alzheimer's or other types of dementia tend to get extremely upset, agitated, and disoriented when forced to move away from their familiar surroundings. One caregiver described it as taking one step forward and a hundred steps back when an Alzheimer's resident has to move from one living arrangement to another. Let's say your father made his initial move from your parents' home into an assisted living community due to his physical needs, and three years later he develops dementia and requires increased care and supervision. The move from his familiar surroundings at the assisted living community would be traumatic. If, however, the assisted living community you chose had a dedicated Alzheimer's wing, the surroundings would still be somewhat familiar (e.g., common areas) and would ease the transition to a different apartment in a different wing. This is a delicate decision, and the timing of such transitions is critical. Each situation is unique, so you, your parents, and their caregivers and personal physician must carefully examine all of the circumstances of each situation before making a final decision.

When visiting an Alzheimer's wing or dedicated community, be sure to note whether the wing is located anywhere other than on the ground-floor level. Access to the upper levels of a building creates a very dangerous environment for your parents if they suffer from Alzheimer's disease or any other type of dementia. I've heard far too many horror stories about Alzheimer's sufferers wandering, becoming confused and disoriented, and dying as a result of falling or jumping out of a second- or third-story window.

The Healing Power of Music...
Waking the Spirit

If you are searching for a dedicated Alzheimer's wing or dedicated community, it would be a great benefit and asset if the activities program for these residents included a healthy dose of music therapy. One of the peer reviewers of my book, Sister Roseann E. Kasayka, Ph.D., was a pioneer, advocate and great believer in the tremendous healing power of music for persons living with dementia.

Sister Roseann passed away suddenly in 2006 but she will never be forgotten. I was so inspired by her passion and dedication for helping people deal with this terrible disease that I would be remiss if I did not mention her here. She was a fantastic lady and it was a privilege and an honor to have her input and her enthusiastic endorsement of this book.

Sister Roseann felt that singing, dancing, and playing music was the pathway to which people living with Alzheimer's and other forms of dementia could communicate and express themselves again. Her research found that music therapy reduced their anxiety and frustration levels and increased their level of self-esteem. What she discovered was that all of these wonderful people were struggling each and every day to express themselves verbally and physically, and frustrated by their inability to communicate in any meaningful way, were living a life of involuntary emotional and spiritual incarceration. She found that music therapy freed them of their captivity by awakening their power of expression through singing, dancing, beating a drum, playing the piano or any other instrument. It could be as simple as tapping their hand on a table to the beat of the music. Through the music, the residents were communicating with each other and having meaningful group interactions. From Sister Roseann's viewpoint, it was an awakening of the spirit. They were feeling alive again, looking into each other's eyes, listening, looking, laughing... living. Being a music lover and amateur musician myself, I can relate to what these folks are feeling. Whenever

I'm feeling down, I'll pick up a guitar and sing. It is extremely thera-peutic, like going to see an old friend. It's an exercise that seemingly al-ways heals the mind, body and soul.

Bono, the singer/songwriter from the legendary band U2, once said, *"It's such an extraordinary thing, music ... It's the language of the spirit. If you believe that we contain within our skin and bones a spirit that might last longer than your time breathing in and out — if there is a spirit, mu-sic is the thing that wakes it up. And it certainly woke up mine. And it seems to be how we communicate on another level."*

A Sisters Love and Dedication Brings Hope and Understanding

Sister Roseann Kasayka, Ph.D. was a person who showed an extraordi-nary amount of love and dedication to her profession. In the December 2006 newsletter of the National Religious Retirement Office, William L. Keane, M.S., M.B.A. wrote an amazing dedication to Sister Roseann, who was his mentor. Because I could not write it any better, he has al-lowed me to include a portion of it here:

> *During her last years, Roseann was a strong advocate and speak-er on the subject of spirituality and Alzheimer's disease. She always ended her talks with the beautiful music of Shaina Noll and her "Songs for the Inner Child", sharing her five affirmations about per-sons with Alzheimer's disease. She would profess ... "I believe ...*
>
> *1. persons with Alzheimer's are full, living human beings with a rich past, growth-filled present and evolving future;*
>
> *2. persons with Alzheimer's disease have the ability to celebrate life and enjoy beauty, goodness and truth;*
>
> *3. persons with Alzheimer's disease are the enlightened ones, given to us to remind us how really to live and grow;*

4. persons with Alzheimer's disease challenge us to walk a common spiritual path with them; and

5. that we must learn the language and the space of the person with Alzheimer's, and go to their space rather than asking them to come back to our space."

Sister Roseann's five affirmations offer us all a great deal of hope and understanding with regard to this disease. She believed with all her heart that this disease was not a curse; but a special journey taken by people who have the ability to enjoy and celebrate life in very different way.

Option Seven
Nursing Care Facilities

We all have our own perceptions of nursing homes. Let me briefly share with you my first. Long before I got into consulting in the long-term care industry, my perception of a nursing home was that of a prison. I can recall a single-story nursing home in my hometown that looked very much like one. I think the windows even had bars. As a young child, I went inside once with my mother to visit a friend of the family. My mom and I were buzzed into the nursing home from the outside, and walked through an endless maze of doors that locked behind us as we passed through. I looked over my shoulder as the doors shut one by one. It was an awful experience. I remember looking up at my mom and asking, "Are they going to let us out of here?"

I vividly remember the awful stench in the air as we walked down the cold tile floors of the long, wide hallway. My mom's friend shared a small semi-private room with a woman who was moaning on the other side of the curtain. My mother's friend complained that she hadn't seen a nurse in hours and was in a great deal of pain. The look of anguish on her face was one I'll never forget. My mom was furious at the lack of attention her friend was receiving, and expressed this to the nurse in so many words. I told myself then and there, at age seven, that I would never, ever, live in a nursing home; I'd rather die first. I think most Americans share this point of view. Let's face it: nursing homes have long been perceived as God-awful places where old folks go to die.

Fortunately, not all nursing care facilities are like that. There are many nursing care facilities that provide the quality care your parents deserve. The key is to know how to find them.

With the arrival of alternative housing and care options available to seniors, such as assisted living, the role of the nursing home in the long-term care industry has changed dramatically over the past several years. To survive this transition, many nursing care facilities are recognizing that they must not only meet the physical needs of their residents, but also their emotional needs. Many facilities are taking a page out of the assisted living manual and trying to provide a more comfortable residential and home-like atmosphere. Several years ago I visited a nursing care facility that was halfway through this type of renovation. Because the building was half completed, it was easy to see the dramatic changes they were implementing. Wall-to-wall carpeting now graced the hallways and rooms that were previously covered with cold gray tile. Brightly colored wallpaper covered the walls that were once a drab green. Decorative wooden handrails were added to the hallway walls. Common areas were added in spaces previously occupied by patients' rooms. The centrally located nurses' station, previously enclosed in glass with wire inserts and large metal doors, was replaced with four smaller, nicely decorated, wood-framed nurses' stations, strategically located at each corner of the newly renovated facility. These folks really tried to create a more home-like, residential feel to their accommodations — and they succeeded.

Nearly all new nursing care facilities built today are doing away with the institutional feel that nursing homes have traditionally had, and are including such design items as common areas, fountains, solariums, atriums, and outdoor courtyards. Some newly built facilities even have private rooms with living room/bedroom combinations much like assisted living apartments.

Unfortunately, not all of the nursing homes have changed for the better. The harsh reality is patient abuse still exists in many of our nursing homes; therefore, the question remains: why is physical, mental, and emotional abuse, including neglect, misuse of restraints, and overmedication, still occurring in our nursing homes today?

In July 2000, the Health Care Financing Authority (HCFA), now known as the Centers for Medicare and Medicaid Services (CMS), completed a study on the appropriateness of minimum nurse-staffing ratios in nursing homes and issued a report on their findings to Congress. The study found that most of the neglect and abuse in nursing homes, including malnutrition, dehydration, bedsores, and the use of restraints, could be directly attributed to inadequate staffing; in short, it concluded that lack of adequate staffing is undermining the quality of care in our nursing homes.

I firmly believe in the direct correlation between adequate staffing and quality care. If there's not enough direct care staff available to take care of residents, then a nursing home resident might not get turned or repositioned every two hours and, as a result, may develop bedsores. They might not be fed properly, which could result in weight loss or inadequate nutrition. Their hygiene needs might not be met; consequently, they might lie in their own urine or feces. They might not be given a daily walk or the necessary range-of-motion exercises and, as a result, could develop muscular deterioration.

According to the HCFA study, fewer than half of the nation's nursing homes have enough staff to meet the needs of their residents, confirming what industry experts have known for years: there is a major staffing crisis in the nursing home industry.

So what caused this crisis? Over the years, I've talked with a number of intelligent and caring nursing home administrators who have had to struggle with many factors, some of which are really out of their control. These are briefly outlined below. It's important to discuss these issues so all of us are educated as to where the problems lie, and gain a better understanding of what the nursing homes are going through.

Three major trends have given rise to this staffing crisis in our nation's nursing care facilities:

1. A Sicker and More Dependent Resident – Today's nursing home residents require more care and assistance than ever before. Tremendous growth in other senior housing and care options—assisted living, Alzheimer's/dementia care, adult day care, home care, and Continuing Care Retirement Communities—has forced nursing homes to care for sicker, more dependent residents who typically need care and/or supervision twenty-four-hours a day.

2. A Reduced Labor Pool of Qualified Direct Care Staff – To fully understand the staffing crisis, we need to understand how the nursing home industry has evolved over the past ten years. As nursing home residents have progressively needed more and more care, staffing levels have remained relatively unchanged. The greater responsibility of caring for these sicker and more dependent residents with the same number of direct care staff has become increasingly demanding on nurses and nurses' aides, both physically and emotionally.

This, coupled with the fact that direct care nursing staff are the most underpaid professionals on the planet, can drive anyone away from this profession. The shortage of qualified nursing staff is most evident with Certified Nurses' Aides (CNAs) who provide 80–90 percent of the care and assistance to nursing home residents. The median rate paid to CNAs in 2008 was $10.07 per hour—less than the median hourly wage rates of receptionists ($12.22), crossing guards ($10.92), bus drivers ($13.49), and accounts payable clerks ($14.18).

This is no joke. The individuals whom we trust to care for our aging parents and help them live with as much independence and dignity as possible are among the lowest-paid professionals in America. In addition, many nursing care facilities don't even offer health care and retirement benefits to their CNAs, and if they do offer benefits, the monthly premiums and co-payments are usually so expensive the CNAs can't afford them.

Due to extremely demanding work, low wages, and the negative image that nursing homes have, it's no surprise that nationwide enrollment numbers in nursing programs have decreased by nearly 20 percent over the past five years. As larger numbers of nurses begin to retire, there will be even fewer nurses to take their place, which will make the staffing crisis an even bigger problem.

3. A Reimbursement System and Regulatory Environment that are Incompatible with Today's Long-Term Care Environment – The current Medicaid and Medicare reimbursement systems promote cost containment, which puts a great deal of undue pressure on nursing homes to cut costs. Because the nursing home industry is so labor intensive, this usually means cutting staff. The Medicaid program is the primary source of funding for the majority of America's nursing care facilities. Medicaid covers nearly 68 percent of all nursing home residents in the United States, while Medicare accounts for another 9 percent.

In response to sicker, more dependent nursing home residents, and the varying levels of care they need, Medicare and many state Medicaid programs have switched to a case-mix reimbursement system, which pays higher rates for residents who need more care, rather than one standard rate for all residents, regardless of how much care they need. Pursuant to the Balanced Budget Amendment, Medicare incorporated these changes in 1997. While this reimbursement system does provide more funds to nursing homes that care for sicker residents, the system fails in that it doesn't require nursing homes to increase their staffing levels to meet the additional demands of those residents.

Under this flawed system, the incentive for the nursing home is to staff as low as they possibly can and pocket the difference. Thus nursing homes are not using the additional revenue generated to hire the additional staff necessary to meet their residents' increased needs. In my opinion, the case-mix reimbursement system must be fixed so the additional funds received to care for sicker, more dependent residents are actually spent on employing enough staff to meet the heavier care needs. To assure adequate staffing levels, minimum staffing requirements need to coincide with the levels of care the residents require.

To further exacerbate the problem, minimum staffing requirements at both the federal and state levels still remain the same as they were several years ago, despite the fact that nursing home residents are sicker and more dependent than ever before. This has resulted in certified nurses' aides caring for residents with more complex care needs, which is not an ideal situation.

Make no mistake, the shortage of qualified licensed nurses and certified nurses' aides in our nursing homes is a serious issue that our legislators in Washington, D.C., will need to address and address quickly, before our country's long-term care system fails its citizens miserably.

There is no quick fix for this problem, but Congress needs to address this issue now, and with the help of quality organizations like the National Citizens Coalition for Nursing Home Reform (NCCNHR) and the American Association of Homes and Services for the Aging (AAHSA), the seriousness of this staffing crisis may finally get the attention it deserves. Due to these organizations' efforts to create awareness and concern over adequate staffing ratios, most state regulations now require nursing care facilities to post their staffing patterns and ratios and disclose them to their prospective residents prior to admission.

With time, better-educated consumers will help drive staffing up to the desired levels. If the nursing care facility is aware that staffing levels are going to be a factor in a prospective resident's decision, they'll be forced to increase them to the highest level possible. Included on the CD that came with this book is the "Checklist to Conduct a Telephone Survey of a Nursing Care Facility." This checklist is specifically designed to gather staffing information from each facility you and your parents' survey, and just by completing this survey process, you'll be doing your part to help battle the nationwide staffing crisis.

Inadequate staffing is not the only factor contributing to substandard care and patient abuse. A nursing home might have an adequate staffing ratio, but its direct care staff might not be adequately trained to care for an aging population. A nurse's aide who is not properly trained to handle patients with dementia has no business working in a nursing home. Nearly all of the patients in nursing homes are over age eighty, and nearly half of all people over eighty are likely to have some form of dementia. During the latter stages of Alzheimer's disease and other types of dementia, patients can develop speech and behavioral problems that an uneducated staff can interpret as abnormal mental behavior, which, in their minds, can only be handled with medication or restraints. I've heard many stories about patients, who were medicated beyond their physicians' orders, and patients who were tied up in four-point restraints for an entire day, forced to lie in their own waste, crying from the pain of open sores on their arms and legs where the restraints were attached. All this abuse just because the caregivers didn't understand that the patient required specialized care and handling that they were not trained to deal with.

I hope I haven't frightened you, because nursing homes really have a rightful place in the long-term care continuum. Highly skilled nursing care and rehabilitation services will always be in demand, and the nursing home setting is the only suitable option available for this type of care. There are many quality nursing care facilities providing the very best care money can buy; everyone should be aware, however, of the abuse being committed by some individuals who dare to call themselves "caregivers." As long as you do your homework and are careful in your selection, everything will be just fine.

It's also important to remember that a nursing care facility will only be necessary if your parents need twenty-four-hour supervision and are primarily bedridden. Be sure to investigate all the other housing options in this book before having to choose this most institution-like setting. Regrettably, there are some areas of the country where a nursing home may be the only option available to seniors because they can't afford anything else. Some states, for example, still don't provide Medicaid reimbursement for assisted living services to help low-to-moderate income people pay for this type of housing and care. Our nation's lawmakers need to address this huge problem today.

So what does all this mean to you and your parents? How do you make sure they select a nursing care facility that provides the utmost quality of care and maximizes their independence, self-esteem, and dignity?

Just follow the "Five-Step Process to Selecting the Best Senior Housing and Care Option" in Chapter 6 and everything should work out fine.

Choosing a nursing care facility for a parent will be the most difficult housing and care choice you and your parents will make. It will undoubtedly require the most time and diligence, due to the patient abuse still existing in the industry. The "Checklist to Conduct a Telephone Survey of a Nursing Care Facility" and the "Checklist to Conduct a Tour of a Nursing Care Facility," both on the CD, will help you identify which facility meets the quality care standards necessary to satisfy your aging parents' needs. The time you spend calling and visiting the nursing care facilities in your parents' desired area of residence will be well worth it.

As with other housing options, nursing home residents will sign a residency agreement, which outlines the terms and conditions of their stay at the nursing home, including the daily room rate and what services it includes. Most daily rates will include a basic bundle of services including all nursing and personal care, meals, and activities. The residency agreement will also outline all other services available to residents for an additional charge. It should also include what is often referred to as a "Patient's Bill of Rights," which identifies your parents' individual rights. Remember: the residency agreement is a legal and binding contract that your parents will be signing, so please have their attorney and/or eldercare consultant review the agreement before signing anything!

Advantages of a Nursing Care Facility

▸ A wide array of highly skilled care is available in this setting;

▸ Twenty-four-hour skilled care and monitoring is provided, giving family members peace of mind.

Disadvantages of a Nursing Care Facility

▸ Institutional setting with mostly semi-private accommodations;

▸ Overall lack of privacy, which diminishes an individual's dignity and pride; and

▸ The long-standing perception that nursing homes are places where people go to die.

How Much Does it Cost to Live in a Nursing Care Facility?

The cost of living in a skilled nursing facility depends on the level of care your parents need, whether they choose private or semi-private accommodations, and the market where the facility is located. Most nursing care facilities offer skilled nursing care, with respiratory and rehabilitation services included in their service packages. Intermediate nursing care services, which, in the past, were assisted living services provided in an institutional nursing home setting, are now provided in the preferred residential setting, such as assisted living and Alzheimer's/dementia care communities. Because of this natural shift, I'll discuss only what it will cost your parents if they require skilled nursing care in a nursing care facility.

Most recent publications I've read say that nursing home care, on average, costs $158 per day or about $57,700 per year. The only logical explanation for this absurdly low-ball figure is that the sample must have included a large number of intermediate care rates. Again, I'll quote only the rates charged for skilled nursing care.

Rates for skilled nursing care in a semi-private room (in 2008 dollars) range from about $120–$275 per day, with an average of about $185 per day. Rates for skilled nursing care in a private room range from about $140–$350 per day with an average of $209 per day. Based on this average, it would cost your parents approximately $76,285 per year to live in a private room in a skilled nursing care facility. Isn't this an amazing number? And this is an average! You can now better understand why long-term care insurance is so vital to both your parents' estate planning and your own family's. If your parents had no long-term care policy covering skilled nursing care, the money they worked so hard to save for their retirement would quickly be depleted at the rate of $76,285 per year.

Who'll Pay the Bills?

Long-Term Care Insurance

Please refer to Chapter 9, which discusses the ins and outs of long-term care insurance policies and their proper place in the long-term care reimbursement arena, including the varied levels of coverage available to both you and your parents.

Medicare

As with home health care services, the Medicare program is quite restrictive of the amount and length of nursing home care provided, and will pay for a very limited amount. To get Medicare benefits for a nursing home stay, your parents must have been inpatients in a hospital for at least three days, and have been discharged no more than thirty days prior to entering a nursing home. As with home health care services, a physician must prescribe or certify that your parents need skilled nursing care or rehabilitation that can only be provided in a skilled nursing facility. If your parents qualify, Medicare will pay 100 percent of the charges for the first twenty days; for day twenty-one through day one hundred, your parents must pay $128 per day (the 2008 co-pay amount, which increases annually), while Medicare pays the difference. After the hundredth day, your parents will pay for everything out of their own private funds.

Medigap and Other Supplemental Insurance

You've probably heard about the various private supplemental insurance policies, such as Medigap, specifically designed to supplement Medicare benefits. I remember my mother asking me whether it was worth it for her to obtain this supplemental insurance. It seems an insurance salesman had been calling her frequently, telling her she had to have this insurance or she wouldn't get the long-term care benefits she needed. Was the salesman right? Well, supplemental insurance policies such as Medigap do help cover deductibles and co-pays that Medicare doesn't cover. From the standpoint of long-term care coverage, Medigap may cover the $128 per day co-pay that your parents would have to pay for day twenty-one through day one hundred, but, just like Medicare, there's no benefit after the hundredth day.

Most of the services not covered by Medicare will not be covered by Medigap either. Basically, in exchange for the additional monthly insurance premiums your parents are going to have to pay, they'll receive a $128 per day benefit for eighty days, which equates to a total benefit of $10,240. If your parents already have Medigap insurance, use it; if they don't, they needn't buy it. Regarding your own retirement planning, you can decide for yourself whether the premiums are worth it to you; if you already have long-term care insurance, it might not. It depends on the length of the "elimination period" in your policy. See Chapter 9 for a discussion of what this means.

Medicare HMOs

A Medicare HMO is a managed-care organization that has contracted with Medicare to provide all of Medicare's benefits to its plan members. From the perspective of skilled nursing care, Medicare HMO members will usually receive the same benefits as someone qualifying for Medicare coupled with the Medigap supplemental policy: full benefits for the first hundred days of their nursing home stay, assuming that a physician prescribes or certifies their need of skilled nursing care or rehabilitation that can be provided only in a skilled nursing facility. Most Medicare HMOs don't require a three-day hospital stay prior to admission.

If your parents are members of a Medicare HMO plan, be aware that the coverage is more complex and much more restrictive than that of Medicare or a Medigap supplemental policy. For example, you must receive care from a provider that is part of the HMO network or you might not receive your full benefit. Also, if your parents move to another area to be closer to you or other family members, they could lose their benefits. Please review your parents' policy with their attorney or eldercare consultant prior to making any decisions regarding meeting their future housing and care needs.

Medicaid

The Medicaid program is the primary source of funding for the majority of America's nursing care facilities. Medicaid covers nearly 68 percent of all nursing home residents in the United States, while Medicare accounts for another 9 percent. Jointly funded by federal and state governments, the Medicaid program provides financial assistance to people with lower incomes and limited resources. The administration of the program is handled at the state level; therefore, the specific eligibility requirements will vary from state to state. The nursing care facility should be familiar with the regulations of the state in which they're located, and should be able to tell you whether or not your parents would qualify for assistance.

Other Things to Consider

One final important point: If you, as an adult child, are ever faced with the difficult task of moving your parents into a nursing care facility, try to make the transition as easy as possible. Visit them early and often. The frequent presence of loved ones helps reduce the feeling of isolation and loneliness, which can otherwise lead to depression and giving up on life altogether. They need reassurance that their family members still care for them. During visits, get involved in helping care for your parents. Learn about their care plan and help them with their daily effort to get well or deal with their condition. Your presence and your becoming a familiar face with the direct care staff can only make things better and help your parents' outlook a bit brighter. Chapter 7 discusses in detail how you can help your parents cope with their new environment.

Option Eight

Continuing Care Retirement Communities (CCRCs)

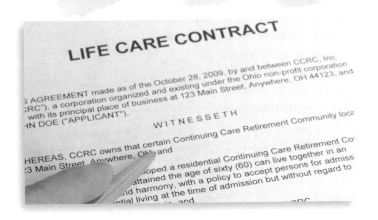

LIFE CARE CONTRACT

S AGREEMENT made as of the October 28, 2009, by and between CCRC, Inc.
RC"), a corporation organized and existing under the Ohio non-profit corporation
with its principal place of business at 123 Main Street, Anywhere, OH 44123, and
HN DOE ("APPLICANT").

WITNESSETH

HEREAS, CCRC owns that certain Continuing Care Retirement Community loca
3 Main Street, Anywhere, OH and

oped a residential Continuing Care Retirement Co
attained the age of sixty (60) can live together in an
d harmony, with a policy to accept persons for admiss
tial living at the time of admission but without regard to
and

Continuing Care Retirement Communities can be an attractive option for your parents because they offer the full continuum of housing and care on a single campus setting. CCRCs typically offer every level of housing and care described herein, from independent living to skilled nursing care.

The size of a CCRC campus can range anywhere from fifty living units to more than 500. Total living units are defined as the total number of independent living, assisted living, Alzheimer's/dementia care, and skilled nursing care accommodations. For example, a typical CCRC may consist of 240 independent living apartments, cottages, or townhouses, twenty assisted living apartments, twenty Alzheimer's/dementia care apartments, and eighty skilled nursing beds. The CCRC above has a total of 360 living units. CCRCs may also have home health care services available in the community, with a home health agency office located right on campus. CCRCs may have adult day care, hospice, and respite programs on their campuses as well.

In exchange for a one-time initial entrance fee and a monthly service fee, your parents are guaranteed a lifetime of housing and supportive and health care services for the rest of their lives. The fees vary depending on the type of contract your parents execute with the CCRC.

There are primarily three types of contracts:

Extensive or "life-care" contract – Residents receive full health care benefits for as long as they need them, without paying additional fees for health care or experiencing substantial increases in their monthly service fee other than cost-of-living adjustments.

Modified contract – Residents may receive a specified or limited amount of health care (e.g., a certain number of days) at no additional charge; however, once they've gone beyond the specified amount of care, additional fees will be incurred. Another form of modified contract may involve the resident receiving health care services at discounted rates (e.g., 10 percent off the current daily skilled nursing rate).

Fee for service or "rental" contract – Residents are responsible for all costs of additional health care services, as needed.

Because of the life-care concept and its provisions, people who want to live in a CCRC must meet certain physical and financial requirements. Your parents must be able to function independently at the time of their admission, and demonstrate the financial resources necessary to meet the CCRC's fee requirements.

Like other senior housing options, CCRCs require your parents to sign a contract called a residency agreement. This agreement describes the terms of their residency at the CCRC and specifies such items as the payment of the initial entrance fee, its respective refund provisions, the payment of the required monthly service fee, and the services to be provided in exchange for that fee. The agreement also lists any additional services offered by the CCRC that your parents can purchase for an additional fee, and specifies when a resident must be transferred to the next level of care such as assisted living or nursing care. Each resident will be required to undergo periodic health evaluations to determine whether they need additional care or assistance provided at the other wings or locations on the CCRC campus. Make sure your parents understand exactly when they'll have to transfer to another level of care. No one enjoys unpleasant surprises, especially those that affect our independence.

Many CCRCs in the marketplace call themselves life-care communities, but do not offer life-care contracts, so make sure you and your parents review the contract together with your parents' attorney or eldercare consultant, to ensure that everyone understands the terms and conditions of the contract. Worth repeating: Do not sign any legal contract until you have reviewed it with your parents' attorney or eldercare consultant.

In exchange for a monthly service fee, a resident of a CCRC will typically receive the following basic bundle of hospitality and supportive services:

▸ One meal per day in a dining area (additional meals can be purchased for an added monthly charge)

▸ Weekly housekeeping, laundry, and linen services (laundry and linen services commonly entail a small additional charge)

▸ Twenty-four-hour security

▸ Scheduled transportation

▸ Maintenance services

▸ Emergency call system, either wireless or with emergency pull cords in the apartments

▸ Activities programs, and

▸ Utilities (usually excludes telephone and cable TV)

As time goes by, your parents will likely need assistance with various activities of daily living or other health care services. Under the extensive or "life-care" contract, any additional care and assistance will be made available to them on-site at no additional charge. Also, if both of your parents move into a CCRC, they may remain together in the same community setting, even if one spouse is transferred to the assisted living or skilled nursing wing.

Most CCRC campuses include large central dining areas, a host of common areas for residents to gather and socialize, including card rooms for bridge and poker, billiard rooms, beauty and barbershops, ice-cream parlors, gift shops, convenience stores, bank branches, and post offices. Most also offer a number of craft areas for such activities as pottery, weaving, and woodworking. Some CCRCs have fitness centers and/or swimming pools used for exercise and/or physical therapy programs. A few even have putting greens on the grounds so your parents can improve that all-important short game. Most CCRCs have an array of activity programs that provide each resident the opportunity to participate to the degree they wish.

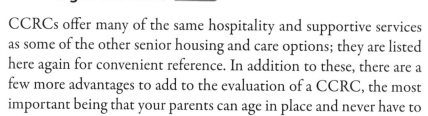

Advantages of a CCRC

CCRCs offer many of the same hospitality and supportive services as some of the other senior housing and care options; they are listed here again for convenient reference. In addition to these, there are a few more advantages to add to the evaluation of a CCRC, the most important being that your parents can age in place and never have to move again.

► **Meals served in central dining area** – You might be concerned about your parents' cooking and/or eating habits; good nutrition is vital to their good health.

▶ **Housekeeping and laundry services** – You no longer need to worry about your parents trying to keep up with these burdensome tasks.

▶ **Twenty-four-hour security** – You might be concerned about your parents' neighborhood deteriorating.

▶ **Scheduled transportation to/from shopping, church services, doctors' appointments** – You might be concerned about your parents' driving capabilities.

▶ **Maintenance services** – Home maintenance will no longer be your parent's responsibility. For something as simple as replacing a light bulb, for example, your parents need only phone the maintenance director, who'll have someone come replace it.

▶ **Twenty-four-hour emergency care, with emergency call system available** – This provides you peace of mind, knowing that help is available to your parents should a medical emergency arise; skilled nursing care is always available right on the community campus.

▶ **Apartment design** – The apartments are specifically designed to accommodate a senior's needs. They include grab bars in the bathroom and tub areas, as well as kitchen counters and cupboards that are strategically placed at a lower height to make them more accessible. Raised toilet seats are a popular design feature, making it easier for residents to get on and off the toilet.

▶ **Opportunity for social interaction with peers** – Living alone at home can lead to isolation and loneliness; living in a housing complex and sharing life with peers helps combat loneliness. The more people your parents meet socially, the more friendships they'll form, and the better they'll feel about themselves and their lives.

▶ **The Convenience of Aging In Place** – Because they offer nearly every level of care on a single campus, CCRCs allow residents to age in place. Thus the emotional distress of moving your parents again will not be an issue. Moving them a second time can be very traumatic and emotionally disturbing for them. As the years pass, seniors continually lose friends and loved ones, while also facing the uncertainty of their own inevitable passing. To combat this, seniors seek the comfort of familiar surroundings. Also, as seniors develop cognitive impairment, they become more easily confused and aggravated when exposed to unfamiliar surroundings. If your parents move into a CCRC, they'll likely never have to move again. They might have to move from one setting to another within the CCRC campus (e.g., from independent living to assisted living); however, the familiar surroundings and friendly faces of the professional staff, with whom your parents have already developed a relationship, will create a natural comfort zone, making your parents' transition to a new setting much easier.

► **Eliminates your parents' fear about becoming a future burden** – Because your parents have everything they could need on one campus, the fear of becoming a burden to their loved ones is eliminated. Prepayment of future health care services under an extensive or "life-care" contract means your parents won't have to make any further painful arrangements as their future health deteriorates.

Disadvantages of a CCRC

► **Affordability** – The payment of a substantial initial entrance fee along with a monthly service fee makes the affordability of a CCRC a barrier for many people.

What Will it Cost to Live at a CCRC?

The extensive, or "life-care" contract is what makes the CCRC option unique and attractive to senior consumers. The fees outlined below will relate only to these contracts. Be aware that there are other types of contracts available with lower initial entrance fee structures, but remember that the monthly or ongoing fees will become substantially higher as your parents' care needs increase.

If your parents choose to live in a CCRC, they'll be able to age in place and likely never have to move again. Assisted living and other congregate care communities make no such guarantees, and might ask your parents to leave the community should their level of care and assistance reach a point at which the community feels it can no longer care for them in the current setting. Because of this guarantee, living in a CCRC takes a substantial financial commitment. The size of the entrance fee deposit is primarily based on how refundable it is. The other major determinant is unit size. The majority of life-care contracts you'll find in the marketplace are either 90 percent refundable contracts, or declining refundable balance contracts.

Under the 90 percent refundable contract, a resident who wants to terminate the contract will typically receive a refund equal to the entrance fee paid less 2 percent per month for the first five months of occupancy, or a minimum of 90 percent of the total entrance fee. Under the declining refundable balance contract, a resident wishing to terminate the contract will receive a refund equal to the entrance fee paid less 2 percent per month of occupancy. After 50 months of occupancy, the resident will receive no refund. As you'd expect, a declining refund contract will cost substantially less than a refundable contract. If a resident dies, this will result in the termination of the contract, and any refund due the resident at that point in time would be transferred to the resident's estate. Most CCRCs will not pay refunds until the vacant unit is resold. This is agreed upon between the two parties and outlined in the residency agreement.

Depending on the refundability of the one-time initial entrance fee, the size of the independent living unit, the amount of services included in the contract, and the market in which the community is located, initial entrance fees can range from $50,000 to well over $600,000, while monthly service fees can range from $800–$4,500.

All CCRCs financially qualify their prospective residents before allowing them to move into the community. General guidelines used by most CCRCs require prospective residents to have an annual income of at least one and one-half (1.5) times the annualized monthly service fee. Thus if the service fee were $2,000 per month, your parents would be required to have an annual income of $36,000 per year ($2,000 × 12 months = $24,000 × 1.5 multiplier = $36,000). Were the monthly service fee $2,500, then your parents would be required to have an annual income of $45,000.

Obviously, affordability will be a barrier for a lot of folks who prefer the CCRC option, but, before jumping to the conclusion that the CCRC option is not a possibility given your financial means, compare your parents' current costs of living at home to the monthly service fee. To help overcome the initial "sticker shock" of this option, use Appendix A on the CD to total all your parents' monthly costs of living at home. You might be surprised to discover how much it actually costs them to live at home.

You should also consider what the actual cost would be to care for your parents over their remaining lifetimes and compare this estimate to the entrance fee outlined in the contract. Of course, no one can predict how much care your parents will need in the future. In most cases, CCRC residents will pay the initial entrance fee with the funds they receive from the sale of their primary residence. Most seniors will have their homes fully paid off by this point in their lives. Also keep in mind that your parents will benefit from the one-time capital gains exemption up to a maximum of $500,000.

Who'll Pay the Bills?

The hefty one-time initial entrance fee and the monthly services fees will be paid out of your parents' own private funds. To reduce their exposure to operating losses, CCRCs financially qualify their prospective residents before letting anyone move into the community. Despite this, there are instances of residents running out of money due to a longer-than-expected stay. The residency agreement specifies the terms of your parents' residency at the community, including whether or not they would be required to move out if they were no longer able to pay their monthly service fee. Again, be sure that you and your parents review this agreement with their attorney or eldercare consultant before signing anything. These agreements are fairly standard; however, it's always a good idea to fully understand every nuance in the contract.

Some communities, especially those with not-for-profit sponsors, have benevolent funds established to help residents remain at the community should they ever become unable to pay their monthly service fees. Commonly, more affluent residents make charitable contributions to the benevolent fund, as do family members of residents or former residents, the estates of former residents, and the supporters and trustees of the not-for-profit organization or sponsor. The "Checklist to Conduct a Telephone Survey of a Continuing Care Retirement Community," on the CD, asks whether such a fund exists at each community, so this question will be answered during your prescreening process.

Other Things to Consider

If your parents can afford the substantial entrance fee and the required monthly services fees of a CCRC, then the extensive or life-care contract will probably be their best option, especially if they don't have a solid long-term care insurance policy. The life-care contract is basically a form of long-term care insurance. The management of a CCRC performs the same types of analyses that an insurance company does to determine the level of risk associated with underwriting a long-term care policy to certain older individuals. CCRCs hire actuarial firms to help them estimate how much it will cost to care for individuals entering the community based on a group's age, marital status, and sex, etc. The actuaries help the CCRC price the entrance fees based on their estimate of how much it'll cost them to care for these individuals over their lifetimes.

I should mention that some CCRCs do require their residents to purchase long-term care insurance as criteria for acceptance. These CCRCs figure this into their analyses when pricing their entrance fees.

Option Nine

Hospice Care

Hospice is the unique concept of care that serves patients with terminal illnesses and whose life expectancy is six months or less should the disease take its normal course. As you might expect, hospice care is usually the final option. The hospice philosophy is to provide compassionate, comfort-oriented care to terminally ill patients in a pain-free environment with the involvement and support of their loved ones. The ultimate objective of hospice care is to ensure that patients live their final days with dignity, self-respect, free of pain, and surrounded by the ones they love.

When Will I Need to Consider Hospice Care?

You'll need to consider hospice care only if your parent has been told that his or her illness cannot be cured and that no further treatment is recommended. Also, your parent should have already come to terms with his or her terminal illness and have decided not to seek any life-extending procedures. In other words, your parent should consider hospice care only when the goal of treatment begins to shift from curing the illness to providing comfort. One of the industry leaders in hospice care told me that some patients, at least outwardly, never accept their imminent demise. For them, it's a natural reaction to fight their terminal illness right to the end. Because of this, many hospices take in patients whether they've outwardly accepted dying or not. For your parent's hospice care to be covered under the Medicare Hospice Benefit, however, he or she must agree in writing not to pursue treatment for curing the terminal illness, and must, after thorough self-examination of mind and spirit, exhibit inner peace and acceptance of imminent demise.

What Types of End-of-Life Services Can a Hospice Team Offer?

Hospice care will help make your parents' final days as comfortable as possible through state-of-the-art pain management and symptom-control. Hospice care focuses on the needs of both patient and family. The hospice team addresses the physical, emotional, social, and spiritual needs of the patient, while addressing the equally important needs of the family by providing information and resources necessary to support them during this very difficult time.

A hospice care program can include, but is not limited to, any of the following services:

- ▸ Palliative care (care focused on comfort rather than cure) and support for the patient, which focuses on alleviating pain and controlling symptoms
- ▸ Skilled nursing care provided by nurses
- ▸ Personal care and assistance provided by home health aides
- ▸ Respite care for family members and caregivers
- ▸ Counseling and support groups for family members and caregivers

- ▸ Training and education for family members and caregivers
- ▸ Bereavement support for family members of all ages
- ▸ Spiritual counseling
- ▸ Volunteer assistance
- ▸ Rehabilitative therapy (only if necessary to achieve a quality end-of-life experience, as hospice would not have a goal to rehabilitate), and
- ▸ Access to various medical equipment and supplies

Who'll Provide Hospice Care Services for My Parents?

Hospice care providers use a team approach to caring for people with terminal illnesses. A team of hospice professionals and volunteers work cooperatively with the patient, the patient's family, and the patient's personal physician to develop a care plan that meets each patient's individual needs for pain management and symptom control. A hospice team typically includes:

- ▸ **Medical director** – A licensed physician who specializes in dealing with terminally ill patients. He or she will be available for consultation with your parent's physician and other members of the hospice team.

- ▸ **Registered nurses (RNs)** are responsible for coordinating the care with your parent's personal physician and hospice medical director to prevent and control symptoms such as pain, breathing problems, and restlessness. The RNs also offer education and guidance to families caring for their loved ones.

- ▸ **Home health aides** assist your parents with activities of daily living and other personal care routines.

- ▸ **Licensed social workers** provide you and your parents with emotional support through counseling and other supportive programs.

▸ **Hospice volunteers** are trained to offer companionship and support to you and your parents in any way possible during this difficult time. For example, they might run errands, go shopping, read a book to your parent, or drive your kids to their baseball game. They're there to help you with the everyday challenges of life.

▸ **Clergy or other spiritual counselors** offer spiritual support and guidance to people of all faiths.

▸ **Bereavement counselors** offer support groups and one-on-one counseling for loved ones of all ages.

▸ **Speech, physical, and occupational therapists,** if needed, can help improve the quality of your parent's end-of-life experience.

Where Are Hospice Care Services Provided?

Hospice care can be provided anywhere your parents currently reside. Whether they still live at home or live at one of the senior housing and care communities described herein, a hospice team can be there to help alleviate pain and maintain comfort throughout their final days. Certain illnesses may prevent your parents from staying at home; however, they'll be able to remain in their home for as long as possible. Naturally, they'll be more comfortable in a familiar environment surrounded by caring family members and friends.

If your parents already live in a senior housing and care community, they'll probably be more comfortable receiving their hospice care while remaining in that community. The familiar environment, including the friendly faces of the care staff, will make the end-of-life transition much easier. Also, the round-the-clock supervision provided at most senior housing and care communities will obviously be a strong factor in deciding whether or not they should remain there. One great thing about hospice care is that the decision regarding where your parents receive their care rests solely with them and their family; and, in most cases, the decision to receive hospice care will not dependent on financial condition, because the government pays for nearly all the services required of a hospice program.

Who'll Pay the Bills?

Medicare covers the cost of nearly all services and supplies for a hospice patient for up to six months. To be eligible for the Medicare Hospice Benefit, a physician must certify that your parent has a terminal illness resulting in a life expectancy of six months or less should the disease run its normal course. Additionally, your parent must also agree in writing that he or she will not pursue treatment for curing the terminal illness. As a Medicare beneficiary, your parent must choose a Medicare-certified hospice in your area in order to receive the benefits listed above.

Under the Medicare Hospice Benefit, your parents may be required to pay five percent of the cost of certain services and supplies such as prescription drugs for pain management and symptom control, short-term inpatient respite care, and certain home care services. The good news: if your parents don't have the financial resources to cover these costs, most hospices are willing to cover that five percent, so your parents won't have to pay for any of the intermittent care. Many hospices are able to fund these out-of-pocket deductibles or co-payments through their established foundations and benevolent funds.

It's important to remember the Medicare Hospice Benefit covers only intermittent care and does not cover continuous twenty-four-hour care in the home. All intermittent services, medications, and supplies provided by the hospice team while making their home visits will be reimbursed by Medicare, but round-the-clock supervision is not covered. Routine round-the-clock supervision and care at home is going to be provided either by a team of family members and loved ones, or by a home health aide hired by your parents. The hospice team will be available twenty-four-hours a day should emergency assistance be required.

If your family is unable to fulfill the round-the-clock supervision responsibility, and your parents have the financial means, they may wish to hire a home health aide to handle these duties. The after-hours services of a home health aide may be covered by your parents' long-term care insurance policy (if they have one) under a home care benefit. If not, they'll probably have to pay for the health aide's after-hours services out of pocket. If a family caregiver is not available, and your parents don't have the means to hire a home health aide, they'll always have the option of moving into an extended care facility, such as an assisted living community or nursing care facility, which is certified under the Medicaid program.

Jointly funded by federal and state governments, the Medicaid program provides financial assistance to people with lower incomes and limited resources. The administration of the program is handled at the state level; therefore, the specific eligibility requirements will vary from state to state. The extended care facility should be familiar with the regulations of the state in which they're located, and should be able to tell you whether or not your parents would qualify for assistance. If your parents meet the financial eligibility requirements of Medicaid and meet the clinical requirements for the Medicare Hospice Benefit, round-the-clock care and supervision is a possibility for them.

Chapter Four

Have "The Talk" with Your Parents Today!

It's hard to imagine our parents as less than self-sufficient. Sitting down and talking with them about their future long-term care needs is an even more agonizing thought. Let's face it; most of us would rather bury our heads in the sand than discuss this subject with our parents. When a difficult situation like this arises, I'm reminded of the TV commercial that depicts a man in overalls expressing his displeasure at dealing with a car salesman by bellowing, in a Southern drawl, "I'd rather be pecked to death by a duck!" When it came to approaching my mom about her future senior housing and care needs, this was my sentiment exactly!

It's time for a reality check, folks. Based on discussions with hundreds of adult children who've gone through this ordeal, talking openly with your parents about their needs for long-term care, and planning for the inevitable before it becomes absolutely necessary, is much better than dealing with it on your own later. Helping your parents prepare for their future housing and care needs will help eliminate any future guilt. The secret is in getting started. The small amount of pain you experience talking about it now will go a long way toward eliminating the pain and guilt you'll experience later if you don't.

You've undoubtedly thought, I never want to be a burden to my children when the time comes that I need care. Well, your parents feel exactly the same way. Research has proven that this is so. The time to talk with your parents about their future housing and care needs is now, while they're in reasonably good physical and mental health. All of your parents' children should be involved in the discussion. Decisions reached as a group are vitally important because the decision will not only affect your parents, but also each member of the family. Group decisions are more likely to be successful than unilateral decisions. Even if some of your siblings can't attend a meeting, keep them informed of any decisions made, preferably in writing. It would be unfortunate if one of your siblings were unaware of your parent's' wishes for housing and care, later resulting in a disagreement over what your parents' wishes really were. Obviously, the final decision is going to reside with your parents as long as they're mentally capable. If your parents are still capable of being involved in the decision-making, their participation makes the entire process much easier.

A wise man once said, "Every battle is won before it's fought." This could not be more applicable than with senior housing and care planning. Let me give you an example. Last year, my friend's mother died suddenly. Her father had developed Alzheimer's disease about four years ago and was requiring assistance with several activities of daily living. Her mother was caring for, and tending to her husband's needs from their home of fifty years. When her mother suddenly died, she and her brother could not agree on what type of housing and care would be best for their dad. It was a very unpleasant experience for both her and her brother. The "guilt factor" was something that played on both of their minds. She told me that she wished they could have sat down earlier with their dad before he developed Alzheimer's disease and discussed what his wishes would have been in this situation. It would've made the decision to move him into an Alzheimer's/dementia care community a much easier one.

Approaches to Bringing Up the Subject

The best way to broach the subject is to be honest and direct. Ask your parents' permission to discuss the topic with them. A couple of good examples to open with: "I'd like to talk with you about how you'd like to be cared for if you got really sick and were unable to care for yourself anymore. Is that okay?" Or, "If you ever got really sick, I'd be afraid of not knowing what kind of care you'd prefer. Could we talk about this now? I'd feel better if we did."

It's extremely important to be a good listener during this discussion. Hear your parents without interrupting, giving your opinion, or telling them what to do. Rather than offer advice, let them work things out for themselves as they talk. As a good listener, you can help your parents explore their situation by asking them open-ended, non-threatening questions like "What specifically concerns you?" or "How do you feel about that?"

To be sure you have a clear understanding of their wishes, periodically repeat back to them what they've said. It's important not to repeat word for word, but rather put it in your own words to confirm your understanding. Pay attention to what's not said, too. Observe their facial expressions, gestures, posture, and other nonverbal clues.

Other opportunities may arise to help break the ice. For example, a perfect opportunity to discuss your parents' future housing and care needs would be when one of their friends or family members suffers a traumatic event that requires them to consider senior housing, care, or assistance. Bring up some "What if?" scenarios: What if Mom couldn't get up and down the stairs anymore? What if Dad couldn't drive anymore? What if both of you suddenly needed help with certain activities of daily living? What would your wishes be if you could no longer live at home without assistance? Are you aware of the different housing and care options? Have you thought about how you'll pay for such housing and care?

Tell your parents how much you love them and how you're willing to work together with them to find answers to these tough questions.

Never Make Promises

Never make promises to your parents such as "We'll never put you in a nursing home" or "You can always come and live with us, we'll take care of you." Circumstances change over time, and what may seem like the best solution now may not be the best solution years from now. Unfulfilled promises can only result in extreme guilt, anxiety, and pain.

Educate Your Parents about Advance Directives

Once the subject is open, if your parents don't already know about advance directives, you'll want to educate them about why they're so advantageous. The Terri Schiavo case should remind everyone of the importance of making your wishes known regarding end-of-life choices. Completing an advance directive is one way to do this. Advance directives are written requests that describe the kind of health care treatment your parents want should they become incapacitated. There are three types of advance directives:

Durable Power of Attorney for Health Care – This allows your parents to appoint another person, called an agent, to make health care decisions for them if they become temporarily or permanently unable to make those decisions for themselves. Your parents can select any adult to be their agent. Since this person will be making important medical decisions for them, they should select someone whom they trust and have confidence in, and who is familiar with their wishes, values, and religious beliefs. Once your parents have chosen someone, they should speak with that person to make sure he or she agrees to accept the responsibility and understands the duties.

Some of the specific powers that may be given to the agent under the durable power of attorney for health care are the power to terminate extreme life-support measures; to donate your parents' organs; to authorize an autopsy; and to direct the disposition of your parents' remains. Under the durable power of attorney for health care, the agent must exercise his power according to your parents' wishes, which your parents have communicated to him in any manner, including orally.

Living Will – This document informs your parents' personal physician or other health care providers whether or not your parents want life-supporting procedures or treatments given to them if they are terminally ill or in a permanent unconscious state. When given to your parents' physician, the living will becomes a part of their medical files; it is binding, unless the physician notifies your parents upon receipt of the document that he or she will not honor it. The living will is probably unnecessary if you have a durable power of attorney for health care with a life-support provision, because the durable power of attorney for health care usually takes precedence over a living will.

Do Not Resuscitate (DNR) Order – A DNR order is a written directive by your parents not to have cardiopulmonary resuscitation (CPR) performed if their hearts stop or if they stop breathing. People with a serious or terminal illness are usually the ones who request DNR orders, which can help reduce a person's suffering, while increasing his or her peace of mind and control over his or her own death.

An advance directive is a great way to make sure that your parents' wishes are carried out should they become too ill to speak. Advance directives can clarify things during a complicated and emotionally trying time. Without them, family members are often left guessing about critical medical decisions. Also, when the family disagrees as to what their parents' wishes might have been, physicians typically continue life support, extending the suffering for everyone involved.

Chapter Five

Four Factors That Will Affect Which Senior Housing and Care Option Your Parents Will Select

Let's assume you've talked with your parents about their future housing and care needs. Also, having read Chapter 3, you and they both know what each senior housing and care option has to offer, including the advantages and disadvantages of each. But what now? Where do you begin?

Factors that Will Affect Your Parents' Decision

Before you and your parents begin your search, it's important to become familiar with the four factors that will affect which senior housing and care option your parents will select.

Your parents' ultimate choice will primarily depend on these four factors:

1. Your Parents' Current Health and Physical Status – How much care and assistance your parents currently need will limit the number of senior housing and care options available to them. If, for example, your parents need assistance with bathing, dressing, and transferring, an independent living community is probably not going to be an option.

2. Financial Position – Your parents' financial position, the availability of public and private financial assistance for each type of care, and whether your parents have a long-term care insurance policy will also affect how many senior housing and care options are available to them.

3. Availability of Quality Senior Housing and Care Options in Your Parents' Desired Area of Residence – The more options available where your parents wish to reside, the better the odds of finding a quality housing and care option that meets their care and assistance needs.

4. Your Parent's Personal Preference – The optimal housing and care option will also depend on your parents' personal preference regarding whether to move in with their adult child, move into a senior housing and care community, or receive care and assistance in their own home.

Each of these factors will in part determine which housing and care option your parents choose. Let's assume, for example, that your mom currently requires various homemaker services as well as assistance with bathing and dressing. She also prefers to remain in her home, but has limited financial resources and doesn't have a long-term care insurance policy. Due to the expensive nature of home care services as the level of care increases, and the lack of public or private assistance for such care over an extended period, your mom might not be able to afford the care and assistance she needs in her own home. She might have to choose another, more affordable, care option such as an assisted living community.

For most seniors, affordability will be the factor driving the decision, so your parents' financial position is likely to be the most influential of the four factors. This is the very reason why private long-term care insurance is such an important consideration. See Chapter 9 for a discussion of such insurance. Having access to long-term care and choosing from several senior housing and care options, regardless of cost, is something every American should be able to do.

Most senior housing and care communities will review your parents' financial position to determine whether they can afford to reside at the community for an extended period. Most home care providers and adult day programs will not; they'll generally provide services for as long as your parents can afford to pay for them.

The information you gather in telephone surveys of all the senior housing and care options in your parents' desired area of residence (see Step 3, Chapter 6) will help them determine how much each option will cost as well as whether any form of public or private financial assistance is available for each. Consult your parents' CPA, financial advisor, or eldercare consultant to determine what types of senior housing and care your parents can truly afford.

Chapter Six

The Five-Step Process to Selecting the Best Senior Housing and Care Option

To determine which housing and care option best meets your parents' care and assistance needs, bearing in mind the four factors listed in Chapter 5, you and your parents should follow this five-step process:

Step One:	Assess your parents' current and future care and assistance needs.
Step Two:	Identify all senior housing and care options available in your parents' desired area of residence.
Step Three:	Conduct telephone surveys of all senior housing and care options.
Step Four:	Conduct in-person tours and interviews of all senior housing and care options that make your parents' short list.
Step Five:	Final evaluation and decision

Step One

Assess Your Parents' Current and Future Care and Assistance Needs

If your parents are still in relatively good health and capable of living independently, then their options will be many and they'll be able to consider all of the senior housing and care options in this book, including the independent living community option. But what if your parents have already experienced a traumatic event such as a fall or a stroke, and need a high level of care and assistance right now? Does Mom or Dad need too much care and assistance to reside in an assisted living community? Trying to figure out exactly what your parents' current and future care and assistance needs are can be confusing and overwhelming. You'll have many practical and emotional concerns, so it's always a good idea to get help from one or more of the following professionals:

Your Parents' Personal Physician – A good place to start is with your parents' personal physician. Most will be able to assess how much care and assistance your parents need. They might also be able to recommend several senior housing and care options available in the area.

Geriatric Care Managers – Another option is to retain the services of a geriatric care manager. These professionals are dedicated to helping seniors and their families select the appropriate senior housing and care option. They'll help you and your parent find the one that meets their individual needs, maximizes their independence, and enhances the quality of their lives. Academic credentials for geriatric care managers range from bachelors' degrees to multiple doctorates in such areas as gerontology, social work, nursing, or counseling.

A geriatric care manager can provide you and your parents a variety of helpful services, including performing an in-home assessment to determine how much care or assistance they might need based on their level of functioning. The care manager can also help arrange for in-home help and services, and determine whether your parents are eligible for any financial assistance. Geriatric care managers will review and discuss all the housing and care options with your parents, including each family member, to make sure everyone fully understands the advantages and disadvantages of each. After your parents select a care option and begin receiving the necessary care, the geriatric care manager will periodically reassess their care and assistance needs to make sure they're receiving the proper amount of care in the proper setting, and will revise the plan if necessary. The cost of a geriatric care manager can range from \$50–\$200 per hour, depending on the types of services rendered, the credentials of the manager, and the area in which your parents are located. Some geriatric care managers may also charge a fee of \$50 to \$300 for the initial assessment.

If you are having trouble locating a geriatric care manager, the National Association of Professional Geriatric Care Managers ("NAPGCM") has made it easy to locate one on its website. The NAPGCM is a volunteer, not-for-profit association with over 2,000 members. Their mission is to advance professional geriatric care management through eduation, collaboration, and leadership.

To find a geriatric care manager near you, go to the NAPGCM website at www.caregiver.org and click on their "Find a Care Manager" feature. Just enter your zip code and the search engine will provide you with a list of all NAPGCM members in your area. If you don't have internet access, you can phone them in Tucson, Arizona: 520-881-8008.

Medical Staff at the Senior Housing and Care Community, Home Care Provider, or Adult Day Program – If your parents are considering a senior housing and care option that provides health care or assistance, the provider will typically have its own medical director on staff (usually a registered nurse) to perform initial assessments of prospective residents or clients, to determine how much care and assistance they need. These initial assessments are usually free of charge. The medical director, often with the input and approval of your parents' personal physician, will develop a customized care plan designed to help your parents live as independently as possible.

Don't Forget Your Parents' Future Needs

When deciding which senior housing and care option best meets your parents' needs, remember to consider their future care and assistance needs, too. For example, having your parents move in with you, only to have them move into an assisted living community shortly thereafter when their care becomes too intense and costly, might not be the best road to travel. Of course, no one can predict what the future will bring, but at least you and your parents will have considered their future needs in your decision. Moving your parents from one place of residence to another can be traumatic, so any attempt to minimize the number of moves would benefit their mental health and attitude. The ability to age in place is an important consideration when making your final senior housing and care decision.

Step Two

Identify All Senior Housing and Care Options Available in Your Parents' Desired Area of Residence

Once you've identified your parents' current and future care and assistance needs, the next step is to become familiar with all the senior housing and care options available in their area. Here are a number of ways to identify the various senior housing and care options:

Let Your Fingers Do the Walking

Your local Yellow Pages is one of the best places to find senior housing and care options. To find all the options available in your area, look under the following categories:

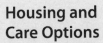

Housing and Care Options

- ▶ Retirement & life-care communities & homes;
- ▶ Assisted living facilities;
- ▶ Residential care facilities;
- ▶ Homes for the Aged;
- ▶ Rest homes;
- ▶ Nursing homes.

Care Options

- ▶ Home health care services;
- ▶ Nurses (for home health care services);
- ▶ Adult day care;
- ▶ Day care centers – adults.

End-of-Life Care Options

- ▶ Hospice care

The Internet

The Internet is a great resource for finding and identifying senior housing and care options in your parents' desired area of residence. Here are a few search engines that can help you begin your search:

- ▸ www.yellowbook.com
- ▸ www.yellowpages.com, and
- ▸ www.bigbook.com

These search engines are very easy to navigate. Just type in one of the senior housing and care categories outlined above as well as the city and state or zip code of your parents' desired area of residence and it will provide you with a list of available options in that area.

Your Local Area Agency on Aging

The United States government has a department called the Administration on Aging. Each state government has its own administration on aging department, which has its work carried out through local area agencies on aging. Every county in each state has at least one area agency on aging, with the exception of some rural areas where one office may serve a multi-county region.

Your local area agency on aging is another good resource for identifying the senior housing and care options available in your area. They can provide you a directory of services, facilities, and communities serving senior citizens in the area and can usually offer good advice on which facilities provide the best care and quality of life. I've found the people working at local area agencies on aging very helpful, but I recommend that you and your parents perform your own due diligence nonetheless and not rely entirely on their word and opinions.

Step Three

Conduct Telephone Surveys of All Senior Housing and Care Options

Once you've identified all the senior housing and care options available in your parents' desired area of residence, the next step is to call each one and conduct a telephone survey to determine if the housing and care option passes what I call "the sniff test." By taking into consideration the four factors in Chapter 5, your parents should be able to narrow the long list of options down to a half dozen or so providers that make up their "short list."

The CD includes nine telephone survey checklists, each specifically designed to gather pertinent information for each type of senior housing and care option, so you and your parents can make an informed decision as to which best meets your parents' care and assistance needs, price range, and personal preference. Print several copies of each checklist, and use them as you would a grocery list.

The nine different types of telephone survey checklists under four different categories of senior housing and care options including their respective appendices (on the CD) are listed below.

1. *Checklists to Conduct Telephone Surveys of Senior Housing and Care Communities*
   ▸ Continuing Care Retirement Communities – Appendix B
   ▸ Independent Living Communities – Appendix C
   ▸ Assisted Living Communities – Appendix D
   ▸ Alzheimer's/Dementia Care Communities – Appendix E
   ▸ Nursing Care Facilities – Appendix F

2. *Checklists to Conduct Telephone Surveys of Home Care Providers*
   ▸ Home Care Agencies – Appendix G
   ▸ Independent Home Care Provider – Appendix H

3. *Checklist to Conduct Telephone Surveys of Adult Day Programs* – Appendix I

4. *Checklist to Conduct Telephone Surveys of Hospice Care Programs* – Appendix J

Discussion of the content and importance of information gathered in the telephone survey checklists is broken out into the four categories of senior housing and care options listed above. Before calling to survey any housing and care option, read the following sections several times. By doing so, you'll gain a thorough understanding of why each question in the surveys is vital to your evaluation and final decision.

Conducting Telephone Surveys of Senior Housing and Care Communities

The checklists for conducting telephone surveys for each of the five types of senior housing and care communities (Located in Appendices B through F on the enclosed CD) will help you and your parents gather all the important information needed to determine whether a particular community is suitable for their housing and care needs. Each of the five telephone surveys is designed to gather information on points such as:

Admission Requirements

What specific age, health, and financial requirements must my parents meet to qualify for admission to the community?

The answers to these questions will tell right away whether your parents would qualify for admission to the community, and whether you should continue the telephone survey.

Is the Community Restricted to Seniors Only?

Many assisted living communities I've visited admit residents of all ages. In most instances, the younger residents at these communities had mental disabilities or mental-health conditions. Depending on your parents' personal preference, this might or might not be the type of environment they're looking for. The goal is to find an atmosphere conducive to preserving their dignity and independence and improving their overall quality of life.

How Much Income Will My Parents Need to Qualify for Admittance to a Community?

This varies from community to community. Obviously, your parents need to have enough income to cover the monthly rental fee, but many communities require prospective residents to have income over and above the monthly rental fee to cover incidental living expenses.

Usually, the more independent the community, the higher the multiple of income to monthly rental fee. For example, most CCRCs require prospective residents to have an annual income of at least one and a half times (1.5) the annualized monthly rental fee, while most assisted living communities require residents to have an annual income at least equal to or one and one-quarter (1.25) times the annualized monthly rental. Refer to Chapter 3 for details on how much each senior housing and care option costs and what it usually takes to financially qualify for admittance.

Are There Any Private or Public Programs Available to Help Cover the Cost of My Parents' Housing and Care?

If your parents' income is limited such that they're unable to qualify for admission to a community, you'll want to find out if the community participates in any public or private programs that can help cover the cost of your parents' housing and care. If, for example, your parents qualify for the Medicaid program, find out if any of the units and/or beds in the community are Medicaid certified. Depending on the state your parents reside in, reimbursement and assistance from Medicaid may be available for assisted living, Alzheimer's/dementia care, and nursing care. The telephone survey checklists are specifically designed to ask these types of questions, including how many of the community's units are Medicaid certified, how many are currently available for occupancy, and, if there's a waiting list, how long is the wait?

When surveying nursing care facilities, find out if any of the nursing care beds are Medicare certified and, if so, how many of them are available for occupancy; also, if there's a waiting list, how long is it? Reimbursement through the Medicare program is very limited when it comes to long-term care: they'll pay only a certain amount for the first hundred days of your parents' nursing home stay (assuming they've met all the conditions for acceptance). Refer to the "Who'll Pay the Bills?" section of the nursing care facility option regarding how your parents may qualify for Medicare reimbursement.

In addition to the government programs, it's always wise to ask whether any other private or public programs are available to help pay the cost of residing at their senior housing and care community. How one qualifies and the amount of assistance varies with the individual program.

Are There Any Physical Requirements to Enter the Community?

In addition to financially qualifying for admission to a community, your parents will likely have to qualify physically. Health and physical requirements vary from community to community, depending on how much care they're capable of providing. At most communities, your parent will have to undergo a health evaluation by both an independent medical professional (your parents' personal physician) and the community's medical director before being admitted.

Ownership/Sponsorship

Is the community privately or publicly owned? Is it a for-profit or not-for-profit organization? What is their mission statement? Is the community sponsored by a religious organization? It's important to know the type of organization you're contracting with, because it could give you an indication of where the organization's focus really is.

Is the Community Privately or Publicly Owned?

Whether a senior housing and care community is privately or publicly owned is a fair question, because there are potential advantages and disadvantages to each type of ownership. If a publicly owned organization (an organization traded on the New York Stock Exchange, NASDAQ, or the American Stock Exchange) owns the community, it's important to understand that the company's corporate and individual shareholders expect a certain return on their investment. If a publicly traded organization fails to meet its shareholders' expectations, the company stock price might suffer, thus making it more difficult and costly for it to obtain additional capital for a community's future needs. How will this affect an organization's ability to operate a senior housing and care community? In simple terms, if the parent organization fails to meet shareholder expectations, the cost of operating the community will become higher, which could affect both the future cost of living there and, more important, the number and quality of services the community provides.

Under public ownership, the community's executive director must answer to a board of directors elected by the shareholders to protect their individual interests. As a result, community residents' needs and expectations might or might not be met. I emphasize that this is not always the case, but everyone should be aware of the possibilities when considering a publicly owned community. Effectively managing investor expectations while not compromising the level and quality of services provided to residents is a never-ending challenge that some organizations are very good at handling, but, under the extreme pressure to meet investor expectations, this is never an easy task. Several senior housing and care organizations have gone public and failed to manage these expectations effectively, which led to those companies' eventual demise and the resultant sale or closing of several hundred senior housing and care communities across the country.

Under private ownership, the housing and care community will not be operated under the public scrutiny of shareholders; their operating decisions might therefore be more focused on meeting the needs and expectations of residents rather than meeting shareholders' expectations of return on investment.

What does this mean, and how should it affect your decision making? Should you never consider a community owned by a publicly owned company? The answer is an emphatic no. Public ownership has its advantages. Provided that the company is in good financial health, a public company has better access to capital to meet the current and future needs of residents, which can provide long-term financial stability to a community. Public companies can also take advantage of economies of scale by entering into purchasing contracts with their suppliers on a regional or national basis, thus lowering overall costs through high-volume buying. By doing so, a publicly held company can generally provide services at a lower cost than a privately owned company can.

In summary, when considering a senior housing and care community, the financial health of the community is more important than whether the community is owned publicly or privately. It's important, however, to understand the differing nuances of public and private ownership. As you'll see later in "Step Five: Final Evaluation and Decision," if a community makes your parents' short list, it's imperative that you and your parents' CPA or financial advisor review the community's current financial statements to determine whether the community is in a position to provide your parents' present and future care and assistance needs.

Is the Community a For-Profit or Not-For-Profit Organization?

The main difference between for-profit and not-for-profit organizations lies in the distribution of their profits. For-profit organizations distribute any profit they earn to their individual equity holders, while not-for-profits are required to use income in excess of expenses for other missions of the organization. The defining characteristic of not-for-profit organizations is that the individuals who control the organization do not have a right to its earnings.

The differences between for-profit and not-for-profit organizations and the manner in which they do business have become less distinct over the years. Generally, I've found the two types of organizations far more alike than they are different. The primary reason is because both are fiercely competing for the same customer. This competition greatly benefits the consumer because it forces senior housing and care communities to offer the optimum level of services at the lowest price.

In the past, not-for-profit organizations had an advantage because most were exempt from paying local real estate taxes due to their not-for-profit/benevolent status. This was a huge annual savings, which for many of the larger communities can be hundreds of thousands of dollars. In recent years, however, more and more cities, in an effort to raise additional capital, have been asking not-for-profit senior housing and care communities to pay their fair share of taxes. In most cases, the cities are asking not-for-profit communities to enter into PILOT (payment in lieu of taxes) agreements, which are agreements to pay a certain lesser amount of taxes negotiated between the community and the city or county tax assessors. PILOT payments are commonly considered user fees paid for city services, such as police and fire protection, provided to the community.

Not-for-profits have also been able to obtain less expensive, tax-exempt, bond financing, which provides for a lower overall debt-service obligation than their for-profit counterparts get. Not-for-profits also benefit from being able to collect charitable contributions to help them offset their obligations.

Some not-for-profit communities establish resident benevolent funds to help residents who are no longer able to pay their monthly fees. The more affluent residents, residents' family members, former residents' estates, and supporting members and trustees of the not-for-profit organization typically make charitable contributions to the fund. These benevolent funds are specifically set up to help residents who've exhausted their assets so they may continue to live at the community for as long as they desire.

Is the Community Sponsored by a Specific Religious Organization? Does the Community Include Residents of All Religious Affiliations?

Depending on your parents' faith and religious beliefs, the answers to these questions may or may not influence their decision to move into a given community.

Management / Operating Experience

How experienced is the organization at operating a senior housing and care community? Many owners of senior housing and care communities hire management companies to operate their communities for them. If a management company operates the community, find out what other communities they operate, and whether they have a good, solid reputation for quality care. This is one of the most important  factors to consider. Communities with experienced, successful management teams should rank much higher on the list than ones that don't.

If the community has been serving the area for any length of time, it will have developed a track record, which others who've lived in the community can vouch for or deny. The fact that a community has been in the business for a considerable time is a good sign, but you should take further steps to confirm the quality of care it provides. Completing the telephone survey is only one step in the five-step process to selecting the best senior housing and care community. All five steps must be completed to fully evaluate a community.

If the community makes it onto your parents' short list, ask the executive director to give you a list of references including physicians, hospital social workers, discharge planners, current and former clients (including family members), and any other references he or she is willing to offer. Follow up with these references to determine whether their reputation for quality housing and care is a good one. Refer to

"Step Five: Final Evaluation and Decision" for more on how to check references.

Licensing, Certification, Accreditation, and Membership

Is the Community Licensed?

Is the community licensed by the state? If so, is its license current and prominently displayed? Independent living communities are not required to be licensed, because they don't provide their residents health care or assistance with activities of daily living. Most states require licensing of assisted living and Alzheimer's/dementia care communities. All states require licensing to operate a CCRC, due to the large initial investment residents make through the payment of entrance fees. Every nursing care facility is required to be licensed in the state in which it operates.

Licensed communities are surveyed (inspected) annually to determine whether they meet the minimum standards outlined in state regulations. Each state establishes its own regulations regarding minimum staffing levels, the amount of care and assistance provided, and standards for quality of care. Health professionals from state survey agencies, usually in the Department of Health, conduct the surveys; operators' licenses are issued or renewed based on the results. Sanctions and remedies are imposed when operators fail to comply with state regulations.

Is the Community Certified?

Some types of services provided in senior housing and care communities, such as skilled nursing care or assisted living services, may be certified to participate in the Medicare or Medicaid programs. Federal laws govern this certification. Annual surveys are conducted to verify these services are being provided in compliance with Medicare or Medicaid standards. State survey agencies also conduct these annual surveys, and cite communities that fail to meet federal guidelines. Every nursing care facility certified to participate in the Medicare or Medicaid program is required to make the results of their last inspection available onsite for public review.

A new, five-star quality rating system was unveiled in December 2008 by the Centers for Medicare and Medicaid Services ("CMS"). This new system was designed to give consumers more useful information to compare nursing care facilities and help them make better, more informed long-term care decisions. In the new system, each nursing care facility is rated from a lowest rating of one star to a highest rating of five stars in three critical areas: (i) health inspection results; (ii) quality measures; and (iii) staffing levels.

> **You can access the new five-star quality rating system and search the database of nearly 16,000 nursing care facilities by city, state, or zip code at www.medicare.gov/NHCompare.**

The five-star quality rating system is a great place to begin your search for nursing care facilities that might meet your parents' needs. Be aware that a great deal of information on this website is provided directly by the nursing care facilities themselves and is not checked for accuracy; therefore, it's important you perform your own due diligence by visiting and touring the facilities as well as completing all five steps to selecting the best senior housing and care option before making your final decision.

Is the Community Accredited?

Senior housing and care communities can attain accreditation by meeting certain standards of quality and excellence set by an accrediting body. Accreditation is different from licensing and certification, in that the process is voluntary. A community's effort to get voluntary accreditation indicates the community is committed to providing its residents the highest possible quality of life by continuously trying to improve its quality of care and services, and consistently proves it by meeting or exceeding performance standards set by the accrediting body.

Here are some of the nationally recognized accrediting organizations you'll need to be familiar with:

▶ **The Commission on Accreditation of Rehabilitation Facilities (CARF)** – Founded in 1966, CARF (www.carf.org) is an international, private, not-for-profit organization that accredits more than 5,000 service providers providing programs and services in adult day services, assisted living, nursing homes, Continuing Care Retirement Communities, behavioral health, employment and community services, and medical rehabilitation. CARF develops and maintains practical standards of performance and quality for all of these programs.

CARF began accepting applications for voluntary accreditation of assisted living communities in July 2000, and this relatively new program is gaining momentum. After the initial inspection of a community, CARF awards it one of three accreditation outcomes based on how well the community graded in various performance areas: a three-year accreditation, a one-year accreditation, or non-accreditation.

In 2006, CARF introduced standards for Person-Centered Long-Term Care Communities ("PCLTCC") to help enhance the quality of life for nursing home residents. The standards present a framework to create an environment where the residents want to live, where personnel want to work, and where both choose to stay.

Also in 2006, CARF introduced standards for dementia care accreditation under a Dementia Care Specialty Program. Dementia care accreditation can be applied for in many settings including adult day services, assisted living, stand-alone Alzheimer's/dementia care communities, nursing homes and Continuing Care Retirement Communities. The Dementia Care Standards developed by CARF help foster a dynamic culture that creates a partnership between the person served (including the person's family and other support systems) and the provider to better the lives of the people living with Alzheimer's and other forms of dementia.

If a CARF-accredited community makes your parents' short list, you can contact CARF to receive performance information on that community. The information you receive will include a summary of the performance areas for which the community is exceeding the standards, as well as those needing improvement; the areas so identified include recommendations for improvement, so the community can meet the standard the next time it is surveyed.

> **For a complete list of CARF-accredited providers and programs, visit www.carf.org. If you don't have Internet access, or you wish to request a specific community's most recent survey results, you can phone CARF in Tucson, Arizona: 888-281-6531.**

▸ **The Continuing Care Accreditation Commission (CARF-CCAC) –** Founded in 1985, the Continuing Care Accreditation Commission was acquired by CARF in February 2003. CARF-CCAC (www.carf.org/aging) acts as the nation's only accrediting body of Continuing Care Retirement Communities ("CCRCs") and other retirement communities. It is an independent, not-for-profit organization whose mission is to inspire excellence in organizations dedicated to serving older adults through aging services continuums using the commission's standards and educational tools for advancing innovation and continuous improvement.

If a community you and your parents are considering is accredited by CARF-CCAC, you'll know the CCRC meets certain standards of excellence in four specific areas: (1) financial resources and disclosure; (2) governance and administration; (3) resident life and services; and (4) resident health and wellness. You and your parents can take comfort in knowing the CCRC's financial position was reviewed thoroughly by the commission's Financial Advisory Panel (FAP). To receive accreditation, a CCRC must meet or exceed certain financial ratios and standards.

CARF-CCAC awards accreditation for five years; a CCRC must, however, submit annual progress and financial reports to demonstrate that it's still in compliance with the standards. After the five-year period has expired, the CCRC must then reapply for accreditation.

> **For more information on CARF-CCAC, including a directory of accredited communities nationwide, visit www.carf.org/aging, or phone them in Washington, D.C., toll-free: 866-888-1122.**

► **The Joint Commission on Accreditation of Health Care Organizations (The Joint Commission)** – Founded in 1951, The Joint Commission (www.jointcommission.org) is the nation's largest health care accrediting body. It is an independent, not-for-profit organization whose mission is to improve the quality of health care for the public by providing accreditation and related services that support performance improvement in health care organizations. The Joint Commission evaluates and accredits more than 15,000 health care organizations in the United States, including home health care agencies, hospice care, and skilled nursing facilities. The Joint Commission surveys (inspects) accredited facilities every three years.

> **If a skilled nursing facility makes your parents' short list, a directory of all Joint Commission-accredited organizations and performance reports from their most recent evaluation can be accessed at The Joint Commission's website: www.qualitycheck.org.**

Their online Quality Check™ lets you access a nursing care facility's latest performance report and see how they rate compared to similar accredited facilities. If a facility is not in full compliance with the applicable standards, the requirements for improvement will be listed in the Quality Report as well as the summary page on Quality Check™.

It should be noted that Quality Check™ is a comprehensive directory that lists nearly all nursing care facilities available today, both accredited and non-accredited. The Joint Commission added non-accredited facilities in order to provide a more complete inventory of nursing care facilities for its users. Nursing care facilities that are accredited by The Joint Commission will display a large Gold Seal of Approval™ under the Accreditation/Certification column on the website.

> **If you don't have Internet access, you can request a facility's Quality Report by phoning The Joint Commission's customer service department in Washington, D.C.: 630-792-5800.**

Is the Community a Member of a Trade Association?

Like voluntary accreditation, membership in a trade association indicates management cares about the type and quality of care provided at their community. It tells me they're continually trying to stay on the cutting edge by keeping abreast of new developments that might help them operate their community more efficiently, and are constantly trying to learn about new ways to improve the quality of care they provide to their residents. Members of trade associations commonly share information and care techniques at least annually at conferences that take place nationwide. These conferences routinely include education sessions that members attend daily.

Some of the more prominent national trade associations:

▸ **American Association of Homes and Services for the Aging (AAH-SA)** – AAHSA (www.aahsa.org) is the association for the nation's not-for-profit long-term care and senior housing providers. Its members include over 5,000 nursing homes, assisted living communities, Continuing Care Retirement Communities, senior housing, and home and community-based service organizations. More than half its members are religiously sponsored, and, at the core of the work of all its members, is a mission to serve older people by providing the means for them to live with the greatest level of self-determination, dignity, and independence possible.

▸ **Assisted Living Federation of America (ALFA)** – ALFA (www.alfa.org) represents more than 7,000 for-profit and not-for-profit providers of assisted living, Continuing Care Retirement Communities, independent living, and other forms of senior housing and services. ALFA is the only trade association exclusively devoted to the assisted living industry and the population it serves.

▸ **American Health Care Association (AHCA)** – AHCA (www.ahcancal.org) is a federation of fifty affiliated state associations representing more than 10,000 for-profit and not-for-profit assisted living communities, nursing facilities, and sub acute care providers dedicated to improving the health of those needing short-term rehabilitative services, long-term skilled nursing care, or assisted living services.

Current Occupancy Rates

The occupancy rate of each senior housing and care community you and your parents survey is information crucial to deciding which community your parents will select. Occupancy rates are important because your parents will make a substantial investment in a particular community by way of monthly fees, and, in the case of a CCRC, a large initial entrance fee deposit. A low occupancy rate may be a "red flag" indicating the community is experiencing financial difficulty. In such a case, your parents' initial and ongoing cash investment in this community would be at risk. Some state regulations require senior housing and care communities to carry a surety bond to protect all resident deposits or other community-held trust accounts. It's important to remember that a personal financial loss isn't the only thing at risk here; your parents' emotional well-being is also at risk. If the community were to close, your parents' emotional health would suffer because they'd have to endure yet another move and, if the community had no insurance to cover their large initial deposit, would most likely have to move at the expense of their children or a government-funded program such as Medicaid.

What is considered low occupancy? The telephone surveys are designed to trigger an explanation from management when occupancy rates are lower than 90 percent. Most senior housing and care operators and managers should be able to successfully operate their communities at occupancy rates of 90 percent or higher. This means they can generate enough cash flow to pay their monthly debt obligations as well as all other monthly operating expenses required to provide the current level of services offered to their residents.

There are some instances in which lower-than-expected occupancy rates would be acceptable. For example, the community might have just opened in the past two years and is still in the midst of its initial fill-up stage. From my experience, most senior housing and care communities should fill up within twenty-four months of opening, regardless of their size. If a community that's been open longer than two years explains a lower-than-expected occupancy rate as a result of being in the initial fill-up stage, it may be a sign the community is struggling in the market, which would make it a possible investment risk. As a general rule, a senior housing and care community should be able to fill an average of three units per month net of any move-outs. For example, if a community had five people move in and two move out in a given month, they would have achieved a net three move-ins for that month. If the community you're surveying is filling less than three units per month (net of any move-outs), then it's probably struggling to make its financial ends meet.

Another instance in which lower-than-expected occupancy rates would be acceptable is when a community is expanding or renovating. In this instance, units are being added to the total number available for occupancy, naturally triggering lower occupancy rates. Again, as long as its units fill at an acceptable rate per month, this alone doesn't indicate a problem with the community.

Low occupancy may also indicate other problems, such as poor quality of care, which would require further investigation. If the explanation of low occupancy appears reasonable, "Step Four" in this chapter offers tips to help you evaluate the quality of care provided at a senior housing and care community and what to look for when conducting an in-person tour. The CD includes checklists you can use during your tour of each senior housing and care option.

If a community makes your parents' short list, it's important to ask the community's executive director or administrator for a copy of their most recent audited financial statements so you and your parents' financial advisor can review their current financial position. Some communities may even have a disclosure statement, which provides prospective residents a wide array of marketing and financial information, including the community's audited financial statements. If your parents are considering a community, a review of its audited financial statements is a must regardless of whether its occupancy rates are high or low. This is covered in "Step Five: Final Evaluation and Decision."

Age of the Community

If you intend to visit and tour a community that has made your parents' short list, the community's age and physical structure will be useful information. It'll help you determine whether the community has been allocating enough of its annual budget to capital improvements. If, for example, a community is ten years old and, upon touring, the building looks like it's thirty years old, you might question why they aren't putting money back into the community by allocating funds for such capital improvements as periodic replacement of carpeting, wall coverings, and furniture. Is it because management feels it's not necessary, or is it because the community is struggling financially? Either way, it may be an indication of how things will be handled in the future. If, on the other hand, a thirty-year-old community appears to have new furniture, wall coverings, and carpeting, then you and your parents can feel better about its financial health, knowing that money is being invested back into the community.

It's also helpful to know whether all the units at the community opened at the same time. The community might have been built in phases; consequently, some sections may be older than others. If it was built in phases, make sure to ask when each construction phase was completed, and, when asking about the available units, note which phase the available unit is in.

Unit Configuration and Range of Fees Charged

For each community, gather as much information as you can about the types of units and/or beds it possesses and which ones are available for occupancy. Get an idea of the size of the units (i.e., square footage) and the range of fees charged for each. When discussing and gathering fee information, of course, get quotes on all the fees, including entrance fees if required, the refundability of such entrance fees, and any monthly or daily fees. Also, find out whether any up-front deposit other than an entrance fee is required, and whether the deposit is refundable upon leaving the community.

Find out whether fees have increased significantly over the past few years. Request a short history of the rate increases management has approved and passed down to the residents over the past three years. This will give you an indication of how much more it will cost to live there in the coming years. Because your parents are likely on a fixed income, this information will be very important in determining the affordability of certain communities.

It's important to ask what happens if your parents funds are depleted to a level where they can no longer pay the fees required for occupancy. Will they be forced to move out? Is a resident benevolent fund available to help supplement their income? Will your parents be allowed to continue living at the community regardless of their ability to pay the required fees in full?

Most communities perform an extensive review of your parents' financial position to make sure they qualify before allowing them residency. Prospective residents financially qualify if they can comfortably pay the fees required to live at the community for the rest of their lives. Some communities even use sophisticated computer software, which takes into account a prospective resident's remaining life expectancy, to determine the estimated length of stay.

Some communities experiencing occupancy problems become so desperate to get residents in the door that they'll relax the financial requirements and admit people who don't have sufficient resources to live there for an extended period of time. These communities allow the residents to remain in their apartments until their funds are depleted, and then make them move out. It's unfortunate that some communities must resort to such tactics to improve occupancy rates. Management is sometimes put under so much pressure to perform that they forget the difference between right and wrong. Communities using such admission practices are few; however, it's important to be aware of their existence. Make sure your parents review their financial position with their accountant, financial advisor, or CPA eldercare consultant to determine how much they can afford before starting their search.

Services Included in the Base Monthly Fee

Each telephone survey checklist includes a list of services typically provided at each type of senior housing and care community. Be sure to check off all services included in the base monthly fee; also, indicate which services are available for an additional charge, so you can easily compare the rates of competing communities.

The services listed on the various checklists include many of those listed below:

▶ Meals per day – circle one: [one] [two] [three]
▶ Scheduled transportation
▶ Twenty-four-hour security
▶ Emergency response system – circle one: [pull cords] [wireless system]
▶ Wireless wander prevention system
▶ Activities
▶ Maintenance
▶ Housekeeping / linen services – circle frequency: [weekly] [biweekly] [monthly]
▶ Utilities – circle one: [electricity] [gas] [water] [telephone] [cable TV]
▶ Assistance with one ADL*
▶ Assistance with two to three ADLs*
▶ Assistance with three to four ADLs*
▶ Assistance with five or more ADLs*
▶ Medication reminders
▶ Medication supervision
▶ Medication administration
▶ Rehabilitation or therapy services (indicate type)
▶ Other (space is provided to describe)

*ADLs are activities of daily living including bathing, dressing and grooming, transferring, walking, eating, and toileting.

Many communities like to quote their base monthly fee and provide no detail on services requiring additional charges. For example, many assisted living communities charge a base monthly fee for the basic bundle of hospitality and supportive services, typically including three meals a day, scheduled transportation, twenty-four-hour security, emergency response system, various daily activities, maintenance, weekly housekeeping and linen services, all utilities (excluding telephone and cable TV) and assistance with one activity of daily living. Any assistance or services needed beyond these basic services will usually require an additional charge.

Each community has a system to capture the added cost of caring for your parents by charging them additional fees as they come to need more assistance. Many communities charge an additional $12–$22 per day if your parents need assistance with two to three ADLs, $23–$33 per day if they need assistance with four to five ADLs, and $34–$44 per day if they need assistance with six or more.

It's important to list all the services available at the community, including those that require an additional charge. For example, does the community offer rehabilitation and therapy services should your parents need them in the future? If not, how are these needs satisfied?

What's the community's policy regarding residents' medications? Are medication reminders provided? How is medicine storage and record keeping handled? Is there a central storage location or do medicines remain in the possession of the resident? Is the community's professional staff permitted to administer medication to residents, or only to supervise its administration? The answers to these questions will vary from community to community. Be sure to carefully document the response of each community you survey.

If your parents are in the early stages of Alzheimer's disease or any other form of dementia, find out whether the Alzheimer's/dementia care wing or stand-alone community has architectural features specifically designed to help memory-impaired individuals cope with their everyday activities. Refer to Chapter 3, Option 6, "Advantages of an Alzheimer's/Dementia Care Wing or Community," for a detailed discussion of these features, which include circular/continuous hallways with specific patterns, colors, and distinct visual cues, enclosed outdoor patios, even lighting throughout the building or wing, memory-enhancement boxes, extra common area space, and line-of-sight bathrooms, closets, and refrigerators. Ask the person you're surveying to specify which design features the community has; and if they're unable to, you can probably cross them off the list.

People with Alzheimer's disease and other forms of dementia are prone to wandering. Keeping track of your parents is an ongoing safety and security issue at any community. To better manage this, many communities that house Alzheimer's/dementia care residents are implementing wireless wander prevention systems to help keep track of their residents and prevent any harm to them or others due to wandering. If a resident wanders away from a supervised area of the community, the wireless monitoring device worn by the resident alerts the caregivers by sounding an alarm. If your parents are in the early stages of Alzheimer's or suffer some other form of dementia, I recommend choosing a community that offers wireless wander prevention.

Assessing and Monitoring Your Parents' Care and Assistance Needs

Resident Care and Assessment Programs

If your parents are considering a community with a health care component, it's important to learn about its care and assessment program. Ask them how they intend to monitor and document your parents' care and assistance needs. If it's a quality community, they'll assess your parents' care and assistance requirements upon admittance, and, based on the results of that assessment, will develop a customized care plan to meet their needs.

After the initial assessment, residents should be re-assessed periodically thereafter. The interval between assessments depends on how much care the resident is currently receiving. For example, residents in reasonably good health who are living in the independent living apartments of a CCRC are usually re-assessed semi-annually, while assessments at assisted living communities are usually performed quarterly. Assessments may occur more frequently if a resident's care needs are extensive or if the resident has recently experienced a traumatic event (e.g., a fall) requiring emergency medical attention.

The community's medical director is usually the person responsible for assessing your parents' care and assistance needs both upon their admittance and periodically thereafter. The final approval of a resident's care plan usually involves several parties: the community's medical director, the resident, the resident's personal physician and, in some instances, the resident's adult children. This eliminates any argument regarding your parents' customized care plan and any future increase or decrease in their care. It's beneficial for the community to involve everyone in approving the care plan, especially if residents' care needs increase to a level at which the community can no longer care for them and requires them to be transferred out to a higher level of care.

For each community you survey, be sure you understand how a customized care plan is developed and approved. If your parents' personal physician or another outside third party is not involved, the community will have the ability to needlessly increase the amount of care your parents receive, and consequently can increase their rates unnecessarily.

Staffing

Adequate Staffing Levels

For housing options with a health care component, it's extremely important to know the current ratio of residents to direct care staff (all registered nurses, licensed practical nurses, certified nurses' aides, therapists, personal care workers, and resident aides and assistants).

To preserve your parents' independence and dignity, the senior housing and care community needs a sufficient number of direct care staff available to meet their scheduled and unscheduled care and assistance needs. I strongly believe in the direct correlation between quality care and adequate staffing levels; therefore, it's crucial for you to know the community's current ratio of residents to direct care staff. Volunteers may also be included as direct care staff, provided their education and training meet the minimum requirements of staff positions at the community.

Based on my exposure to senior housing and care communities nationwide, for each resident to receive the optimum attention he or she needs and deserves, the ratio for each level of care by shift should be no more than those in the table below. I should emphasize that these are ideal ratios, and point out that no single staffing ratio is appropriate for any given level of care, because each community has its own unique resident population with differing needs and levels of acuity. Thus the ratios in the table below are targets.

It's also important to understand that the majority of communities in the market today are not likely to meet these desired ratios. This is especially so regarding skilled nursing care, for the reasons listed in the "Nursing Care Facility" section of Chapter 3. Until the issue of inadequate direct care staffing levels is addressed by industry leaders and legislators alike, the desired ratios below are targets that I'd want adopted at any senior housing and care community caring for my parents. The closer the community is to these ratios, the better.

Desired Ratios of Residents to Direct Care Staff for Each Level of Care by Shift			
Level of Care	**Morning**	**Evening**	**Night**
	7 a.m. to 3 p.m.	3 p.m. to 11 p.m.	11 p.m. to 7 a.m.
Assisted Living	Maximum of 10 to 1	Maximum of 12 to 1	Maximum of 25 to 1
Alzheimer's/ Dementia Care	Maximum of 5 to 1	A maximum of 5 to 1	Maximum of 10 to 1
Skilled Nursing Care	Maximum of 5 to 1	Maximum of 10 to 1	Maximum of 15 to 1

Even though most communities are unlikely to meet these targets, at least you'll have the ratios of all the communities in your parents' desired area of residence. With this information, you and your parents will be better able to make informed decisions as to which community might best meet their needs. Until government and industry leaders address the problems of long-term care delivery systems, the desired ratios will remain just that—desired.

It's also important to know how many licensed nurses are on duty during each shift at every level of care (i.e., assisted living, Alzheimer's/dementia care, and skilled nursing care). As the acuity or complexity of care increases, outcomes get less predictable, requiring an advanced level of knowledge on-site. A licensed nurse partners with other health care professionals as a member of an inter-reliant team to meet the residents' care needs. The presence of licensed nurses, whether registered or licensed practical nurses, can provide you and your parents a level of comfort, knowing there's an on-site professional who's trained and experienced in handling medical emergencies. Their presence also assures you that the certified nursing aides, personal care workers, or resident assistants are receiving the necessary supervision throughout the day. In order for each person to receive the optimum attention he or she needs and deserves, the ratio of resident to licensed nurses for each level of care by shift should be no more than those in the table below.

Desired Ratios of Residents to Licensed Nurses for Each Level of Care by Shift			
Level of Care	**Morning** 7 a.m. to 3 p.m.	**Evening** 3 p.m. to 11 p.m.	**Night** 11 p.m. to 7 a.m.
Assisted Living	Maximum of 30 to 1	Maximum of 50 to 1	Maximum of 70 to 1
Alzheimer's/ Dementia Care	Maximum of 15 to 1	A maximum of 25 to 1	Maximum of 35 to 1
Skilled Nursing Care	Maximum of 15 to 1	Maximum of 25 to 1	Maximum of 35 to 1

Licensed nurses include all registered nurses (RNs) and licensed practical nurses (LPNs) or licensed vocational nurses (LVNs) as they are called in Texas and California.

It's been my experience that many stand-alone assisted living communities fail to staff a licensed nurse during the night shift; they have a nurse on call in case of emergency instead. In my opinion, there should always be at least one licensed nurse on site throughout the day, including the night shift. If my parents were paying these significant monthly fees to live at one of these communities, I would expect at least one licensed nurse to be there twenty-four-hours a day.

It's worth mentioning that the quantity of people working at a community has nothing to do with the quality of people working there. The direct care staff ratio you gather in a telephone survey is just the initial test of a care and assistance program. During the survey, you'll gather information that'll help you determine whether the direct care staff has the qualifications, education, and training necessary to perform the duties of competent caregivers, covered below under "Staff Recruitment, Qualifications, and Training." To determine firsthand whether the quality of staff is sufficient to meet your parents' needs, you should tour the senior housing and care community. Refer to "Step Four" of this chapter for tips on how to evaluate the quality of the staff at each community you visit.

Volunteer Program

Does the community have a volunteer program? The use of volunteers is a great sign for many reasons. First of all, if a person is a volunteer, you can take comfort in the fact that this person would not be there if they didn't truly care about the residents and genuinely want to help take care of them in any way possible. Secondly, the use of volunteers can help take the pressure off the community's paid professional staff and can expand the amount of services available to its residents. Volunteers also provide the residents with more exposure to human interaction. This increased exposure will help make your parent's transition to a senior housing and care community an easier one to make.

Staff Recruitment, Qualifications, and Training

Recruiting, Screening and Hiring Process

Your parents will want to make sure the people assigned to meet their care and assistance needs are not only professionally qualified but also have the personalities suited to handling their psychological and emotional needs.

What steps does the community take to screen and select its employees? Are background checks performed? Are references checked? In today's world, you can't afford to hire anyone without a proper background check. To be certain that it doesn't hire anyone with a history of criminal activity, it's important that the community verify, from several third-party sources, that each candidate has the responsibility, character, and moral fiber necessary to take on the task of caring for your parents. The importance of checking potential employees' references and conducting thorough background checks can't be overstated.

Most senior housing and care communities conduct background and reference checks and put their candidates through a rigorous interview process that may include an on-the-job exam. This can be best described as a "dress rehearsal" in which, under the direct scrutiny of a supervisor, the prospect actually does the tasks that he or she would be called upon to do as a staff member. This helps the community determine whether candidates have the skills necessary to perform their everyday tasks. During the interview, a quality senior housing and care community looks for candidates who evidence such traits as commitment, empathy, patience, flexibility, and sense of humor. They must also have energy and enthusiasm for their work, but must at the same time be able to project a feeling of calm. Overall, the senior housing and care community is looking for people who genuinely appreciate working with aging adults. This helps ensure that the people hired to take care of your parents are well rounded and fully qualified to help preserve your parents' independence as long as possible.

Training and Continuing Education

Is the professional staff required to complete specific training in caring for seniors? If so, have them specify what types of training. The continuing education of a community's staff is especially important with regard to caring for people with Alzheimer's and other forms of dementia. During the latter stages of these conditions, people can develop speech and behavioral problems that an uneducated staff might interpret as mental abnormalities that can only be handled with medication or restraints. Many documented cases of abuse took place just because the caregivers didn't understand that the resident's condition and needs required specialized care and handling that they weren't trained to deal with.

In Case of Emergency

What happens if my parents need emergency medical care? Is a registered nurse on staff twenty-four-hours a day, seven days a week to handle emergencies?

A registered nurse on staff twenty-four-hours a day would be a huge advantage should a medical emergency occur; however, due to cost constraints, this isn't possible at some senior housing and care communities. These communities can make up for the lack of a round-the-clock nurse by having other systems in place should your parents need emergency medical assistance. For example, do the bedrooms and bathrooms have emergency pull cords? If not, what other emergency response equipment do they have to identify when your parents might need such assistance?

Some communities have incorporated wireless emergency response systems: residents wear wireless communication devices around their necks and can press a button whenever they need emergency assistance. Once activated, these devices send a signal to the nurses' station or front desk, alerting them that a resident needs assistance. Some systems can even identify the resident's precise location. This wireless system is far more effective than emergency pull cords, because the call button is located on the resident's person and not in one specific area of the apartment. What happens if your mom falls down in the bedroom and is unable to get up to pull the emergency cord? Many communities are now switching to this improved technology to eliminate such situations. If the community doesn't have this technology yet, ask them if they're considering switching to it soon.

Furthermore, ask the executive director to explain the specific steps taken by the community when responding to a resident's medical emergency. Has the community made arrangements with a nearby hospital or emergency response unit to facilitate a quick response and transfer of residents needing emergency medical attention?

Questions and Complaints

What if my parents or I have a concern or complaint about the housing and/or care being provided? Is someone in the administrative offices assigned to handle such inquiries? What specific steps must be taken to address and ultimately resolve the problem?

Most senior housing and care communities handle complaints in much the same way; however, it's important to know how each community handles them. If the problem isn't too serious, the family typically discusses it first with the executive director who, based on the findings of an investigation, will offer a solution to resolve the problem. Many problems can be resolved; some can't.

If the problem or complaint is more serious, the family should contact appropriate outside agencies and organizations. If the community or home is licensed or certified, file a complaint with the state survey agency that regulates it. These agencies typically operate within each state's Department of Health. If the community is accredited, file a complaint with the accrediting organization as well.

If the complaint involves theft, fraud, physical or mental abuse, or any other criminal activity, contact your local police department and file a police report.

Long-Term Care Ombudsman Program

To help resolve your complaint you may also use a long-term care ombudsman, who is an advocate for residents of nursing homes, assisted living communities, and other long-term care facilities. These ombudsmen are trained to resolve problems and assist residents with any complaint against a long-term care community. Under the federal Older Americans Act, every state is required to have an ombudsman program to address complaints and advocate for improvements in the long-term care system.

Ombudsmen can help resolve complaints regarding:

▸ A violation of residents' rights or dignity

▸ Physical, verbal or mental abuse, deprivation of services necessary to maintain residents' physical and mental health, or unreasonable confinement

▸ Poor quality of care, including inadequate personal hygiene and slow response to requests for assistance

▸ Improper transfer or discharge of a resident

▸ Inappropriate use of chemical or physical restraints, and

▸ Any resident concern about quality of care or quality of life

While ombudsmen do not have direct authority to require action by a long-term care community, they are responsible for negotiating on a resident's behalf and working with other state agencies for effective enforcement. Nationally, the ombudsman program handles over 264,000 complaints annually and provides information, referrals, and consultations to more than 260,000 people. You may contact the ombudsman program in you area by calling your local or state agency on aging.

You can also contact the National Long-Term Care Ombudsman Program Resource Center (ORC) located in Washington, D.C.: 202-332-2275.

The ORC provides support, technical assistance and training to the 53 state long-term care ombudsman programs and their statewide networks of almost 600 local and regional programs. Funded by the Administration on Aging, the ORC is operated by the National Citizens Coalition for Nursing Home Reform (NCCNHR). They have an informative website: www.ltcombudsman.org, which provides a much more detailed look at the ombudsman program. The site includes an "Ombudsman Locator" that enables you to easily find the ombudsman program nearest you.

Other Pertinent Questions

Special Dietary Needs of Seniors

Does the community have a dietitian on staff to ensure your parents receive not only quality meals, but also meals that are nutritionally balanced? As we grow older, nutrition becomes an ever more important factor in healthy living. A senior's reduced metabolism and decreased physical activity, along with decreased appetite, make it necessary for your parents to obtain the same amount of nutrients from a lower caloric level. Many experts believe that as seniors grow older, poor eating habits and poor nutrition increase their chances of chronic illness.

Fortunately, most senior housing and care communities today hire dietary experts or dietitians who are educated in the area of senior nutrition. Sometimes the dietitian is a full-time employee, but is more commonly a part-time consultant who visits periodically to review the community's meal preparation and to review and approve the menu.

Many senior housing communities dedicate a major portion of their operating budget to the dietary segment of their operations. Many in the industry feel that the best way to residents' hearts and satisfaction is through their stomachs. Well, it doesn't hurt. Many communities promote their dining experience as the "best in town" and direct much of their marketing focus to their culinary excellence. It makes perfect sense: if you were considering moving into such a community, wouldn't one of the more important factors in your decision be the quality of the food and the dining experience?

Should your parents require a special diet, is the community willing and able to prepare meals for them? It's important to know whether the community can accommodate their needs and whether there's any additional charge. Most senior housing and care menus are designed to accommodate most seniors' nutritional needs, but ask the question anyway—it never hurts to ask.

Community Outreach Programs

What type of community outreach programs does the community participate in? Many senior housing and care communities offer their dining and other common areas to the surrounding community for events such as birthday parties, baby showers, high school proms, dances, and other special occasions. Such outreach programs are very helpful and important to the residents as well as to the surrounding communities.

Some of the better community outreach programs are intergenerational, many of them after-school programs for latchkey kids. Most American families today have two wage earners; as a result, the children need supervision after school until their parents arrive home from work. Some senior housing and care communities offer such supervision by participating in after-school latchkey programs, which allows the residents to spend valuable quality time with the children. The kids' ages usually range from six to thirteen. The residents help them with their homework, go for walks, talk, and watch TV, etc. The interaction between the elderly residents and the children benefits everyone. The children energize the residents while recognizing the elders' value and learning the lesson that aging is a natural part of life. Loving bonds are formed, and self-esteem levels increase dramatically for both the seniors and the children. The children's parents also benefit, because it shows them that humane and dignified forms of senior housing and care are being provided right in their own backyard. These programs help teach the children and their parents not to fear these types of senior housing and care communities, that they aren't places where senior go to die, but where seniors go to thrive!

Do the Resident's Have a Voice?

Does the community have a resident council or a resident on the Board of Directors or Trustees? Many communities have resident councils elected by the residents to represent them in discussions with management and/or the Board of Directors of the community. It allows the community's residents to have a voice and be heard regarding any concerns they might have and enables them to continually recommend changes and improve the overall quality of life at the community.

An effective executive director is always a good listener. If he or she actively listens to the concerns of his or her residents and responds to those concerns as best as he or she can, then that's all you can ask. If the community has a resident council, it provides an even better avenue for residents to air their concerns because if they're brought to the attention of the executive director by the resident council, those concerns will likely carry more weight since the council's mission or objective is to voice the concerns of the entire community rather than just one individual. Resident concerns can be as small as empty coffee pots in the dining area to more serious problems such as resident abuse by the community's professional staff.

Philosophy of Care

What's the community's philosophy regarding physical and chemical restraints? I've heard too many horrific tales about nursing care facilities' irresponsible use of physical and chemical restraints to have any tolerance in this matter. Be certain to get a clear, honest answer to this question from the community's executive director or administrator.

The best possible answer to the question is "We do not believe in the use of physical and chemical restraints. Never have, never will." I'd go a step further: have the community put its money where its mouth is and state in the residency agreement that they will not use physical or chemical restraints.

Pets

Does the community allow pets? If your parents are pet owners, this will be an important factor in their decision. Anyone who's bonded with a pet can attest to the benefits of owning pets. Their unconditional love and companionship help us relax, ease our stress and anxiety, and provide us an increased sense of security.

Research has found that seniors who own pets:

- ► Experience lower blood pressure
- ► Take better care of themselves
- ► Experience increased levels of activity
- ► Have an increased sense of security
- ► Experience less depression and loneliness
- ► Experience increased self-esteem, and
- ► Experience increased levels of socialization

The love and affection a pet offers can help seniors adjust to the new living environment in a senior housing and care community. Pets help ease a senior's transition to the new lifestyle by providing a link with the former lifestyle. Further, people love to talk about their pets, so pets help initiate interaction with other residents, allowing residents to form new friendships and relationships faster than they might otherwise.

Some communities participate in visiting pet programs such as "Pets on Wheels" and "Pet Partners." As an alternative to allowing residents to live with their own pet, some keep a community pet; unquestionably, these pets provide much joy to seniors nationwide, but they're not an adequate substitute for the unique relationships people have with their own pets. The importance of pets to seniors has made many communities revise their "no pets allowed" policies.

Marketing Materials

Does the senior housing and care community have marketing materials to send you, describing their services and including the cost of each option? If so, have them mail you and your parents a copy. These materials commonly include floor plans of the various apartments, and might provide additional details of what they have to offer.

Conducting Telephone Surveys of Home Care Providers

The CD contains telephone survey checklists, great tools for calling home care providers. The checklists are designed to help you and your parents gather all the information you'll need to determine whether home care can meet your parents' care and assistance needs.

On the CD, you'll find two different checklists under the following appendices:

- ► Telephone Survey of a Home Care Agency – Appendix G
- ► Telephone Survey of an Independent Home Care Provider – Appendix H

The types of questions you'll ask of home care agencies and independent home care providers are quite different, so we'll examine the contents of both surveys. Read the following sections carefully so you'll understand why each question is so important to your evaluation and final decision.

Should You Hire a Home Care Agency or an Independent Home Care Provider?

When choosing a home care provider it's important to first decide which type you and your parents would prefer contracting with to meet their care and assistance needs. There are two options: you either contract with a home care agency ("Home Care Agency") or hire an independent home care provider ("Independent Home Care Provider"). Each of these two types has clear and distinct advantages and disadvantages, which are discussed in detail below.

The type of home care provider your parents choose is important on many levels and will ultimately depend on their preferences as to convenience, cost, flexibility, control, and whether they're comfortable with handling certain employer duties and responsibilities. To help you and your parents decide, I'll list the advantages each option has over the other, but first, let's refresh your memory regarding the different types of Home Care Agencies and what an Independent Home Care Provider is.

Home Care Agencies

Three main types of Home Care Agencies are available to help your parents, depending on the care and assistance they need. As described under "Home Care Services" in Chapter 3, these are:

- **Home health care agencies** – Home health care agencies provide health care services including skilled nursing care. Some offer the full gamut of home care services, including personal care, homemaker, and companion services. Most, however, limit their services to skilled nursing and one or two other specialties such as rehabilitation and therapy services. Because home health care agencies provide health care services, most states require them to be licensed. Most are Medicare-certified as well, meaning that they meet the minimum federal requirements for quality patient care.

- **Private-duty nursing agencies** – Private-duty agencies can offer the same full spectrum of home care services offered by home health care agencies, including skilled nursing care, personal care, homemaker, and companion services. The primary difference between the two types is that home health care agencies are Medicare-certified, while private-duty agencies are not. Because home health care agencies are Medicare-certified, their services must be provided intermittently over short periods, while private-duty nursing agencies usually provide home care services over longer periods.

+ **Homemaker and home care aide agencies** – These agencies can offer their customers homemaker, companion, and personal care services. Some states require homemaker and home care aide agencies to be licensed and meet the minimum operating standards established by the state.

Independent Home Care Providers

Independent Home Care Providers are caregivers such as nurses, therapists, home health aides, homemaker, and companion workers hired directly by those requiring care or assistance (i.e., your parents). Independent Home Care Providers may also be hired through registries, which are employment agencies that match independent providers with customers.

Advantages of Home Care Agencies over Independent Home Care Providers

▸ **Convenience** – Home Care Agencies have a good number of qualified staff available to meet the needs of their many clients, and, because of this, it's much easier and more convenient to find qualified help on short notice. If your parents choose to hire an Independent Home Care Provider, it's naturally going to take more time and effort to recruit, interview, check references, and conduct background checks of potential caregiver candidates. Additionally, Home Care Agencies have the resources available to send out another nurse or home care worker if your parent's regular nurse or home care worker can't be there due to illness, emergency leave, or vacation. This would naturally be more problematic if your parents hired an Independent Home Care Provider.

▶ **Home Care Agencies assume full liability for all care** – Because the nurses and other home care workers are the agency's employees, the agency assumes full liability for all care and assistance provided to your parents.

▶ **Your parents won't have to assume any employer responsibilities** – Home Care Agencies handle all responsibilities and duties associated with being an employer, including:

  ✓ **Recruiting, interviewing, and conducting the necessary due diligence for each prospective employee** – The agencies, not you and your parents, are responsible for performing the due diligence required when hiring their employees. Each candidate's credentials and background are carefully checked and their references verified. Home Care Agencies are responsible for hiring the most qualified candidates, who not only have the educational and professional credentials but also the personalities necessary for handling your parents' psychological and emotional needs. Most agencies are adept at evaluating which candidates have the skills necessary to succeed in the profession; you and your parents likely do not. Their discriminating hiring practices will, in most cases, assure that the people assigned to care for your parents are well-rounded professionals capable of providing the desired quality of care.

  ✓ **Ongoing supervision and periodic evaluation** – Most Home Care Agencies employ registered nurses who continually supervise of all the home care staff assigned to your parents. As employers, most Home Care Agencies conduct regular employee evaluations, tracking their performance and making recommendations for improvement. Additionally, the supervisor, usually an RN, will periodically visit your parent's home to evaluate and adjust their care plan as needed. This would not be available should your parents hire an Independent Home Care Provider. As part of their array of services, many agencies now offer a "daily check":

the agency's administrative staff will phone your parents' place of residence daily, including holidays, weekends, and nights, to insure that their home care worker is on time and performing the assigned tasks according to your parents' care plan.

✓ **Continuing education and training** – Most agencies insist that employees meet their ongoing education and training requirements. Continuing education and training is vital for caregivers to remain on the cutting edge of care and assistance methods. Most agencies will pay the cost of their employees' education programs.

✓ **No additional employer responsibilities** – If your parents hire a home care worker through an agency, you and your parents won't be burdened with the additional paperwork and responsibility of complying with all state and federal labor, health, and safety regulations, which include employee withholdings and payment of payroll and social security taxes.

Advantages of Independent Home Care Providers over Home Care Agencies

▸ **Lower overall cost** – The overall cost of obtaining home care services through an Independent Home Care Provider is typically going to be lower than Home Care Agencies due to the lack of administrative overhead and more flexibility with how and when services are provided.

▸ **More flexibility** – Most Home Care Agencies charge a minimum of four hours per visit regardless of how long it actually takes the home care worker to provide the contracted services. Independent Home Care Providers typically do not charge a minimum number of hours per visit and, depending on the visit, can be used for just a couple hours per visit or may split a four-hour shift into a morning and evening shift. At a Home Care Agency, there also may be limitations with regard to the type of services each home care worker is permitted to provide. For example, if your parents need both home-maker and personal care services, the agency may have to send two different types of workers to handle the different tasks depending on the individual situation. Remember, if an agency has to send out two workers to handle your parents different home care needs, they'll likely have a four-hour minimum charge for each worker. This is yet another example where less flexibility results in more cost.

► **Total control over choosing the perfect home care provider** – By hiring an Independent Home Care Provider, your parents retain full control of whom they'll choose. Being able to hire the most qualified person, whose personality is the perfect fit for your parents according to their own best judgment, is a big advantage over contracting with a Home Care Agency. Although agencies are good at finding and screening qualified candidates with the personality necessary for handling all the needs of aging adults, they still might not be able to provide the perfect person. With some agencies, your parents might be allowed to choose only the type of home care worker, but not the individual who'll provide the services. Still, your parents have the right to request the assignment of another worker should they not get along with the one the agency assigns, but they might find such a "trial and error" process frustrating and stressful.

Conducting Telephone Surveys of Home Care Agencies

The "Checklist to Conduct a Telephone Survey of a Home Care Agency" (Appendix G on the CD) is designed to help you and your parents get all the information you need to determine whether a Home Care Agency can meet their care and assistance needs.

Type of Home Care Agency

Which of the three types will best meet your parents' needs?

- ▸ **Home health care agency**
- ▸ **Private-duty nursing agency, or**
- ▸ **Homemaker and home aide agency**

Be sure to indicate which type of agency you're surveying. For contacting an Independent Home Care Provider, use the "Checklist for a Telephone Survey of an Independent Home Care Provider" (Appendix H on the CD).

Ownership/Sponsorship

Is the agency privately or publicly owned? Is it a for-profit or not-for-profit organization? Knowing the type of organization you're contracting with gives you an indication of where the organization's focus really is.

Is the Home Care Agency Privately or Publicly Owned?

Whether an agency is privately or publicly owned is good question, because there are potential advantages and disadvantages to each type of ownership. If the organization is publicly owned (traded on the New York Stock Exchange, NASDAQ, or the American Stock Exchange), then the company's shareholders expect a certain return on their investment. If a publicly traded organization fails to meet shareholders' expectations, the company's stock price may suffer, making it harder and more costly for the organization to obtain additional capital for the agency's future needs.

A privately owned Home Care Agency doesn't operate under the scrutiny of shareholders; its operating decisions might therefore be more responsive to the expectations of its customers, rather than to shareholders' expectations of return on investment.

Does this mean you should never consider a Home Care Agency owned by a public company? The answer is an emphatic no. Public ownership has its advantages. Provided the company is in good financial health, public companies have better access to capital to meet their customers' current and future needs. Public companies can also enter into purchasing contracts with national or regional suppliers, thereby lowering overall costs by purchasing at higher volume. By doing so, the publicly held company can often provide its services at a lower cost than its private counterparts.

Is the Home Care Agency a For-Profit or Not-for-Profit Organization?

The differences between for-profit and not-for-profit organizations and how they operate their businesses have become less and less distinct over the years; for-profit and not-for-profit organizations are now far more alike than they are different, primarily because each is fiercely competing for the same customer. This greatly benefits the consumer because it forces Home Care Agencies to offer the optimum amount of services for the lowest price.

Operating Experience

Does the provider have experience operating a Home Care Agency? If the agency has been serving the area for any length of time, it will have developed a track record, which others whom the agency has served can verify. The fact they've been in the business for any considerable length of time is a good sign; nonetheless you should take further steps to confirm the quality of care the agency provides. The telephone survey is one step in the five-step process to selecting the best Home Care Agency. You'll need to complete all five steps to fully evaluate an agency.

If the agency makes your parents' short list, ask the director for a list of references including physicians, hospital social workers, discharge planners, current and former clients (including family members), and any other references they'll offer. Follow up with these references to determine if the agency has a reputation for providing quality home care services. For more on how to check references, refer to "Step Five: Final Evaluation and Decision."

Licensing, Certification, Accreditation, and Membership

Is the Home Care Agency licensed by the state? Whether agencies are required to be licensed depends on the state your parents live in. Most states require licensing of home health care agencies because they provide health care services and are usually certified to participate in the either the federally administered Medicare program or the state-administered Medicaid program.

Most states don't require private-duty agencies or homemaker and home care aide agencies to be licensed or meet specific regulatory requirements. Because most home health care agencies are Medicare-certified, their services must be provided intermittently over short periods, while private-duty agencies can provide home care services over longer periods. Remember, Medicare does not cover long-term care, so if your parents need home care services over an extended period, they'll most likely contract with a private-duty nursing agency or, if they don't need health care services, a homemaker or home care aide agency.

Licensed agencies are required to meet the minimum operating standards established by state regulators. Licensed agencies are surveyed (inspected) annually to determine whether they meet the minimum standards in the state regulations. Health professionals from state survey agencies, typically in the Department of Health, conduct these surveys. Each state sets its own regulations regarding how much home care and assistance can be provided, and its own standards for quality of care. Operators' licenses are issued or renewed based on the surveys. Sanctions and remedies are imposed when operators fail to comply with state regulations.

Is the Home Care Agency Certified?

Most home health care agencies are certified to participate in the Medicare and Medicaid programs. Federal laws govern this certification. Annual surveys are conducted to verify that services are being provided in compliance with Medicare or Medicaid standards. State survey agencies conduct these annual surveys and cite home health care agencies that fail to meet federal guidelines.

Is the Home Care Agency Accredited?

Home Care Agencies can also get voluntary accreditation from a nationally recognized accrediting organization. Home care providers get accreditation by meeting specific standards of quality and excellence set by the accrediting body. Accreditation is different from licensing and certification in that the process in voluntary. A Home Care Agency attempting to get voluntary accreditation tells me they're committed to providing their clients with the highest possible quality of life by continuously trying to improve the quality of care they provide, and is willing to consistently prove it by meeting or exceeding the performance standards set by the accrediting body.

You'll need to become familiar with these nationally recognized accrediting organizations of home health care providers:

▶ **The Joint Commission on the Accreditation of Health Care Organizations (The Joint Commission)** – Founded in 1951, The Joint Commission (www.jointcommission.org), the nation's largest health care accrediting body, is an independent, not-for-profit organization whose mission is to improve the quality of health care for the public by providing accreditation and related services that support performance improvement in health care organizations. The Joint Commission evaluates and accredits more than 15,000 health care organizations in the United States, including home health care agencies, hospice care, and skilled nursing facilities. The Joint Commission surveys (inspects) its accredited organizations every three years.

> **If a Home Care Agency makes your parents' short list, you can access a directory of all Joint Commission-accredited organizations, and performance reports from their most recent evaluations, at The Joint Commission's website: www.qualitycheck.org.**

Their online Quality Check™ lets you access an agency's latest Quality Report and see how they rate compared to similar accredited agencies. If a Home Care Agency is not in full compliance with the applicable standards, the requirements for improvement will be listed in the Quality Report as well as the summary page on Quality Check™.

It should be noted that Quality Check™ is a comprehensive directory that lists nearly all Home Care Agencies available today, both accredited and non-accredited. The Joint Commission added non-accredited facilities in order to provide a more complete inventory of Home Care Agencies for its users. Home Care Agencies that are accredited by The Joint Commission will display a large Gold Seal of Approval™ under the Accreditation/Certification column on the website.

> If you don't have Internet access, you can request a specific Home Care Agency's Quality Report by phoning The Joint Commission's customer service department in Washington, D.C.:
> 630-792-5800.

▸ **Community Health Accreditation Program (CHAP)** – An independent, not-for-profit accrediting body formed in 1965, CHAP (www.chapinc.org) was the first home care accrediting body in the nation to be granted "deemed status" by the CMS (Centers for Medicare and Medicaid Services), for home health in 1992 and for hospice in 1999. To achieve deemed status, an accrediting organization must meet or exceed the Medicare standards set by CMS.

▸ **Accreditation Commission for Healthcare, Inc. (ACHC)** – An independent, private, not-for-profit corporation established in 1986, ACHC (www.achc.org) offers an accreditation program developed by providers for providers, with written, user-friendly standards and interpretations. Nationwide, ACHC accredits over 500 organizations doing business as home health care agencies, home infusion companies, home aide agencies, home medical equipment suppliers, specialty pharmacies, hospices, and companies that specialize in services and products for breast surgery patients.

Is the Home Care Provider a Member of a Trade Association?

Like voluntary accreditation, membership in a trade association tells me management cares about the type and quality of care they provide their clients, and are continually trying to stay abreast of new developments that might help them to improve quality and efficiency. Members of trade associations commonly share information and care techniques at least annually at conferences that take place across the country. These include education sessions that members attend daily.

Here are some of the more prominent national trade associations serving the needs of the home health care industry:

▸ **National Association for Home Care and Hospice (NAHC)** – NAHC (www.nahc.org) is the nation's largest trade association representing the interests of home health care agencies, hospices, home care aide organizations, and other home care providers. Its members are primarily corporations and other organizations, including state home care associations, medical equipment suppliers, and schools. NAHC is dedicated to the proposition that Americans should receive the health care and social services they need in their own homes in so far as is possible.

▸ **American Association for Home Care (AAHomecare)** – AAHomecare (www.aahomecare.org) is dedicated to working to advance the value and practice of quality health care services at home. AAHomecare's membership includes home care providers of all kinds—not-for-profit, proprietary, facility-based, freestanding, and government owned—regardless of the nature of the home care services they provide. Members provide home health services, home medical equipment and supplies, home infusion therapy, and rehabilitation technology services to consumers in their homes. With 3,000 members, AAHomecare is dedicated to advancing the value and practice of quality health care services at home, while building a community of support for the home care industry.

▸ **American Association of Homes and Services for the Aging (AAHSA)** – AAHSA (www.aahsa.org) is the association for the nation's not-for-profit long-term care and senior housing providers. Its members include over 5,000 nursing homes, assisted living communities, Continuing Care Retirement Communities, senior housing, and home and community-based service organizations, more than half of which are religiously sponsored. The mission of all its members is to serve older people by providing the means for them to live with the greatest possible level of self-determination, dignity, and independence.

Types of Home Care Services Offered

The "Checklist to Conduct a Telephone Survey of a Home Care Agency" provides an extensive list of available home care services so you and your parents can easily check off all the services each home care agency offers. The types of home care services are divided into the following categories:

Homemaker / Companion Type Services – These are home-based supervision and monitoring activities that help your parents maintain a safe environment when they can no longer do so alone. The services can include some or all of the following:

- Meal planning and preparation
- Washing dishes
- Monitoring diet
- Preparing grocery list
- Light housekeeping
- Changing linens
- Laundry
- Taking out the garbage
- Assisting with care of house plants
- Assistance with pet care
- Supervising and coordinating home maintenance and lawn care
- Assistance with errands
- Shopping
- Sorting and/or reading mail
- Reading books, newspaper or other
- Letter writing
- Mailing bills and letters
- Taking phone calls
- Answering the door
- Supervising and maintaining medication schedule
- Arranging appointments
- Appointment reminders
- Escorting to doctors' appointments, church services, entertainment, and other activities
- Light assistance with walking, bathing and grooming, as well as
- Providing friendly conversation and companionship

Custodial/Personal Care Services – Custodial or personal care services include assistance with activities of daily living which might include some or all of the following:

- ▸ Assistance with transferring (e.g., getting in and out of bed)
- ▸ Assistance with walking
- ▸ Assistance with bathing
- ▸ Assistance with dressing
- ▸ Assistance with eating, and
- ▸ Assistance with toileting

Skilled Nursing Care Services – Skilled nursing care services provided in the home can include, but are not limited to, such services as:

- ▸ Monitoring and administering of medications (e.g., injections)
- ▸ Intravenous therapy
- ▸ Catheter care
- ▸ Ventilator care
- ▸ Wound care (changing of dressings), and
- ▸ Pain management

Rehabilitation and Therapy Services – People recuperating from a debilitating injury, surgery, or stroke need rehabilitation and therapy services, which are described in detail in the "Home Care" section of Chapter 3; these include but are not limited to:

- ▸ Physical therapy
- ▸ Speech therapy, and
- ▸ Occupational therapy

Other Home Care Services -

▸ **Medical social services** – Licensed medical social workers typically provide short-term counseling services to help seniors and their immediate family deal with the physical, emotional, and financial difficulties that may slow the individual's rate of recovery or interfere with his or her ability or willingness to follow the care plan.

▸ **Nutrition services** – Space is provided on the telephone survey to list any and all other services offered by the home care provider. Such services might include nutrition services; the agency may have a nutritionist on staff to assist and counsel seniors and immediate family members by creating a special or restricted diet based on clients' needs.

Does the Home Care Agency offer live-in or twenty-four-hour home care?

Many Home Care Agencies offer live-in or twenty-four-hour companion, custodial, or skilled nursing services that provide your parents round-the-clock supervision. Be sure to ask what types of services the live-in home care worker can and cannot provide.

Are there services the Home Care Agency cannot provide?

There may be certain services that an agency or a particular type of home care worker is not permitted to perform. Be sure to document these services in the space provided on the survey. If a home care worker is not permitted to perform a service, additional charges could result because the agency may have to send another type of worker to your parents' home to perform the needed task.

In Case of Emergency

What procedures does the Home Care Agency have in place should your parents experience a medical emergency in their residence? Is a registered nurse on call to meet their needs twenty-four-hours a day, seven days a week? Does the agency offer a wireless emergency response system to help monitor your parents should they need emergency medical assistance?

Some emergency response systems feature a wireless communication device worn around the neck; the wearer can simply press it when in need of emergency assistance. Once activated, it sends a signal to the home care agency's administrative offices or the local emergency response team, notifying them the person needs emergency medical assistance. An emergency response vehicle is then dispatched immediately to the home to investigate the situation. Most home care providers are now offering this service for an additional charge. In most situations, you and your parents would contract directly with the company offering the emergency response service. Thus your parents will not be billed by the Home Care Agency but by the company providing the service. If your parents can't afford to pay for this service, if the home care agency is supported by a foundation or has a benevolent fund, it may help to cover this cost.

Rates Charged for Home Care Services

For each Home Care Agency you survey, gather as much information as you can about the hourly rates for each type of home care worker. The type of worker assigned, whether a registered nurse, homemaker, or physical therapist, depends on the amount and type of care and/or assistance your parents need. Most agencies will provide your parents a written estimate of the total charges, based on a registered nurse's initial assessment of your parents' care needs.

The telephone survey provides space to record the hourly rates for services provided by the following home care personnel:

- ▸ Registered Nurse (RN)
- ▸ Licensed Practical Nurse (LPN)
- ▸ Certified Nurses Assistant (CNA)
- ▸ Home Health Aide (HHA)
- ▸ Homemaker
- ▸ Companion
- ▸ Live-in
- ▸ Medical Social Worker
- ▸ Nutritionist/Dietitian
- ▸ Physical Therapist
- ▸ Occupational Therapist, and
- ▸ Speech Therapist

Columns are provided for writing the hourly rates for weekdays, nights, and weekends. Naturally, the rates for a live-in will be daily, not hourly, rates.

It's important to find out if the agency has a minimum charge per visit. Many require a minimum number of hours charged for each visit, regardless of how much time is actually spent at the client's home.

The person answering your survey questions can probably tell you what type of home care worker will be assigned to your parents, based on your description of their current physical and mental status. It's a good idea to get fee information for all personnel anyway, in case this individual's assessment is inaccurate.

Be sure to get a list of items or services that might require additional charges. Hidden charges might include overtime, taxes, and emergency response system, etc.

If your parents' income and resources are limited, find out if any types of public or private financial assistance are available to help cover the cost of their care. Medicare will help pay for a very limited amount of home care services. It will partially cover the cost of skilled nursing care and therapy services provided in the home for the initial two to three weeks, but after that, your parents will be on their own. Medicare will cover only the cost of home care that is intermittent (short-term). Medicare will not cover the cost of home care services providing custodial/personal care or homemaker/companion services.

Your parents may be eligible for assistance through the Medicaid program for a specific period of time. Jointly funded by federal and state governments, Medicaid provides financial assistance to people with lower incomes and limited resources. The administration of the Medicaid program is handled at the state level. Therefore, the specific eligibility requirements as well as the actual dollar amount of assistance and length of time a person may receive it vary from state to state. Any Home Care Agency you're surveying should be familiar with the regulations in the state its home care offices are located in, and should be able to provide you information on whether and for how long your parents would qualify for assistance.

If an agency is unable to offer you any helpful information, contact your state's Medicaid agency or Department of Health and Human Services for information on the requirements for participation in this program. To better serve their citizens' long-term care needs, many states have, over the past several years, expanded their coverage of home care services through the Medicaid program in an effort to emphasize community-based care, as opposed to placing people in nursing homes. Many have revamped their Medicaid programs to not only provide reimbursement for skilled nursing services in the home, but also for custodial or personal care services. To receive reimbursement under this program, you parents must select a Medicaid-certified Home Care Agency. These agencies are required to meet federal standards for cost and quality of care.

Home care can be expensive; many state leaders are now realizing, however, that in some instances it can be a lower-cost alternative to hospitalization and institutional care. Funds available through the Medicaid program are limited; therefore, states that have expanded the number of home care services covered by Medicaid can provide these services only to a pre-approved number of people, which caps the financial exposure on each participating state's budget.

Other public or private programs may be available in your parents' area to help provide them some level of financial assistance. The Home Care Agency you're surveying should be aware of any such programs.

As with many not-for-profit senior housing and care communities, some not-for-profit home care agencies have created benevolent funds to help lower-income people receive the care they need. To receive assistance from the benevolent funds, a person must first prove that one has exhausted all other options and truly needs the care and assistance. Many agencies raise funds from individuals and businesses alike, and receive appropriations from towns and cities to help provide specific services to resident taxpayers.

Assessing and Monitoring Your Parent's Care and Assistance Needs

Patient Care and Assessment Program

If your parents need health care or personal care services, be sure to ask the Home Care Agency about its care and assessment program and how they intend to monitor and document your parents' care and assistance needs.

Most agencies offer a free in-home assessment of your parents' care and assistance needs. They'll typically send out a registered nurse who'll meet

with you and your parents to evaluate their home environment, health status, and other factors. Based on this meeting, the RN will develop a care plan tailored to meeting your parents' specific needs; attached to the plan will be an estimate of the cost to provide these services. When an agency is developing a care plan for your parents, they, their personal physician, you, and any other interested family members should be involved, which will make it much easier for your parents to accept.

After their initial assessment, clients are continually re-assessed periodically thereafter. Assessments will occur more frequently if a person's care needs are extensive or if the person recently experienced a traumatic event—a fall, for example—requiring emergency medical attention.

Staff Recruitment, Qualifications, and Training

Recruiting, screening, and hiring process – You and your parents must make sure that anyone assigned to meet their care and assistance needs is not only professionally qualified, but also has a personality suited to handling their psychological and emotional needs.

In addition to checking their candidates' backgrounds and references, many Home Care Agencies require them to pass a written exam and a rigorous interview process that may include an on-the-job clinical exam. In essence, this is a "dress rehearsal" in which the prospect performs the tasks he or she would be called upon to perform under the scrutiny of a supervisor (usually an RN). This helps the agency determine whether the candidate has the skills necessary to perform these tasks. During the interview process, prudent agencies will look for candidates with qualities such as commitment, empathy, patience, flexibility, and a sense of humor. They must have energy and enthusiasm for their work, but must, at the same time, be able to project calmness. Overall, the agency wants people with a genuine appreciation for working with aging adults. This process helps insure the people hired to care for your parents are well rounded and fully qualified to help preserve your parents' independence for as long as possible.

Training and Continuing Education

Is the Home Care Agency's professional staff well trained in caring for seniors? Continuing education for an agency's staff is especially important in handling and caring for our aging population. If the agency is licensed or certified, its employees must complete specific continuing education requirements established by state or federal regulations. In addition, many agencies establish their own professional development requirements, which each employee must complete periodically. Such in-house programs help assure that employees at every level are current on all new home care procedures, treatments, equipment, and resources.

Staff Supervision

Is the home care worker assigned to my parents supervised and periodically evaluated? If so, who is responsible for supervising the home care services and what are his or her qualifications? How often will the supervisor visit my parents' residence?

Most Home Care Agencies assign a qualified supervisor to all their home care workers to monitor the quality of care their clients receive, which helps ensure the consistency, quality, and appropriateness of your parents' care. The supervisor, usually an RN, will periodically visit to evaluate your parents and adjust their care plan if needed. If the agency you're surveying doesn't do this, cross it off your list.

Many agencies have added a daily check to their repertoire of services: a member of the administrative staff phones your parents every day, including holidays, weekends, and nights, to insure that their home care worker is on time and performing all assigned tasks according to your parents' care plan.

Staffing Issues

What happens if the home care worker assigned to my parents is ill or on vacation? How will a suitable replacement be assigned to temporarily handle their care and assistance needs? What happens when my parents' regular caregiver leaves the agency and a new one must be assigned to handle the responsibility of their needs?

In both situations, most agencies send a supervisor to your parents' home to introduce each new caregiver, assuring a smooth transition and making sure everyone is comfortable with the change. The supervisor will familiarize the replacement worker with all the duties and responsibilities in your parents' customized care plan.

Employee Bonding and Professional Liability Insurance

Are Home Care Agency employees bonded and insured? In a perfect world, employee theft would never happen, but in this world it does, so bonding of employees entering your parents' residence is important. Bonding is a type of insurance; the agency pays a fixed annual premium, and if an employee is found guilty of any wrongdoing, the patient is reimbursed from the bond. Most agencies bond their employees.

Do all licensed professional staff (i.e., RNs) carry malpractice insurance? Professional liability insurance, which includes malpractice insurance, protects the agency from any claims made by their patients alleging negligence in the rendering of, or the failure to render professional services. Most reputable Home Care Agencies will carry professional liability insurance to protect them from the possibility of one of their nurses committing a negligent act.

Home Care Agencies that carry professional liability insurance and bond their employees will allow you and your parents to receive adequate financial retribution should any negligent acts be committed by the agency.

Questions and Complaints

What if my parents or I have a concern or complaint about the services they receive? Is someone at the agency's administrative office assigned to address such inquiries? If there's a problem or complaint, what specific steps must be taken to resolve it?

Most Home Care Agencies handle complaints in much the same way, but it's important to know how each agency handles them. If the problem isn't too serious, the family will usually first discuss it directly with the home care worker. If the problem or complaint is more serious, the family should notify the supervising RN, who will follow up with the worker and, based on the findings of an investigation, offer a solution to the problem.

Most problems can be resolved (for example, there's a personality conflict and a replacement worker is assigned); others cannot. If the problem is serious and can't be resolved to your satisfaction, you should contact other appropriate outside agencies and organizations. If the Home Care Agency is licensed or certified, file a complaint with the state survey agency that regulates the home care industry in your state—usually the state's Department of Health. If the agency is accredited, you should also file a complaint with the accrediting organization.

If your complaint involves theft, fraud, physical or mental abuse, or any other criminal activity, contact your local police department and file a police report.

Marketing Materials

Does the agency have marketing materials they could send describing their services including the respective cost of each option? If so, have them mail you and your parents a copy.

Conducting Telephone Surveys of Independent Home Care Providers

The "Checklist to Conduct a Telephone Survey of Independent Home Care Providers" (Appendix H on the CD) is designed to help you and your parents gather all the information you'll need to determine whether an Independent Home Care Provider can meet your parents' care and assistance needs.

Time Commitment

Before calling to survey an Independent Home Care Provider, it's important to precisely define your parents' care and assistance needs, in essence creating a job description detailing the home care worker's responsibilities and duties, including the number of hours required daily and/or weekly. This will allow you to easily prescreen your applicants by telephone, ascertaining whether they have the necessary qualifications and experience and whether they can commit the necessary time.

Decide how many hours of care and assistance your parents will require each day, and the specific time of day when the caregiver will be needed. It might be in the mornings, to help your parents with bathing or dressing; at midday, to help with homemaker tasks; or evenings, to help prepare and serve dinner. Each person's needs are unique, and must therefore be defined and understood before interviewing prospective caregivers. Remember to consider your parents' future care and assistance needs, so that a change in personnel won't be necessary shortly after employing the desired home care provider. Any change in your parents' routine will be a mental and emotional challenge. Trying to determine your parents' current and future care and assistance needs can be confusing and overwhelming, so get the help of a professional such as your parents' personal physician and/or a geriatric care manager.

How many hours per day can you commit to caring for my aging parents? Might other obligations affect the amount of time you can spend with them? When surveying prospective caregivers, ask the candidates how many hours they can commit to assisting and caring for your parent each day of the week including the time of day. It's also important to find out what other obligations the candidates have in their life that might affect the potential time spent with your parents. For example, the candidate may have a second job or they may be a part-time student trying to obtain their degree. This is important when considering whether a candidate is able to commit enough time to your parents.

Qualifications and Experience

What experience do you have in providing home care services in this community? The telephone survey is designed to identify what types of home care services a candidate is willing and qualified to perform, and to ascertain their level of experience (none, moderate, or extensive) at performing these tasks for aging adults. The checklist provides you a wide-ranging list of services that your parents might or might not need. As with the "Checklist to Conduct a Telephone Survey of a Home Care Agency," this checklist divides the types of home care services into the following categories:

Homemaker / Companion Services – These are home-based supervision and monitoring activities that help your parents maintain a safe environment when they can no longer do so alone. The services might include some or all of the following:

- Meal planning and preparation
- Washing dishes
- Monitoring diet
- Preparing grocery list
- Light housekeeping
- Changing linens
- Laundry
- Taking out the garbage
- Assistance with care of house plants
- Assistance with pet care
- Supervising and coordinating home maintenance and lawn care
- Assistance with errands
- Shopping
- Sorting and/or reading mail

- Reading books, newspapers, other
- Letter writing
- Mailing bills and letters
- Taking phone calls
- Answering the door
- Supervising and maintaining medication schedule
- Arranging appointments
- Appointment reminders
- Escorting to doctors' appointments, church services, entertainment, and other activities
- Light assistance with walking, bathing, and grooming, as well as
- Providing conversation and companionship

Custodial / Personal Care Services – These services entail assistance with activities of daily living, which might include some or all of the following:

- Assistance with transferring (e.g., getting in and out of bed)
- Assistance with walking
- Assistance with bathing
- Assistance with dressing
- Assistance with eating, and
- Assistance with toileting

Skilled Nursing Care Services – These services may include:

- Monitoring and administering of medications (e.g., injections)
- Intravenous therapy
- Catheter care
- Ventilator care
- Wound care (e.g., changing of dressings), and
- Pain management

Rehabilitation and Therapy Services – People recuperating from a debilitating injury, surgery, or stroke need rehabilitation and therapy services, which include but are not limited to:

- Physical therapy
- Speech therapy, and
- Occupational therapy

These are described in detail in the "Home Care" section of Chapter 3.

The telephone survey checklist also provides space for listing all other home care services offered by the Independent Home Care Provider.

Are you open to the idea of twenty-four-hour live-in care? You and your parents might be interested in hiring someone to provide round-the-clock supervision. If so, ask the candidate if he or she would consider moving in with your parents if acceptable provisions for room and board were available. A candidate who's interested in live-in care could save you and your parents' considerable costs, as the provision for room and board would partially offset the daily rates charged by the caregiver for their services.

Before you consider hiring a live-in caregiver, ask yourself the following questions to determine whether your parents can provide adequate accommodations:

► Does my parents' home or place of residence have a spare bedroom or other suitable accommodations for the caregiver (e.g., a mother-in-law suite)?

► Is the room furnished?

► Is there adequate closet space?

► Will the caregiver have a private bathroom or must he or she share one?

► Will the caregiver have adequate privacy?

► Will the caregiver have a separate phone line?

► What kitchen/food privileges will the caregiver have?

Ultimately, the caregiver decides whether the accommodations are adequate. For this type of arrangement to succeed, the caregiver's privacy must be respected. Also, expectations should be clearly established regarding working hours, food, telephone, and visitors. Caregivers should not be expected to be "on-the-clock" twenty-four-hours a day; they should be given adequate time off during the day for their personal needs. In some cases, live-ins have very flexible hours; they'll work a morning and evening shift each day and have the rest of the day to do whatever they please. In this type of arrangement, the live-in may have a second job or attend school during off hours; each case will be unique, depending on your parents' care and assistance needs.

To determine the fair market value of room and board, you'll need to research the market rate for room rentals in your parents' area, and include a month's assessment for food. You would then deduct this amount from the caregiver's monthly salary.

Sharing a home with a caregiver will take some getting used to, but this type of arrangement has worked out very well for many aging adults. Both parties stand to gain something of considerable value: your parents get home care services with round-the-clock supervision at a considerable cost savings, while the caregiver gets a place to live and a respectable paycheck.

Are there services you can't or won't provide? Perhaps the candidate despises light housekeeping or might feel uncomfortable reading the newspaper to your parents. Be sure to document any services that he or she won't perform in the space provided on the survey.

Do you have any health or physical limitations that would prevent you from meeting the physical demands of my parents? The answer will depend on your parents' current care and assistance needs. If they need help getting in and out of the car, tub, or bed, the candidate needs to be physically capable of lifting and transferring them from place to place. Is the candidate able to do this?

Providing Transportation for Your Parents

Does the candidate own a car and have a current driver's license and car insurance? Is he or she willing and able to provide transportation and escort your parents to appointments and/or functions? Would the candidate be willing and able to drive your parents' car if required?

One of the most common worries adult children have is their parents' impaired driving ability. Hiring a home care worker who can provide transportation would be a major benefit. The answers to the questions above will determine whether the candidate can provide this service. If you've agreed to let the caregiver use your parents' car (rather than his or her own) to meet their transportation needs, make sure the candidate is comfortable driving that type of car, which, for one reason or another, the candidate might have difficulty driving.

Education, Training, and Licensing

What training and education have you completed to help meet my aging parent' needs? Caregivers need to learn many specialized skills before they're truly ready to deal with the everyday needs of an aging adult. Document all of the training programs the candidate completes each year.

Are you trained in lifting and/or transferring seniors from place to place?
Depending on how ambulatory (able to move about) your parents are, they might at some point need assistance with transferring. Lifting and transferring an aging adult into a bed, an automobile, or a tub without injury to client or caregiver isn't easy; it's an acquired skill. If your parents need help with transferring, make sure the candidate has completed some training in how to lift and/or transfer an aging adult from place to place.

Are you trained to handle people with Alzheimer's or other forms of dementia? As our parents grow older, they might have or might develop cognitive impairments such as Alzheimer's or other forms of dementia. It's important to know whether the candidate has completed any specific training in handling and caring for people suffering such impairments. Have the candidate specify what types of training. Every person in the business of caring for our aging population should complete some formal training in handling people with Alzheimer's and other forms of dementia. The caregiver needs to understand the person's mental condition and how to react to it; otherwise, he or she might misinterpret certain behaviors as violent or abusive, which could result in the caregiver's quitting or even reacting with mentally or physically abusive behavior.

Are you a licensed nurse? Should your parents need skilled nursing care or assistance with certain activities of daily living, they'll most likely require the services of a licensed nurse such as an RN or LPN. Like most licensed professionals, licensed nurses are required to complete a minimum amount of continuing education or training each year. Ask the candidate to describe the specific types of training he or she must complete annually, including the number of hours.

Assessing and Monitoring Your Parents' Care Needs

Precisely how will you assess and monitor my parents care needs? If your parents' care needs require the services of a licensed nurse, ask the candidate how he or she will monitor and document their care and assistance needs. RNs are capable of such assessments, evaluating your parents' home environment, health status, and other factors. Based on this evaluation, the RN will develop a written care plan tailored to meeting your parents' specific care and assistance needs.

It's important that your parents, their personal physician, you, and other interested family members are involved in this care plan, which will make it much easier for your parents to accept.

After their initial assessment, your parents' condition should be re-assessed periodically thereafter. Assessments will occur more frequently if your parents' care needs are extensive or if they have recently experienced a traumatic event (e.g., a fall) requiring emergency medical attention.

In Case of an Emergency

What would you do if my parents experienced a medical emergency? The candidate's answer should make you feel comfortable that this person is watching over your aging parents. The correct answer is an immediate call to 9-1-1 to request an emergency medical-response team. The next answer would be to reveal all medical training the candidate has completed, including CPR, and how he or she would use this training under the pressured urgency of a medical emergency.

Other Pertinent Questions

Precisely what would you do to help promote and preserve my parents' independence and dignity? The candidate's answer to this powerful question will be paramount in determining whether this person has the "right stuff" to be your parents' caregiver. Allow the candidate ample time; his or her answer could take many forms, but they should all express the same general theme. The way to promote and preserve the independence and dignity of our aging population is through human contact, care, and nurturing; to offer a helping hand when needed, to listen intently when they have concerns, to respect their privacy, and to always offer them friendly conversation and companionship. Your parents' home is a place that provides them with warmth, comfort, and security. The caregiver's objective will be to try to preserve this for as long as possible while helping your parents achieve a meaningful, dignified, and fulfilling lifestyle.

What made you choose this type of work? The candidate's response will give you a further indication of what this person is all about. When I was a high school sophomore, confused about what I wanted to do with my life, I asked my dad for advice on what type of degree to pursue. As he so often did, Dad offered me some very wise advice. He said, "Son, whatever you choose to do with your life, make sure you love what you do and have a genuine passion for it. Living your everyday life with passion is the best advice I could ever give you. If you do this, you'll never work a day in your life."

Whom would I want taking care of my mom or dad? Someone who absolutely loves his or her work; someone who recognizes our seniors as strong, vibrant members of society, people who live with purpose and make valued contributions to their families and communities; someone who's genuinely caring and passionate about helping others.

Why did you leave your last job? This standard interview question can elicit some interesting information. Interviewees are trained not to respond with negativity or criticism of their former employers; however, sometimes things slip out indicating the candidate doesn't have the patience or personality to deal with aging adults.

What would you do if you were ill and unable to come to work? This is one of the disadvantages of hiring an Independent Home Care Provider rather than a Home Care Agency. Naturally, there'll be times when the independent worker your parents hire is ill or on vacation. When this occurs at a Home Care Agency, the agency assigns a replacement caregiver to meet your parents' needs until their regular caregiver is ready to return to work.

When hiring an independent provider, there's no perfect answer, unless the caregiver can provide you with a replacement to handle the responsibilities while he or she is ill or on vacation. All you can ask is they notify you promptly of any illness (e.g., the night before) and vacation plans (e.g., six months in advance), so you can arrange for someone else to take care of Mom or Dad.

What are your attitudes toward smoking, alcohol, and drugs? People with alcohol and drug problems are less productive and likely to miss more days of work than those without substance-abuse problems. Your parents' attitude toward smokers will probably depend on whether they are, or once were, smokers. Whether a person smokes has nothing to do with how productive or caring he or she is on the job.

Are you bonded and insured? If a candidate is bonded, your parents will be insured against all losses that may occur due to theft. If the candidate is a registered nurse, ask whether he or she carries malpractice insurance.

Are you familiar with any of the trade associations that represent the interests of the home care industry? If the answer is yes, ask the candidate to describe any involvement. Membership in trade associations tells me the candidates love their work and genuinely care about what they're doing, that they want to stay abreast of new developments that could help them provide more effective care and assistance.

Members of trade associations share information and care techniques at least annually at conferences that take place nationwide. These include daily education sessions that members attend. Unfortunately, the high cost of membership keeps most Independent Home Care Providers from become members of home care trade associations, so membership is primarily made up of Home Care Agencies, home care equipment suppliers, and schools. Even though hefty membership fees prevent an individual from participating, it's a plus if the candidate is aware of such organizations and stays in touch with their membership and agenda.

Here are some of the more prominent national trade associations serving the needs of the home health care industry:

- ▶ National Association for Home Care and Hospice (NAHC)
- ▶ American Association for Home Care (AAHomecare)
- ▶ American Association of Homes and Services for the Aging (AAHSA)

These organizations are profiled in the "Conducting Telephone Surveys of Home Care Agencies" section of this chapter.

Compensation and Benefits

What hourly rate do you need for your services? The candidate might or might not respond directly; instead, he or she might deflect the question back to you by asking, "What do you plan on paying your best candidate?"

To prepare yourself for this, you'll have to do a little research to determine what home care workers in your area are currently demanding. Look at salary surveys at the library or on the Internet, and browse the classified ads in your local newspaper to get an idea of how much home care workers with various skill sets are getting. These figures will give you a starting point for negotiating compensation with candidates during in-person interviews. Remember, the purpose of the initial telephone survey is to screen the candidates down to a select few whom you'll interview in person.

When asked, "What are you planning on paying your best candidate" during the phone survey, you can respond in one of two ways. You can either indicate the range of hourly wage rates you gathered from your research or you can just deflect it back to the candidate and tell them you're still in the process of gathering comparable home care compensation information in the area.

What type of benefits package are you looking for? As with compensation, the candidate might prefer to ask you, "What do you plan to offer your best candidate?"

Sometimes, to hire the best, you'll have to offer a generous hourly wage and a solid benefits package as well. At the very least, a standard package includes health insurance. More attractive and more expensive packages also offer dental coverage, life insurance, or even a pension plan.

If their hourly wage is high enough, not all Independent Home Care Providers will demand a benefits package. Each candidate's compensation and benefit demands are driven by his or her own unique set of circumstances. Some candidates might, for example, have working spouses who have a benefits package covering the entire family. Such a candidate will likely negotiate a higher hourly rate in lieu of benefits. Others might forego a higher wage for decent health insurance with lower monthly premiums, co-payments, and deductibles.

As with compensation, you'll need to research how much it will cost your parents to give a prospective employee each benefit option. The people responsible for taking care of our aging population are some of the nation's lowest-paid workers. As a result, many Independent Home Care Providers are not even offered benefits; it's just assumed that their wages are sufficient to obtain their own health coverage. Often, these workers earn just enough to feed their families and keep a roof over their heads. Health insurance usually becomes a victim of priorities. Just remember, if you want to hire the best caregiver possible to take care of Mom or Dad, you'll have to offer a generous hourly wage and a decent benefits package. Consult your parents' CPA when trying to figure out what the total monthly and annual costs would be to hire an Independent Home Care Provider with the skills necessary to meet your parents' care and assistance needs.

Résumé

Can you send me a résumé of your qualifications and experience?
If, after completing the telephone survey, you feel the candidate has
the potential to be your parents' caregiver, ask for a résumé so you can
prepare for an in-person interview. Tell the candidate you'll call in the
next few days to set up a date and time for the interview. Next is "Step
Four: Conducting an In-Person Interview of a Home Care Provider."
Go to that section of the book to find out how to structure your interview and get tips on evaluating a candidate during the interview process.

Conducting Telephone Surveys of Adult Day Programs

The CD includes a telephone survey checklist for adult day programs (Appendix I), which is designed to help you and your parents gather all the information you'll need to determine whether adult day services is suited to meeting your parents' care and assistance needs. The survey will give you vital information on:

Admission Requirements

Does the program have specific age, health, or physical requirements to qualify for admission? The answers will tell you right away whether your parents would qualify for admission and whether to continue the survey.

Is the adult day program restricted only to seniors? As with some assisted living communities, some adult day programs admit individuals of all ages. In some that I've visited, the younger people had mental disabilities or mental-health conditions. Based on your parents' personal preferences, this might or might not be a factor in their decision.

Some adult day programs might not be qualified to accept or handle participants with physical or mental conditions such as incontinence, limited mobility, or the early stages of Alzheimer's disease or other forms of dementia.

Types of Adult Day Programs Offered

How would you best describe your program? It's very important to match your parents' current care and assistance needs with the services the adult day program offers. Are they social needs, physical needs, or cognitive needs?

Determine which of the following best describes the program:

- ▶ **A Social Program**
- ▶ **A Health Care and/or Rehab Program, or**
- ▶ **An Alzheimer's/Dementia Care Program**

The program administrator's answer will help you determine whether the program will satisfy your parents' preferences and needs. There are adult day centers that offer all three types of programs. In such a case, make sure the programs dealing with people with cognitive disorders and chronic health problems are in separate parts of the building. Some group environments could be harmful to your parents' morale. If they have no cognitive problems, they might prefer not to be spending their entire day with seniors who have Alzheimer's or other forms of dementia. Most adult day programs offer activity programming designed to deal with this issue.

Ownership/Sponsorship

Are the owners and/or sponsors of the program privately or publicly owned? Is the program owned and/or sponsored by a for-profit or not-for-profit entity? What is its mission statement? Is the program sponsored by a specific religious organization? Knowing the organization you're contracting with could give you an indication of where its focus really is.

Operating Experience

How experienced is the owner and/or sponsor at providing adult day services? How long has the program been serving the community?

An adult day program that's been serving the area for any length of time will have developed a track record, which can be corroborated by people who've been served by the program. That they've been in the business for any considerable length of time is a good sign; however, you should take further steps to confirm the quality of care provided by the program. Completing the telephone survey is only one step in a five-step process to selecting the best adult day program. You must complete all five steps to fully evaluate a program.

If a program makes the final cut, ask the director for a list of references including physicians, hospital social workers, discharge planners, current and former clients (including family members), and any other references they're willing to offer. Follow up with these to determine whether the program has a good reputation for providing quality adult day services. For more on how to check references, refer to "Step Five: Final Evaluation and Decision."

Age of the Building

If an adult day program makes your parents' short list and you intend to visit and take a tour, the age of the building where the services are provided will be useful information. It will help you determine whether the provider has been allocating enough of its annual budget to capital improvements. If, for example, the building is ten years old and looks like it's thirty years old, you might question why they're not putting money back into the program for such capital improvements as periodic replacement of carpeting, wall coverings, furniture, fixtures, and equipment. Is it because management feels it's unnecessary, or because the program is struggling financially? Either way can be an indication of how things will be handled in future. If, on the other hand, the building is thirty years old and looks like new, with new furniture, wall coverings, and carpeting, then you and your parents can be assured that management is investing money back into the program. This might not be as important as when your parents are considering moving into a senior housing and care community, but it deserves some attention. Your parents will want to choose the adult day program that has the best facilities available.

Licensing, Certification, Accreditation and Membership

Is the adult day program licensed by the state? Whether or not an adult day program is required to be licensed depends on the state where your parents live. Most states require licensing of adult day programs that provide health care and/or rehabilitation services. Licensed adult day programs must meet the minimum operating standards established by state regulators. Each state establishes its own regulations regarding the types of services that can be provided and specific standards for quality of care. Licensed agencies are surveyed (inspected) annually by health professionals from state survey agencies, typically in the Department of Health, to determine whether they meet the state's minimum standards. Operators' licenses are issued or renewed based on the outcome. Sanctions and remedies are imposed when operators fail to comply with state regulations.

Is the adult day program certified? Medicare does not cover adult day services, but in some states, some adult day services are covered by Medicaid. To participate in a state-administered Medicaid program, adult day programs must be licensed by the state and certified by the Medicaid program. State laws govern licensing of adult day services, while federal laws govern certification. Annual surveys are conducted to verify that these services are provided in compliance with Medicaid standards. As with state licensing, state survey agencies conduct the annual surveys for the Medicaid program and cite communities that fail to meet state guidelines.

Is the program accredited? Adult day programs can get voluntary accreditation from a nationally recognized accrediting organization if they meet the standards of quality set by the accrediting body. Accreditation differs from licensing or certification in that it's voluntary. If a program attempts to get voluntary accreditation, it tells me the people running it are committed to providing their clients with the highest possible quality of life, continuously trying to improve the care and services they offer, and consistently proving it by meeting or exceeding the performance standards set by the accrediting body.

Accreditation of adult day services is a relatively new process; the first adult day programs received accreditation in 2000. Accreditation can be received through the Commission on Accreditation of Rehabilitation Facilities (CARF). The standards for adult day services were jointly developed by CARF and the National Adult Day Services Association (NADSA) in 1997 and published in 1999.

For an adult day program to receive accreditation through CARF, it must demonstrate it meets the certain standards of quality and excellence jointly developed by CARF and NADSA by completing an on-site survey by trained representatives from CARF. During the survey, the adult day program is asked to demonstrate its conformance with the CARF standards. After meeting the necessary criteria and receiving accreditation, the adult day program will be re-surveyed periodically thereafter to make sure it's maintaining the standards of quality and excellence.

> **For more information about CARF and its accredited adult day programs, phone them at 520-325-1044 or visit their website: www.carf.org.**

Is the provider of adult day services a member of a national or state trade association? Like voluntary accreditation, membership in a trade association indicates to me that management cares, that they try to stay abreast of new developments and techniques that could help them provide services more efficiently, and that they're constantly trying to improve the quality of care. Members of trade associations share information and care techniques at least annually at conferences that take place nationwide. These conferences typically include education sessions that members attend daily.

Here are two of the more prominent national trade associations that serve the needs of the adult day services industry:

- **National Adult Day Services Association (NADSA)** – NADSA (www.nadsa.org) serves as the national voice for adult day care providers and consumers alike. It seeks to promote quality adult day services as an essential component of community care. Based in Seattle, Washington, NADSA is a private, not-for-profit organization committed to providing its members effective national advocacy, educational and networking opportunities, technical assistance, research, communication services, and professional development. To more effectively speak for and support the development of adult day services, NADSA is growing and changing along with the industry. After several decades as a constituent unit of The National Council on the Aging (NCOA), NADSA, which is wholly owned by its membership, has formed as an independent national organization dedicated solely to representing adult day services. A collaborative working relationship will be maintained with NCOA, a leading representative organization of older Americans.

- **American Association of Homes and Services for the Aging (AAHSA)** – The association for the nation's not-for-profit long-term care and senior housing providers, AAHSA's (www.aahsa.org) membership numbers more than 5,000 nursing homes, assisted living communities, Continuing Care Retirement Communities, senior housing and home and community-based service organizations, including those that provide adult day services. More than half its members are religiously sponsored; central to the work of all its members is a mission to serve older people by providing them the means to live with the greatest possible level of self-determination, dignity, and independence.

Types of Slots Available and Current Utilization

A typical provider of adult day services offers both full- and half-day programs, which your parents can choose depending on their situation. The provider has a maximum number of slots available in each program. Adult day programs are staffed and budgeted to operate with a certain minimum number of participants. During your telephone survey, be sure to ask for the maximum number of slots for each program and for the number currently filled. Low utilization of the maximum number of available slots may indicate that the program is in financial trouble. Low utilization at an adult day program isn't quite as alarming as low occupancy rates at a senior housing and care community, because your parents won't be making as substantial an investment.

If an adult day program were to close due to financial difficulties, your parents would only have to select another program in their area. Conversely, should a senior housing and care community close, your parents would not only lose their initial investment but would also have to deal with choosing another community, moving, and getting acclimated—a great strain on their mental and emotional well-being. Low utilization of an adult day program should still be a red flag, indicating that something might be wrong: the program is struggling financially, or the quality of care and assistance it provides isn't what it should be.

What is considered low utilization? The telephone surveys are designed to trigger an explanation from management if utilization rates are lower than 90 percent. Most adult day service operators and managers should be able to run their programs at utilization rates of 90 percent or higher. Successfully operating their program means they can generate enough cash flow to pay their monthly debt obligations as well as all monthly operating expenses required to provide the current level of services to participants. In certain parts of the country, the weather affects the adult day business as much as anything else does, so you should expect some seasonality in utilization rates.

Base Fees for Adult Day Services

Adult day programs may charge by the hour, half day, full day, or by the week. Many programs have a minimum and a maximum charge per day as well. I've found that adult day fees generally range from $40–$80 per full day, with an average of $65 per day. In addition to the daily fees, you should find out whether an initial deposit is required and, if so, whether it's refundable.

The telephone survey is designed to obtain information on whether there are any additional services for which added fees are charged. For example, what is the charge for extended hours if needed, and is there a charge for transportation to and from the adult day program?

About half of the adult day programs I've encountered provide transportation to and from the program free of charge. Additional charges for transportation typically range from $8–$15 per day for round-trip transportation; others charge by the mile (e.g., 50¢ per mile).

If your parents' income and resources are limited, find out whether any public or private financial assistance is available to help cover the cost of their adult day services. Medicare doesn't cover adult day services, but in some states, Medicaid does. The adult day program director you're surveying should be familiar with Medicaid program requirements and regulations in his or her state, and should be able to tell you whether your parents would qualify for financial assistance and for how long. If the director can't give you information on the requirements for participation in this program, get it from your State Medicaid Agency in the State Department of Health and Human Services.

There might be other public or private programs in your parents' area that could provide financial assistance. The adult day provider should be aware of these.

Like other not-for-profit senior housing and care options, some not-for-profit adult day programs establish benevolent funds to help lower-income people get the care and assistance they need. To receive financial assistance from such funds, your parents must first prove they've exhausted all other assistance options and truly need the care and assistance. Many adult day programs receive charitable contributions from individuals and businesses in the community, as well as appropriations from towns and cities to help provide specific services to resident taxpayers.

Types of Adult Day Services Available

Each telephone survey checklist includes a list of services usually provided at an adult day program. Be sure to check off all services included in the base daily fee; also, indicate which services are available for an additional charge. This way, you'll be able to easily compare the rates of the competing adult day programs in your parents' area.

The types of adult day services a program offers may include:

- One, two, or three meals per day
- Transportation to/from home
- Activities
- Assistance with one ADL*
- Assistance with two to three ADLs*
- Assistance with three to four ADLs*
- Assistance with five or more ADLs*
- Medication reminders
- Medication supervision
- Medication administration
- Rehabilitation or therapy services
- Family support programs

ADLs are activities of daily living, including bathing, dressing and grooming, transferring, walking, eating, and toileting.

Types of Activity Programs Offered to Participants

Adult day programs can provide your parents daily stimulating socialization, fun, and enrichment through activity programs, which commonly take up the majority of a program's day. The activities may be recreational, educational, or therapeutic in nature. There's ample space on the telephone survey to list all the activities the program offers. Many of the recreational programs are designed to promote independence and self-esteem.

Some activities offer educational opportunities such as how to stop smoking, lessons in playing bridge, a course on mature driving, or a presentation on the ins and outs of Medicaid. Other activities are disguised therapy programs, which include art, music, and dance.

Many adult day programs feature activities that offer their seniors community integration opportunities such as frequent outings to movies, plays, museums, libraries, zoos, shopping centers, swimming pools, and bowling alleys.

 Like other senior housing and care options, some adult day programs offer intergenerational programs. One center I visited operates both an adult day center and a child day care center on the same campus. Each day, the seniors and children participate in supervised activities together. These include seniors rocking infants or creating art projects with preschool children. Others offer intergenerational programs for latchkey kids. Instead of children participating in the after-school latchkey program at their school, they're brought to the adult day program to spend the afternoon with the seniors. The latchkey kids' ages typically range from six to thirteen. The seniors help them with their homework, go for walks, talk, watch TV, and whatever else they want to do. The interaction between elderly participants and young children benefits everyone. The children energize the older adults while recognizing the elders' value and learning that aging is a natural part of

life. Loving bonds are formed, and the self-esteem of both seniors and children increases dramatically.

The adult day program should not only meet your parents physical needs for care and assistance but should also meet their intellectual and social needs by providing them with a place they can go to have an interesting, enjoyable day filled with companionship and the opportunity to make new friends.

What is the program's policy regarding participants' medications?

Are daily medication reminders provided to participants? How is medication storage and record keeping handled? Is there a central location, or do medications remain in the possession of the participants? Is the program's professional staff allowed to administer medications to participants, or are they allowed only to supervise the administration of medications? The answers to these questions will vary from program to program. Be sure to carefully document the response of each adult day program you survey.

Does the program offer family support services?

Many adult day programs provide support and resources to families and caregivers. The support groups offer caregivers a setting where they can discuss such things as the difficulty of coping with a family member who has Alzheimer's disease or is recovering from a stroke. These services can help you and your family deal with and overcome the numerous challenges of caring for an aging loved one.

Does the program offer overnight respite services?

Some adult day programs offer adult children a break from their evening or weekend caregiving duties by offering overnight respite services. This gives the caregiver a chance to get away for a special weekend or weeknight by having a familiar, qualified staff person offer the elder participant quality overnight care and supervision, as well as stimulating activities in a familiar environment and routine. Adult day programs usually offer these services a certain number of weekends per year; some even offer an entire week of overnight respite care so caregivers can take a much needed vacation.

Are there any services the adult day program can't provide?

There may be services that an adult day provider is not permitted to perform. Be sure to list these in the space provided on the telephone survey. Depending on their response, a given adult day program might not be able to meet your parents' needs.

If the adult day program offers an Alzheimer's / dementia care program, what design and security features does it offer?

If your parents are in the early stages of Alzheimer's or other forms of dementia, find out whether the building has any architectural features designed to help memory-impaired individuals cope with their everyday activities. Design features include continuous/circular hallways with patterns, colors, and distinct visual cues, enclosed outdoor patios, even lighting throughout the building or wing, and line-of-sight bathrooms, closets, and refrigerators. For more information, see Chapter 3, Option 6, under "Advantages of an Alzheimer's/Dementia Care Wing or Community." Ask the person you're surveying to specify the program's design features; if they're unable to do so, cross them off your list.

People who have Alzheimer's and other forms of dementia are prone to wandering, which is an ongoing safety and security issue. Some adult day programs offering Alzheimer's/dementia care programs use wireless wander prevention systems to help keep track of their participants and prevent harm due to wandering. If a participant wanders off from a supervised area of the building, the wireless monitoring device worn by the participant sounds an alarm, alerting the caregivers. If your parents are in the early stages of Alzheimer's or other forms of dementia, I highly recommend selecting a program that offers the wireless wander prevention system.

Assessing and Monitoring Your Parents' Care and Assistance Needs

Participant Care and Assessment Program

If your parents are considering an adult day program that offers personal care, health care, or Alzheimer'/dementia care, be sure to ask the program director about their care and assessment program. Ask him or her to specify how they'll monitor and document your parents' care and assistance needs. A quality program will assess your parents' needs upon their admittance to the program, and, based on the results of this initial assessment, will develop a care plan tailored to meet their needs.

Be sure that your parents, their personal physician, you, and other interested family members are involved when the adult day program develops its care plan. This will keep everyone informed of your parents' progress and will make it easier for them to accept the plan.

Some adult day programs also offer family members counseling and education on their parents' situation. These programs provide invaluable information on how adult children and other family members can be of help and support in their loved ones' quest for independence and dignity.

After their initial assessment, participants should be re-assessed periodically thereafter. The interval between assessments depends on how much care the participant is currently receiving. Assessments may occur more frequently if a participant's care needs are extensive or if he or she has recently experienced a traumatic event (e.g., a fall) that needed emergency medical attention.

Subsequent updates or revisions to the written care plan are reviewed and approved by the participants' personal physician, the participants themselves, their adult children, and other family members. The adult day program will send you and other family members a copy of the initial care plan, including all subsequent changes made to the plan as your parents' care needs increase or decrease.

Staffing

Adequate Staffing Levels

The staff of an adult day programs typically includes a multidisciplinary team of licensed nurses, aides, personal care workers, activities coordinators, therapists, social workers, and administrative personnel. To maintain your parents' independence and dignity, the program they choose will need to have an adequate number of direct care staff to meet their care and assistance needs. There is a direct correlation between quality care and adequate staffing levels; when conducting your telephone surveys, it's extremely important to find out what the current ratio of participants to direct care staff is for each program you survey. Direct care staff includes all employees having face-to-face contact with the participants: all registered nurses, licensed practical nurses, certified nurses' aides, therapists, and personal care workers. Volunteers may also be included, as long as their education and training meet the minimum requirements of staff positions at the center.

Based on my exposure to adult day programs nationwide, for each person to get the proper care and attention he or she deserves, the ratio of participants to direct care staff should be no greater than the ratios outlined below:

▸ **Social Programs** – A maximum ratio of eight participants to one direct care staff

▸ **Health care and/or Rehab Programs** – A maximum of six participants to every one direct care staff

▸ **Alzheimer's/Dementia Care Programs** – A maximum of four participants to one direct care staff

If the participant to direct care staff ratios are within these parameters, the staffing at the adult day program may be sufficient to meet your parents' care and assistance needs; it's important, however, to remember that the quantity of people working at an adult day program has nothing to do with the quality of those people. Gathering ratios of participants to direct care staff in your telephone survey is just an initial test. To see if the quality of people working at the center is sufficient to meet your parents' needs, you'll need to tour the adult day program. See "How to Conduct an In-Person Tour of an Adult Day Program" for tips on evaluating staff quality during your tour. This is step four of the five-step process to selecting the best senior housing and care option for your parents.

Volunteer Program

Does the adult day program use volunteers? The use of volunteers is a great sign for many reasons: first, you can be assured that a volunteer wouldn't be there unless he or she truly cared about the participants and genuinely wanted to take care of them; secondly, volunteers can help take the pressure off the program's paid professional staff and expand the services available to participants. Volunteers also give participants more exposure to human interaction, which can help ease your parents' transition to the program.

Staff Recruitment, Qualifications, and Training

Recruiting, Screening, and Hiring Process – You and your parents must make sure that the people assigned to meet their care and assistance needs are not only professionally qualified, but also have the personalities necessary for handling their psychological and emotional needs.

Quality professional staff is the key to an effective adult day program; therefore, most adult day programs check their candidate's backgrounds and references and put them through an extensive interview process during which the program director looks for a candidate with such qualities as commitment, empathy, patience, flexibility, and a sense of humor. They must have energy and enthusiasm for their work and at the same time must be able to project calmness. The program looks for people with a genuine appreciation for working with aging adults. The process ensures that the people hired to care for your parents are qualified to provide quality adult day services and help your parents live independently while maintaining their dignity as long as possible.

Training and Continuing Education

Is the program's professional staff required to complete specific training in giving care and assistance to seniors? Have them specify what types of training. Continuing education is vital for an adult day program's professional staff, especially if the program cares for aging adults with Alzheimer's and other forms of dementia.

If the program is licensed or certified, its employees must complete continuing education requirements established by state or federal regulations. Many adult day service providers also establish their own set of continuing education and professional development requirements, which employees are required to complete periodically. These in-house programs help keep their employees, at all levels and disciplines, up-to-date on all new care and assistance procedures, treatments, equipment, and resources.

In Case of an Emergency

What if my parents need emergency medical care while at the adult day program? Is a registered nurse on staff at all times during business hours, seven days a week, to handle such emergencies? Ask the program director to explain the specific steps taken by the adult day staff when responding to a participant's medical emergency. Has the community arranged with a nearby hospital or emergency response unit to facilitate a quick response and transfer of participants in emergencies?

Do the bathrooms at the center have emergency pull cords should a medical emergency occur while your parents are in the bathroom? If not, what other emergency response equipment do they have to identify when your parents might require emergency assistance?

Questions and Complaints

What if my parents or I have a concern or complaint about the services? Is someone in the program's administrative office available to handle such inquiries? If there is a problem or complaint, what formal steps must be taken to address and ultimately resolve the problem?

Most adult day programs handle complaints in much the same way, but it's important to know how each program handles these situations. If the problem isn't too serious, the family usually discusses it first with the program director who, based on the findings of an investigation, will offer a solution. Most problems can be resolved; some cannot.

If the problem or complaint is more serious, the family should contact the appropriate outside agencies and organizations. If the program is licensed or certified, file a complaint with the state survey agency responsible for overseeing it. The state survey agencies are usually operated within each state's Department of Health. If the community is accredited, file a complaint with the accrediting organization. If a complaint involves a theft, fraud, physical or mental abuse, or any other criminal activity, contact your local police department and file a police report.

Other Questions and Concerns

Special Dietary Needs of Seniors

Does the program have a dietitian on staff to ensure your parents are not only receiving quality meals, but meals that are nutritionally balanced? As we grow older, nutrition becomes increasingly important to healthy living. A senior's reduced metabolism and decreased physical activity, along with decreased appetite, means your parents need to derive the same amount of nutrients from fewer calories. Many experts believe that as seniors get older, poor eating habits and poor nutrition increase the chances of suffering a chronic illness.

Like other senior housing and care options, many adult day programs have dietitians or dietary experts educated in senior nutrition. Often, the dietitian is hired as a part-time consultant to periodically review the program's meal preparation and review and approve the menu.

Is the program able to prepare special meals for your parents if their physician recommends a special diet? It's important to know whether the program can accommodate their needs and whether there'll be any additional charge for this service.

Philosophy of Care

What's the program's philosophy regarding physical and chemical restraints? I've heard too many horrific stories about caregivers' irresponsible use of physical and chemical restraints. Be sure to get a clear and honest answer from the program director. The best answer is "We do not believe in the use of physical and chemical restraints. Never have, never will." I would go even further: have the organization put its money where its mouth is and, if it's not already there, state in their enrollment agreement that they will not use physical or chemical restraints.

Marketing Materials

Can the adult day program send you marketing materials describing the services they offer, including the cost of each option? If so, have them mail you and your parents a copy.

Conducting Telephone Surveys of Hospice Care Programs

The CD includes a telephone survey checklist for hospice care programs (Appendix J). The survey is designed to help you and your parents gather all the information you'll need to determine whether a hospice care program is qualified to meet your parents' end-of-life needs. The survey helps you gather vital information on:

Licensing, Certification, Accreditation, and Membership

Is the hospice care program licensed by the state? Most states require licensing of hospice programs. Licensed programs must meet the minimum operating standards established by state regulators. Licensed agencies are surveyed (inspected) annually to determine whether they meet the minimum standards established in state regulations. Health professionals from state survey agencies, usually in the Department of Health, conduct these surveys. Each state establishes its own regulations regarding how much hospice care and assistance can be provided, as well as standards for quality of care. The regulations also set minimum standards for the qualifications, education, and training of the professional staff working at the hospice. Operators' licenses are issued or renewed based on these surveys. Sanctions and remedies are imposed when operators fail to comply with state regulations.

Is the hospice program certified? In all fifty states and the District of Columbia, a hospice program can apply for certification to become eligible for reimbursement from the federally administered Medicare program. In forty-six states and the District of Columbia, a hospice program can apply for certification to become eligible for reimbursement from a state-administered Medicaid program.

Most hospice programs are certified to participate in the federally administered Medicare program; a small but growing percentage are certified to participate in the state-administered Medicaid program. Like licensing, certified hospice programs are surveyed (inspected) annually to verify that hospice services are provided in compliance with Medicare or Medicaid standards. As with state licensing, state survey agencies conduct these annual inspections and cite hospice programs that fail to meet federal or state guidelines.

Anyone over sixty-five years of age who is receiving social security benefits automatically receives Medicare Part A. The Hospice Benefit is under Medicare Part A. If your parents qualify for Medicare coverage, which is likely if they're over sixty-five, Medicare will cover nearly all of their hospice care costs under the Medicare Hospice Benefit, so unless your parents have some other means or coverage to pay for hospice care, they should select a Medicare-certified program.

Because most hospice care programs are Medicare-certified, it's important to remember that for services to be covered, they must be provided intermittently (i.e., the hospice staff cannot be at your parents' home twenty-four-hours a day). Medicare doesn't cover long-term care, so if your parents require someone such as a homemaker or companion to be at their home after-hours, they'll likely have to pay for these services themselves. In most cases, family members work together as a team to meet such after-hours needs for their loved ones in order to avoid the additional out-of-pocket expense.

Remember that your parents' standard Medicare coverage will continue to pay for those medical conditions unrelated to their terminal illness, so your parents' receiving the Medicare Hospice Benefit doesn't mean they forfeit their regular benefits for prescriptions and other costs.

Is the hospice accredited? Hospice care programs can also get voluntary accreditation from a nationally recognized accrediting organization by meeting specific standards of quality and excellence set by the accrediting body. Accreditation differs from licensing and certification in that it's voluntary. A hospice's interest in voluntary accreditation indicates that it's committed to providing patients the highest quality end-of-life experience, continuously trying to improve its quality of care and services, and consistently proving it by meeting or exceeding the accrediting body's performance standards.

The most prominent accrediting organization of hospice providers is the Joint Commission on the Accreditation of Health Care Organizations (The Joint Commission). Founded in 1951, The Joint Commission is the nation's largest health care accrediting body. It's an independent, not-for-profit organization whose mission is to improve the quality of health care for the public by providing accreditation and related services that support performance improvement in health care organizations. The Joint Commission evaluates and accredits more than 15,000 health care organizations in the United States, including home health care agencies, hospices, and skilled nursing facilities. The Joint Commission surveys (inspects) its accredited organizations every three years.

> If one of your parents is terminally ill and wants more information on the hospice care programs in the area, a directory of all Joint Commission-accredited organizations and performance reports from their most recent evaluations can be accessed at The Joint Commission's website: **www.qualitycheck.org.**

Their online Quality Check™ lets you access a hospice care program's latest Quality Report and see how they rate compared to similar accredited programs. If a facility is not in full compliance with the applicable standards, the requirements for improvement will be listed in the Quality Report as well as the summary page on Quality Check™.

It should be noted that Quality Check™ is a comprehensive directory that lists nearly all hospice care programs available today. It lists both accredited and non-accredited hospice care programs. The Joint Commission added non-accredited facilities in order to provide a more complete inventory of hospice care programs for its users. Hospice care programs that are accredited by The Joint Commission will display a large Gold Seal of Approval™ under the Accreditation/Certification column on the website.

> **If you don't have Internet access, you can request a specific hospice care program's Quality Report by phoning The Joint Commission's customer service department in Washington, D.C.: 630-792-5800.**

Is the hospice a member of a trade association? Is the hospice a member of a national or state trade association? Like voluntary accreditation, membership in a trade association tells me the hospice truly cares about the quality of care they provide to their patients; that they're continually trying to stay abreast of new developments that might help them provide high quality care and assistance more efficiently. Trade association members share information and comfort techniques at least annually at conferences that take place nationwide; these typically include education sessions that members attend daily.

Here are some of the more prominent national trade associations serving the needs of the hospice care industry:

▸ **National Hospice and Palliative Care Organization (NHPCO)** – The oldest and largest not-for-profit membership organization representing hospice and palliative care programs and professionals in the United States, its membership currently includes more than 3,000 hospice organizations. NHPCO (www.nhpco.org) is committed to improving end-of-life care and expanding access to hospice care, profoundly enhancing quality of life for the dying and their loved ones.

▸ **National Association for Home Care and Hospice (NAHC)** – The nation's largest trade association representing the interests of home care agencies, hospices, home care aide organizations, and other home care providers, its members are primarily corporations and other organizations including state home care associations, medical equipment suppliers, and schools. NAHC (www.nahc.org) is dedicated to the proposition that Americans should receive the health care and social services they need in their own homes in so far as is possible.

Type of Hospice Setting

In which settings can the hospice care program provide its services? Since 80–90 percent of today's hospice care is provided in the home, most programs are capable of providing their services in the familiar setting of your parents' own home. In fact, most will come to wherever your parents reside, whether at home or in any of the other senior housing and care communities discussed in this book.

Does the program have a dedicated inpatient hospice facility should my parents require care that can no longer be provided in the home? Dedicated inpatient hospice facilities, sometimes referred to as "hospice houses," offer your parents round-the-clock supervision by a professional staff specifically trained in caring for terminally ill patients.

Some hospice programs have affiliations or contracts with hospitals or other extended care facilities (e.g., assisted living communities or nursing homes) should your parents require additional care that can no longer be provided at home. Be sure to identify these programs and inquire into their reputations.

For-Profit or Not-for-Profit

Is the hospice care provider a for-profit or not-for-profit organization? The main difference between for-profit and not-for-profit organizations lies in the distribution of their profits. For-profit organizations distribute any profit they earn to their individual equity holders, while not-for-profits are required to use income in excess of expenses for other missions of the organization. The defining characteristic of not-for-profit organizations is that the individuals who control the organization do not have a right to its earnings.

Over the years, the differences between for-profit and not-for-profit organizations and the way they operate their businesses have become less and less distinct. Now, for-profit and not-for-profit organizations are far more alike than they are different, primarily because each is competing for the same customer. This fierce competition greatly benefits the consumer by forcing hospice care providers to offer the optimal amount of services for the lowest price.

Operating Experience

What experience does the hospice have operating a hospice care program in the community? If the program has been serving the surrounding area for any length of time, it will have developed a track record, which can be corroborated by others who've been in the program. Having been in the business for a considerable length of time is a good sign, but you should take further steps to confirm the quality of care the program provides. Completing the telephone survey is only one step in a five-step process to selecting the best hospice care program; you must complete all five-steps to fully evaluate a hospice program.

Ask the hospice director for a list of references including physicians, hospital social workers, discharge planners, current and former clients (including family members), and any other references they're willing to offer. Follow up with these to determine whether the program has a good reputation for providing quality hospice care services. For more on checking references, refer to "Step Five: Final Evaluation and Decision."

List the Types of Hospice Care Services Offered

The "Checklist to Conduct a Telephone Survey of a Hospice Care Program" contains a list of typical hospice care services, so you and your parents can easily check off and compare the services each provider offers its patients.

Services may include, but are not limited to:

- Pain control and symptom management services
- Assistance with activities of daily living such as bathing, dressing and grooming, transferring, walking, eating, and toileting
- Skilled nursing services
- Limited homemaker/companion services
- Respite care for family members and caregivers (under Medicare regulations, respite care must be provided to caregivers for five days of every benefit period (usually ninety days)
- Counseling and support groups for family members and caregivers
- Training and education for family members and caregivers
- Bereavement support for family members of all ages
- Spiritual counseling
- Rehabilitative therapy (only if necessary to achieve a quality end-of-life experience, as rehabilitation would not be a hospice goal), and
- Access to all necessary medical equipment and supplies

The checklist provides space to indicate whether the service is covered under the Medicare Hospice Care Benefit or whether there's an additional charge for it, allowing you to easily compare the cost of each hospice care program.

What other types of after-hours services are available? If your parents need them, some hospice care services may be available after the

9 a.m. to 5 p.m. workday. These services are usually not covered under the Medicare Hospice Benefit, so be sure to note any additional charge for each. After-hours services commonly include homemaker, companion, and personal care services.

Get a list of all items or services that might require additional charges. Additional charges might include the cost of an emergency response system. If your parents can't afford to pay for such a system, some hospice programs may cover this cost through one of their foundations and/or benevolent funds.

What out-of-pocket costs should my parents expect to pay for your services? Under the Medicare Hospice Benefit, your parents may be required to pay five percent of the cost of certain hospice services and supplies, such as prescription drugs for pain management and symptom control, short-term inpatient respite care, and some home care services. In most instances, the hospice will cover the remaining five percent of the cost so your parents won't have to pay anything for intermittent care.

It's important to remember the Medicare Hospice Benefit covers only intermittent care and does not cover continuous, twenty-four-hour care in the home. If your parents require round-the-clock supervision, family members will usually be responsible for meeting this need during the evenings and weekends.

If your family is unable to assume responsibility for round-the-clock supervision, and your parents have the financial means, they might wish to hire a home health aide to handle these duties. A home health aide's after-hours services may be covered by your parents' long-term care insurance policy under a home care benefit. If not, they'll probably have to pay for the after-hours services out-of-pocket. If your parents don't have the financial means to hire a home health aide and a family caregiver is not available, they retain the option of moving into a Medicaid-certified extended care facility, such as an assisted living community or nursing care facility.

Jointly funded by federal and state governments, the Medicaid program provides financial assistance to people with lower incomes and limited resources. The administration of the Medicaid program is handled at the state level, so the specific eligibility requirements vary from state to state. An extended care facility should be familiar with the regulations in its state and should be able to tell you whether your parents will qualify for assistance. If your parents meet the financial eligibility requirements of Medicaid and meet the clinical requirements for the Medicare Hospice Benefit, round-the-clock hospice care and supervision is a possibility for them, as it is for anyone who wants it.

Does the program have a foundation or benevolent fund? Many not-for-profit hospice care programs establish foundations and/or benevolent funds to help lower-income people receive the end-of-life dignity they deserve. To receive financial assistance from the benevolent funds, your parents must first prove they've exhausted all other assistance options and truly need the care and assistance. Many hospices raise funds from individuals and businesses in the community, and receive appropriations from towns and cities to help provide specific services to resident taxpayers.

Are any other types of public or private financial assistance available to help pay the cost of my parents' hospice care? If your parents' income and resources are limited, find out whether any public or private financial assistance is available to help cover the out-of-pocket cost of your their hospice care. The hospice should be aware of any programs available to help your parents pay for their home care needs.

Are there any services the hospice cannot provide? There may be services that a hospice care program is not permitted to perform. Be sure to list these in the space provided on the survey.

What happens when my parent's comfort needs can no longer be managed at home? Under these circumstances, a hospice will transfer your parents to its dedicated inpatient hospice facility. If they have no facility of their own, they'll probably have affiliations or transfer agreements with certain local hospitals or extended care facilities that have dedicated inpatient hospice units. In either case, these dedicated inpatient hospice facilities can offer your parents round-the-clock supervised care by a professional staff specifically trained to deal with terminally ill patients.

Who'll be assigned to my parents' hospice team? For each hospice program you survey, find out what human resources are available to serve your parents' physical, emotional, social, and spiritual needs during this difficult time. What type of hospice worker is assigned—a registered nurse, homemaker, or physical therapist—depends on the amount and type of care and assistance your parents need to have the best possible end-of-life experience. Most providers will assign the hospice staff based on an initial assessment of your parents' care and comfort needs. This assessment is typically conducted by one of the program's RNs. The hospice program will also have support staff available to meet the equally important needs of the family.

The telephone survey provides a list of hospice care team members, so you can easily check them off as they're mentioned. There's also space to write every team member's role and responsibilities in meeting your dying parents' many needs as well as your own.

- ▶ **Medical director** – A licensed physician who specializes in dealing with terminally ill patients. He or she will be available to your parent's physician and other members of the hospice team for consultation.

- ▶ **Registered nurses** are responsible for coordinating the care with your parent's personal physician and hospice medical director to prevent and control their symptoms of pain. The RNs also offer education and guidance to the families caring for their loved ones. The RNs are typically certified in hospice and palliative care (i.e. special licensing). A typical hospice care team will consist of two RNs, each with differing responsibilities. One is the Patient Care Manager RN. The Patient Care Manager will make the home visits to your parent's place of residence to assess and coordinate your parent's care and comfort needs in person. The other is the Supervisor RN. The Supervisor RN is responsible for supervising and assessing the performance of the entire hospice care team. This provides the hospice care team with an unbiased, independent assessment of each team member's performance.

▶ **Home health aides** assist your parents with activities of daily living and other personal care routines.

▶ **Licensed social workers** provide you and your parents with emotional support through counseling and other supportive programs.

▶ **Hospice volunteers** are trained to offer companionship and support to you and your parents in any way possible during this difficult time. For example, they may run errands, go shopping, read a book to your parents, or drive your kids to their baseball game. They're there to help you with the everyday challenges of life.

▶ **Clergy or other spiritual counselors** offer spiritual support and guidance to people of all faiths.

▶ **Bereavement counselors** offer support groups and one-on-one counseling for loved ones of all ages.

▶ **Speech, physical, and occupational therapists, if needed** – These specialists can improve the quality of your parent's end-of-life experience.

In Case of Emergency

What procedures are in place should my parents experience a medical emergency in their residence? Is a registered nurse on call to meet your parents' needs twenty-four-hours a day, seven days a week? If the program is Medicare certified, twenty-four-hour availability is required. As with other senior housing and care options, emergency response systems are available to hospice care patients. Such a system allows the patient to wear a wireless communication device around their neck, which he or she can press when in need of emergency assistance. When activated, it sends a signal to the emergency call service, alerting them their client needs emergency medical assistance. The service then contacts the hospice team, which will be the first to respond. An RN from the team will be dispatched immediately to your parents' place of residence to investigate. Some hospice care programs now offer this service for an additional charge. In most situations, you and your parents would contract directly with an emergency response company for this service. If your parents can't afford to pay for it, the hospice program's foundation or benevolent fund may help cover the cost.

What if my parent was in acute pain and wanted additional pain medication? It's important to know what specific steps a hospice would take to suppress any acute pain your parents might experience that their current medication couldn't control. In the situation above, the on-call hospice nurse would be telephoned; he or she has the power to provide with additional pain medication up to the dosage previously approved by the medical director. If additional medication beyond the previously approved level were deemed necessary, the nurse would be required to contact the medical director or your mother's personal physician for approval of the increased dosage.

What procedures are in place to handle my loved one's death? The death of a loved one is always painful and stressful. The best way to cope with such difficult times is to know exactly what steps are going to take place in advance. This way, everything that happens immediately after the death occurs without surprise or consequence. Most hospice care deaths are handled as follows:

The family or the extended care facility calls the hospice nurse to notify them of the patient's death. If the patient lives in an extended care facility, the family will be contacted first, and then the hospice. The hospice nurse immediately comes to the home or extended care facility to arrange for the deceased patient to be picked up by the funeral home. (An emergency medical services ambulance is not usually used in these situations.) A coroner does not perform an autopsy unless the family requests it. Some hospice programs dispatch bereavement counselors, clergy, or other spiritual counselors if needed to help family members cope with their loss.

Assessing and Monitoring Your Parents' Care and Assistance Needs

It's important to ask hospice care providers about their care and assessment programs. Ask each to specify how they'll monitor and document your parents' care and assistance needs.

Would an initial care assessment be performed prior to entering into a contract? Most hospice care programs offer a free in-home assessment of your parents' care and assistance needs. The hospice sends a registered nurse to meet with you and your parents and evaluate their home environment, health status, and other factors. Based on this meeting, the RN develops a care plan tailored to meet your parents' comfort needs.

Would my parents' personal physician be involved in developing the final care plan? When the agency develops a care plan, it's important that your parents, their personal physician, you, and other family members be involved, which will make your parents' end-of-life experience much easier to accept.

How often will my parents' need for pain control and symptom management be assessed? After the initial assessment, patients are re-assessed periodically thereafter. The entire hospice team meets weekly or biweekly to re-examine each patient's care plan. The entire team's input and expertise is considered, allowing them to devise the best possible care plan.

Staff Recruitment, Qualifications, and Training

You and your parents will want assurances that the people assigned to meet their hospice care needs are not only professionally qualified, but also have personalities appropriate to handling their psychological and emotional needs.

What steps does the hospice take to screen and select its employees? Are background checks performed? Are references checked? In today's world, you can't afford to hire anyone without a proper background check. To be certain that it doesn't hire anyone with a history of criminal activity, it's important that the hospice verify, from several third-party sources, that each candidate has the responsibility, character, and moral fiber necessary to take on the task of caring for your parents. The importance of checking potential employees' references and conducting thorough background checks can't be overstated.

Many programs not only check the backgrounds and references of their candidates, but also require them to pass a proficiency test and undergo a rigorous interview process. The hospice needs to determine whether a candidate has the caring skills necessary to perform their everyday tasks. During interviews, reputable hospice care programs look for candidates with such qualities as commitment, empathy, patience, flexibility, and a sense of humor. They must have energy and enthusiasm for their work, but must at the same time be able to project calmness. Overall, the hospice care provider wants people with a genuine appreciation for working with terminally ill patients. This process helps assure that the people hired to care for your parents are well rounded and fully qualified to help make your parents' end-of-life experience as comfortable and pain-free as possible.

Is the hospice staff trained to care for terminal ill patients? What types of training did they complete? Registered nurses are generally required to have two to five years of nursing experience before being allowed to enter the hospice field. In many programs, RNs are certified in hospice and palliative care. Certified Hospice and Palliative Nurse (CHPN) certification, which has been available since 1999, indicates the nurse is competently trained to care for terminally ill patients.

Nursing assistants may attain certification as CHPNAs (Certified Hospice and Palliative Nursing Assistants). This certification is designed to complement the process for registered nurses described above.

Medical directors (i.e., physicians) may also attain certification in Hospice and Palliative Care Medicine. To be eligible, physicians must meet substantial requirements, including achieving certification in a prior major specialty, working as a member of an interdisciplinary team of health care professionals for more than two years, and participating in the active care of at least fifty terminally ill patients during the past three years.

Are your employees required to complete a minimum of continuing education or training annually? Continuing education is especially important for a hospice program's professional staff in handling and caring for terminally ill patients. A licensed or certified program is required to have its employees complete continuing education requirements established by state or federal regulations. Continuing education is a requirement for all hospice staff, regardless of area of practice. Make sure the person you're interviewing is specific in describing the continuing education of staff.

In addition to these requirements, many hospice care programs establish their own set of professional development standards or competencies, which each of their employees is required to meet periodically. Such in-house continuing education programs help assure that employees of all levels and disciplines stay up-to-date on new and improved procedures, treatments, equipment, and resources.

If the program uses volunteers, are they required to complete any specific training to work with terminally ill patients and their families? Hospices were originally founded and operated by volunteers, so it's only natural for volunteers to continue playing a vital role in hospices. Many train their volunteers as they do their employees, to handle the physical and emotional challenges likely to occur when caring for terminally ill patients and their families. In Medicare certified programs, volunteers must complete training to participate.

Staff Supervision

Will all members of the team assigned to my parents have ongoing supervision and periodic evaluation by a qualified supervisor? Who is responsible for supervising services, what are his or her qualifications, and how often will the supervisor visit my parents' place of residence?

Most hospice programs assign a Supervisor RN to each of their hospice care teams in the field to monitor the quality of care patients receive in their places of residence. The Supervisor RN makes sure the services are carried out in accordance with your parents' written care plan. This helps assure the consistency, quality, and appropriateness of their care. If the program is licensed or certified, a supervisor is required to make periodic visits with every discipline of the hospice care team. The frequency of these visits depends on the discipline. For example, home health aides may require supervision every two weeks, while other team members, such as bereavement counselors, may require supervision only twice a year. A supervisor must visit every discipline of the team at least every six months.

Staffing Issues

Naturally, there'll be times when the hospice care worker assigned to your parents is ill or on vacation. How will a suitable replacement be assigned to temporarily handle their hospice care and assistance needs? What happens when your parents' regular caregiver leaves and a new one is assigned to take responsibility for all their needs?

In both instances, most hospice programs send a supervisor to your parents' home to introduce each new caregiver. This helps assure a smooth transition and make sure everyone is comfortable with the change in personnel. Typically, the supervisor familiarizes and orients the replacement worker with the duties and responsibilities in your parents' customized care plan.

Employee Bonding and Professional Liability Insurance

Are all your employees bonded and insured? The bonding of employees entering your parent's place of residence is an important protection. In a perfect world, employee theft would never happen, but this world isn't perfect. Bonding is a type of insurance: in exchange for an annual fixed premium, the hospice is protected if any employee commits a fraudulent or dishonest act. If a hospice employee is found guilty of any wrongdoing, the patient is reimbursed from the bond. Most hospices bond their employees.

Does your licensed professional staff (physicians and RNs) carry malpractice insurance? Professional liability insurance, which includes malpractice insurance, protects the hospice from any claims made by patients alleging negligence in the rendering of, or failure to render, professional services. Most reputable hospices carry professional liability insurance to protect them from the possibility of one of their physicians or nurses committing a negligent act.

Hospices that carry professional liability insurance and bond their employees ensure that your parents will receive adequate financial compensation should any employee commit negligent acts.

Questions and Complaints

What if my parents or I have a concern or complaint about the care being provided? Is someone at the program's administrative office available to handle such inquiries? What specific steps must be taken to address and ultimately resolve the problem?

Most hospice programs handle complaints in much the same way, but it's important to know how each program handles these situations. In discussions with various hospice programs, I've found that if the problem isn't too serious, the family first discusses it with the hospice care worker. If it's more serious, families contact the Supervisor RN about their concern. The Supervisor RN follows up with the hospice care team and, based on the findings of their investigation, offers a solution.

Most problems can be resolved (e.g., there's a personality conflict, so a replacement worker is assigned); others cannot. If the problem is serious and is not resolved to your satisfaction, you should contact the appropriate outside agencies and organizations. If the hospice program is licensed or certified, file a complaint with the state survey agency that regulates the hospice industry. The state survey agencies typically operate within each state's Department of Health. If the hospice is accredited, you should also file a complaint with the accrediting organization. If your complaint involves a theft, fraud, physical or mental abuse, or any other criminal activity, contact your local police department and file a police report.

Marketing Materials

Does the hospice care program have marketing materials describing their services? If so, have them mail you and your parents copies of these materials.

Step Four

Conduct In-Person Tours and Interviews of All Senior Housing and Care Options on Your Parents' Short List

Once you complete all the telephone surveys, your parents should be able to narrow the field to a select few senior housing and care options based on their needs, price range, and personal preferences. The next step is to conduct in-person tours and interviews of those lucky enough to make your parents' short list. As with the checklists to conduct telephone surveys, the CD provides checklists to help you and your parents with these in-person tours and interviews.

Here are the different types of checklists and their respective appendices on the CD:

1. Checklists to Conduct In-Person Tours of Senior Housing and Care Communities
  - Continuing Care Retirement Communities – Appendix K
  - Independent Living Communities – Appendix L
  - Assisted Living Communities – Appendix M
  - Alzheimer's/Dementia Care Communities – Appendix N
  - Nursing Care Facilities – Appendix O

2. Checklist to Conduct In-Person Interviews with Home Care Providers – Appendix P

3. Checklist to Conduct In-Person Tours of Adult Day Programs – Appendix Q

4. Checklist to Conduct In-Person Interviews with Hospice Care Providers – Appendix R

The importance of the information gathered during in-person tours or interviews for each category is discussed below. Read these sections carefully before your tour or interview so you know exactly what to look for.

Conducting In-Person Tours of Senior Housing and Care Communities

The checklists for touring for each of the five types of senior housing and care communities (Appendices K through O on the CD) will help you and your parents gather all the information you'll need to determine whether a given community is the best option to meet their housing and care needs. Make several copies of these checklists and use one to document your observations at each community. Afterward, you and your parents can easily compare all the communities you visited.

Never Give Fair Warning

Rule #1: Never call to make an appointment for a tour—always make unannounced visits. That way, you'll be able to tour the community knowing it's operating as it would on any normal day. Sometimes, when visits are scheduled, marketing directors will have flowers brought in, have special meals prepared, and have their professional staff on their best behavior because prospective residents are coming in. When visits are unannounced, it's very difficult to hide any deficiencies.

As you tour a community, be sure to write a comment for every area on the checklist so you and your parents can keep a clear record of each visit, including all your observations. If you don't take time to note them while they're fresh and clear in your mind, you won't remember them later. In visiting hundreds of senior housing and care communities, I've found the best way to fill out a checklist is to sit in one of the community's common areas immediately after the tour and write down everything I just observed. I do this while I'm still there so that if an additional question comes to mind while I'm writing, I can easily ask someone, or ask to see something again if I want to. The checklist covers such important factors as:

Location, Location, Location

Resale value isn't the issue here, but there are some important factors to consider when comparing communities: as you drive to each one, observe its proximity to:

► Area health care providers such as hospitals, outpatient centers, and your parent's personal physician and dentist

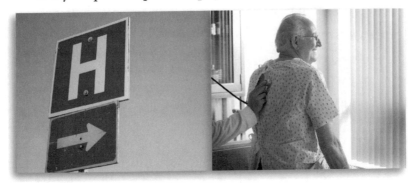

► Churches or synagogues

► Retail shopping centers

► Cultural activities

► Parks and other entertainment, and

► Major highways, airports, and other forms of transportation

Most senior housing communities offer their residents scheduled transportation to and from doctors' appointments, church services, shopping trips, and cultural and entertainment activities. Proximity to a hospital is probably the most important of the factors above.

Is the community near major highways, airports, and other forms of transportation? This is an important factor because your parents will want to live in a community that's easily accessible so their beloved family and friends can visit them as often as possible.

Site Assessment

As you arrive, what's your impression of the property on which the community is located? How would you rate its general aesthetic quality? Are the grounds well maintained? Is it quiet? Is it inviting?

The type of property your parents are going to be comfortable with depends on their personal taste and what kind of property they're accustomed to living in. Not all communities have nice wooded lots with comfortable buffers from the highway, but this might not be the environment your parents desire. If they're from a large metropolitan city and have lived in a big-city environment all their lives, they probably wouldn't be comfortable living on a quiet wooded lot.

Is the community's building located near a highway? This is important because traffic noise might be a problem for some of the living units. I've performed assessments of marketing departments at several senior housing and care communities because they were experiencing problems with overall occupancy. In one instance, a community was having difficulty selling a block of units adjacent to a highway. In this case, the low occupancy wasn't the marketing department's fault, but the developer's, for locating the units too close to a busy, noisy roadway. Be aware of these types of issues when shopping for apartments.

Exterior and Architectural Design

What's your impression of the building's exterior and architecture? Does the community have a residential, home-like feel or a more institutional feel? Does the building appear to be in good physical condition?

Many recently built senior housing and care communities use the Victorian mansion-style architecture, complete with high-pitched roofs and wraparound porches. This type of design promotes a comfortable home-like feel, a far cry from the ugly brick boxes built in years past.

Is there enough parking for residents and guests? Is garage space available for residents to store their vehicles? Even if your parents are driving little or not at all, it'd be nice if there were space for them to store their car, so out-of-town family members or friends could use it while visiting.

Interior Design and Décor

As you enter the building, what's your impression of the interior? Do you and your parents find it attractive? Does it make the community feel residential and home-like?

If you walk into a community that has gray tile flooring in the hallways, I recommend doing an immediate about-face and walking out the door. The days of institutional senior housing and care communities are over. Such facilities must either change their ways or lock their doors forever; no one deserves to live in that type of environment.

Are the carpeting and flooring suitable for an aging population? While touring, make a point of looking down now and then to take note of the floors and carpeting. Notice not only whether they're in good shape and look nice, but also whether they're suitable for an aging population. What's suitable? Most senior housing and care communities nowadays install non-skid tile floors and carpeting, which are tight and firm to walk on, helping prevent falls and providing easy walking for residents. If the community has such flooring, it indicates cognizance of the population they're serving. Make sure the community you're touring has this type of tile and carpeting.

Does the building's interior have special design features to make aging adults' lives easier? Be on the lookout for any senior friendly design features. For instance, many senior housing and care communities have handrails throughout their hallways and common areas for residents who need help walking.

If your parents are in the early stages of Alzheimer's or other forms of dementia, ask the tour guide to point out all specific architectural features designed to help memory-impaired individuals cope with everyday activities. Such design features include continuous/circular hallways with certain patterns, colors, and distinct visual cues; enclosed outdoor patio; even lighting throughout the building or wing; memory-enhancement boxes; extra common area space; and line-of-sight bathrooms, closets, and refrigerators. These are discussed in detail in Chapter 3, Option 6, under "Advantages of an Alzheimer's/Dementia Care Wing or Community."

Lighting / Natural lighting

Does the community have good, even lighting? Is there enough natural light in the building? Many recently built senior housing and care communities are designed to maximize natural lighting through strategically placed interior windows and skylights. Atriums and solariums have also become more frequent additions.

Research has shown that lack of sunlight can negatively affect our biorhythms, mood, and health, and has proven that our bodies need sunlight just as they need clean air and water. We who live in the northern

United States can attest to how mood and energy levels are affected by scarce sunlight during the long winter months. This is sometimes referred to as the "winter blues." Based on the work of Dr. Norman Rosenthal and his research team at the National Institute of Mental Health, science now explains this phenomenon. When people are exposed only to the dimness of artificial light, their pineal glands overproduce melatonin, a hormone that makes us drowsy and signals our bodies when its time to go to sleep. The less our exposure to natural light, the more melatonin we produce, which makes us want to go to sleep or just mope around. Without sunlight, we don't feel the urge to tackle the day's challenges. The research indicates we need at least two hours of natural light each day to function normally. Consider how important exposure to sunlight can be for our aging population.

Various research performed on the effects of natural light has found that daily exposure to natural light can:

- Boost energy levels
- Improve mood and attitude
- Reduce eyestrain and increase visual acuity
- Increase cardiac efficiency
- Lower blood pressure
- Lower cholesterol
- Promote weight loss, and
- Activate the synthesis of Vitamin D, a major factor in the absorption of calcium and other minerals that help us maintain bone density and avoid osteoporosis

The bottom line is: A community with an interior design that exposes residents to as much natural lighting as possible can help support and nurture the aging process. When selecting a housing option, make sure the community you're considering offers adequate exposure to natural light.

Cleanliness is Next to Godliness

Is the building clean and free of unpleasant odors? Throughout your tour, use your sense of smell at all times. One of the consistent traits of a top-notch community is they're always impeccably clean. It's unacceptable for anyone to live in a community where the stench of urine is a constant presence all day long. While touring the community, observe the carpeting and furniture to verify it's clean and free of stains.

Wheelchair Accessibility

Is the building designed for wheelchair accessibility? Are ramps available for easy access? Are all the bathrooms wheelchair accessible? A community with a wheelchair-accessible design doesn't always feel residential or homelike, but allowing residents to extend their independence far outweighs that lack of residential appeal. Observe whether or not the hallways are wide enough for two wheelchairs to pass. If the building has more than one floor, make sure to note if there's an elevator available for residents physically unable to use the stairs.

Resident Apartments with Senior Friendly Design

Bathroom design in most senior communities now incorporates large shower stalls rather than bathtubs; a shower stall with a molded or pull-down seat is much safer to get in and out of than a slippery tub. Raised toilet seats and grab bars are also popular features, making it easier for residents to get on and off the toilet.

Senior apartments are also designed to locate countertops, cabinets, and shelving at lower heights, so your parents can easily reach them. Windows are also lower, allowing residents to easily see the ground from the couch, chair, or bed.

Is the living space conducive to an independent lifestyle? If your parents are still physically active and able to live independently, the apartment they choose should be spacious enough to meet their needs. Senior housing and care communities are fairly consistent as to the amount of living space in an apartment; as a general rule, the more independent the resident, the larger the space. The primary reason for this is afford-ability. The more care and assistance needed, the higher the cost of care per day. If living spaces are smaller, apartments become more affordable to more seniors in the market area.

Furnished Apartments?

Are the apartments furnished, or are residents allowed to bring their own furniture and other belongings from home? Most senior hous-ing and care communities allow residents to bring their own belong-ings from home; if, however, your parents wish to purchase a furnished apartment, some communities offer them for an additional charge.

Safety and Security

Are there emergency pull cords in bedrooms and bathrooms in case of medical emergency? If not, what emergency response equipment does the community have to indicate that my parents require such as-sistance? Does it have the wireless system, with which residents wear a call button on their person? This is safer and much more effective if a resident falls and can't get up.

Is there a wireless wander prevention system to keep track of resi-dents who are prone to wandering? People with Alzheimer's and oth-er forms of dementia tend to wander, which is an ongoing safety and security issue. Many communities housing Alzheimer's/dementia care residents now offer wireless wander prevention systems to help keep track of residents and prevent harm due to wandering. If a resident were to wander off from a supervised area, the monitoring device the resi-dent wears would sound an alarm and alert the caregivers. If the com-munity has this system, ask for a demonstration; if they don't, ask what other safeguards are in place to help keep track of wandering residents.

While touring, did you notice a security guard in the complex? Are all exits clearly marked and all doors equipped with alarms? What type of security system does the community have? Most senior housing and care communities have at least one security guard on site twenty-four-hours a day. More often than not, communities use outside security agencies that are experienced at securing multi-unit housing complexes and health care facilities.

Does the community have a sprinkler system? What about smoke detectors and carbon monoxide detectors? Are fire hoses and extinguishers easily accessible? Ask the director or administrator how often fire drills are conducted and whether you can review their emergency evacuation plan. Most communities can provide this on request.

Common Areas

How much common area space is available for residents to mix and mingle? Is there a library or solarium? It's always gratifying to walk into a senior housing and care community and find the residents enjoying themselves in the company of others in the common areas. They may be sitting around a table playing cards, talking politics in the TV room, or discussing the previous night's ball game over coffee in the dining area. They're telling jokes, laughing, carrying on, and exhibiting the types of behavior one might see at a party with family and friends.

Whenever I visit a community, the residents always like to find out who the new guy is. They're eager to converse, so I sit down and talk with them for a while. What these folks have experienced and the stories they have to tell always capture my attention. Occasionally, while working very long hours, I asked myself why I got into this line of work. These special moments with residents always reminded me that my efforts were undeniably worthwhile.

Helen Keller said,
"The best and most beautiful things in the world cannot be seen, nor touched ... but are felt in the heart."

This is precisely why I believe senior housing and care communities are so vital to our society today and forevermore. They help our seniors' get busy living and not dying. These wonderful communities provide our aging loved ones with the opportunity for socialization, interaction, and communication with others that they would not otherwise experience living at home. Oftentimes, it gives them a reason to get up in the morning and helps add to their self-worth and self-esteem. From my experience, if the residents are socializing and appear happy and comfortable, then it's probably a good bet this community will find its way on to your parent's short list.

Outdoor Courtyard

Does the community have a courtyard so my parents can enjoy the great outdoors? Exposure to sunlight can help support and nurture the aging process; an outdoor courtyard can therefore be a valuable asset to a community. Most outdoor courtyards have walkways that are beautifully landscaped with trees, shrubs, and flower beds. Some have areas for barbecue grills, picnic tables, chairs, benches, and gazebos, and some even have designated areas where residents can plant their own flower or vegetable gardens.

While touring the outdoor courtyard, it's important to be aware of these points:

- ▶ **Is the courtyard enclosed with a security fence?** The courtyard should have some type of enclosure to prevent wandering off the community grounds.

- ▶ **Is the walking area level and smooth to prevent unnecessary falls?** Uneven walking surfaces such as gravel or cobblestone are not the best for seniors. A smooth, non-glare concrete or rubberized surface is ideal for aging adults.

- ▶ **Is there an indoor/outdoor transition area?** Our eyes become more sensitive to light as we get older, and it can take several minutes for an aging adult's eyes to adjust to bright sunlight. Some communities have shaded transition areas, such as porches or awnings, just before entering the courtyard, giving residents' eyes an opportunity to adjust.

Other Amenities and Activities

What other amenities or activity programs does the community offer? Some communities have swimming pools, spas, and exercise rooms available to residents. Others have billiard and card rooms, beauty and barber shops, woodworking shops, and some even have ice cream parlors. Most have activity rooms where residents can perform a variety of activities including arts and crafts.

The Nintendo Wii video game system has become a popular addition at many senior housing and care communities and adult day programs. These video games have revitalized seniors both mentally and physically. The Wii (pronounced "wee") allows residents to do something they may not have been able to do in years such as go bowling or play tennis. No bowling balls or tennis rackets are used; instead, the residents need only swing a small hand-held controller to simulate the rolling of the bowling ball or the swinging of the tennis racket. Physical therapists love the Wii because it motivates the residents to get on their feet, and swinging their arms puts more muscles to use and helps the residents regain and maintain their center of balance.

Many communities schedule group outings such as trips to the opera, ball games, movies, or other forms of entertainment. It's important that the community offer opportunities for social interaction, mental stimulation, and recreation. The degree to which your parents participate in these is, of course, up to them.

Professional Staff and Quality of Care

Is the staff friendly and courteous to you? From the time you enter a community till the time your leave, it's extremely important for you to observe the behavior of the professional staff. Make a point of seeing how they interact and communicate with the residents.

Is the staff friendly, courteous, and caring toward the residents, showing them the respect they deserve? Observe whether they address residents by name; their doing so might indicate that the staff cares enough to develop relationships with the residents.

Do the residents look happy and well cared for?

While touring, observe the residents' faces. An expression can tell you more than a thousand words. Do they look happy? Are the residents interacting and socializing in the common areas, or are they all in their apartments, doors shut, evidencing no desire to come out? Are the residents clean, well groomed, and adequately dressed? If the opportunity arises, talk with some residents about how they like living at the community; especially, ask them what they think of the staff.

Does the community conduct periodic resident satisfaction surveys?

In an effort to satisfy their residents' wants and needs, most senior housing and care communities conduct periodic resident satisfaction surveys to get valuable feedback on the accommodations, personnel, dining experience, social activities, as well as the quality of care they're receiving. Such surveys usually ask residents to grade the direct care staff on friendliness, attentiveness, and response time. If the community you're visiting conducts resident satisfaction surveys, ask them to give you copies of the three most recent survey results. The feedback coming directly from the current residents should provide you some valuable insight as to what your parents can expect should they move into this community.

Nutritionally Balanced Meals, Food Quality, and Overall Dining Experience

Is the central dining area attractive and suitable for everyday dining?
Your parents are going to eat in this room nearly every day! Do they find it appealing? Some CCRCs will have both formal and informal central dining areas on their campus.

Is there a private dining room for entertaining visiting family and guests?
These are great when your parents want to entertain family and friends

in private. The décor is usually elegant, with a large chandelier over a spacious dining table—always a very popular feature with residents.

Is there a good selection of items on the menu? Take some time to review the daily menu. Ask to see the lunch and dinner menus for the entire week. Is there a good selection? If the community has a Dietitian, ask to speak with them about their nutrition program. Ask them to explain how the program meets the nutritional needs of its residents keeping in mind a senior's lower caloric intake. Make sure the Dietitian provides you with a clear, concise, and logical response before accepting the menu as nutritionally balanced. Is the community capable of preparing special meals for your parents to accommodate a special diet if required?

Ask to tour the kitchen. As you walk through, observe whether it's reasonably clean. Note whether there are separate areas for (i) food preparation, (ii) food storage, and (iii) dish washing and trash disposal.

All quality kitchens will have separate areas for these functions.

Ask the person giving you the tour whether you and your parents can have lunch or dinner in the central dining area. By sampling the food, you can appraise its quality. Have everyone order something different, so you can evaluate several types of meals in one sitting. Is the quality acceptable? Remember: your parents will be eating this food almost every day.

Guest Apartments

Are furnished guest apartments available for overnight stays? Many senior housing and care communities have furnished guest apartments so prospective residents can stay overnight or for several days to get a feel for what it's like to live there. The guest apartments are also available for out-of-town family members who come to visit.

An overnight or extended-weekend stay is a wonderful way to expose your parents to a community, allowing them to "test drive" it before they commit. Staying in one of the guest apartments allows them an opportunity to meet the residents, get to know the executive director and the other professional staff, as well as eat a number of meals in the dining room. They might even make some friends along the way and decide they like it enough to move in!

Renewal and Replacement

Does the community look like it's kept up, renovating and replacing items such as carpeting, wall coverings, furniture, fixtures, and equipment? If everything looks like new, you'll know that management is putting money back into the community. During your telephone survey, you'll have learned the building's age, so you'll be able to tell whether management is doing its job renewing and replacing items. Does the community look its age or does it look better? Check to see whether the carpeting is worn, whether the furniture in the common areas is worn or outdated, and whether all the TV sets in the common areas are in excellent working condition with good picture and sound.

Were You Given the Complete Tour?

Did you get a full tour of the entire community? Were you given access to anything you wanted to see without violating the residents' privacy? Be wary of a tour guide trying to avoid a specific area for one reason or another; he or she might be hiding something. You needn't be overly cynical or mistrustful, though; the person giving you the tour might have a good reason for not showing you something, but you should be aware of the possibility of their trying to hide a possible blemish in the community.

Overall Thoughts and Impressions of the Community

Before you leave, be sure to jot down any other observations you think are relevant to your parents' decision. Also, write down your thoughts and impressions of the community as a whole. After observing the types of people living there, you should be able to answer the question, "Will my parents fit in well with the rest of the residents here?"

The tour checklists allow you to grade the various areas of the community on a scale from one to ten, with one being the worst grade and ten the best. Again, do complete the checklist while you're there at the community, so you and your parents can have a clear record of your visit.

Conducting an In-Person Interview
with a Home Care Provider

After using the telephone surveys to thoroughly prescreen all the candidates, the next step is to call the home care provider and schedule an in-person interview. Depending on whether your parents are considering hiring a Home Care Agency or an Independent Home Care Provider, the interview process will be different. The structure of the interview and the points to consider will be the same, but, getting the interview is not. How you'll get an interview for each of the options is discussed below.

In-Person Interview of a Home Care Agency

Some agencies are more accommodating than others when it comes to your choosing a home care worker, but most will agree to your request to meet and interview the home care worker who'll be assigned to your parents before the worker's first day on the job. This allows you and your parents to decide for yourselves whether that worker is a good match to meet their physical and emotional needs.

Most agencies first send an RN to your parents' home to conduct an in-home assessment of their care and assistance needs. Depending on the agency, there might be a charge for this assessment; if the agency charges for in-home assessments, the cost will range from $75–$300. The RN evaluates such things as your parents' home environment, health status, and other factors that might affect their care. Based on the assessment, the RN will develop a care plan tailored to meet your parents' specific needs. Attached to the care plan will be an estimate of the cost of providing the services it specifies.

Once the assessment is completed and the care plan developed, an agency will then try to match one of their home care workers with your parents, based on their individual needs. Once the worker has been identified, the agency usually contacts the family to discuss the worker's background, qualifications, and experience. At this time, you can schedule a meeting to allow you, your parents, and other family members an opportunity to meet and interview the worker before he or she begins the assignment. If your parents feel that the assigned home care worker isn't a good match, the agency will look for another with the skills and qualifications necessary to meet your parents' needs. The initial interview with a home care worker is usually free of charge, but most agencies will charge a small fee ($25–$50) if you request additional interviews.

Some agencies complete the interview process prior to the in-home assessment. To do this, the agency pre-assesses your parents' needs by telephone, and will then try to assign a home care worker who best meets their needs. Once a home care worker with the appropriate skills is identified, the agency contacts the family to discuss the worker's background, qualifications, and experience and to schedule an interview. Once your parents approve the home care worker, the agency will then send an RN to conduct the in-home assessment. From the agency's business perspective, why should they waste an RN's time on an in-home assessment and developing a care plan if they're unable to assign an acceptable home care worker? It really doesn't matter which way your parents complete the process, as long as they find the appropriate person to meet their care and assistance needs.

In-Person Interview of an Independent Home Care Provider

If an independent provider makes your parents' short list, setting up an interview is as simple as calling the candidate and setting a time and a place for the interview. The candidate has made it this far in the process, so he or she has obviously made a good impression on all of you, answering all the telephone survey questions to your satisfaction regarding time commitment, qualifications and experience, and salary and benefit requirements. Now it's time to find out whether the candidate is truly the right person for the job. It's time for the candidate to meet the parents!

Call the candidate and schedule an in-person interview with you and your parents. Choose a time when other family members will also have the opportunity to meet the candidate and provide support and feedback. Distribute copies of the completed telephone survey to participating family members so they can review the candidate's qualifications and experience prior to the interview. Also, have the candidate send a résumé, which might provide you more detail on his or her experience in assisting and caring for aging adults. You'll need the résumé anyway, to do your background investigation if the candidate becomes a finalist. Background investigations are discussed in Chapter 6, Under "Step Five: Final Evaluation and Decision."

The Interview and How to Evaluate It

You'll need to evaluate specific things during the in-person interview to make sure the candidate is right for the job. Your main objective is to determine whether the candidate has the right personality to handle your parents' psychological and emotional needs. A candidate who's made it this far in the selection process should have the necessary skills to perform their job; now it's just a matter of finding the person with whom your parents feel most comfortable.

Here are some questions to ask yourself while interviewing a candidate:

- ▸ Will this person get along well with my parents?
- ▸ Will his or her demeanor and personality mesh well with my parents?
- ▸ Does the candidate seem enthusiastic about getting the job and caring for my parents?
- ▸ Do I like and feel that I can trust this candidate?
- ▸ Will the rest of the family like and trust this candidate?
- ▸ Does he or she appear physically able to handle the duties of caring for and assisting my parents (e.g., lifting and transferring them from place to place)?
- ▸ Will this candidate be able to respond to a medical emergency calmly and quickly?
- ▸ Do I believe this candidate is the right person for the job of caring for my parents?

Questions to Ask Home Care Providers During In-Person Interviews

While interviewing home care providers, it's important to ask the questions that will confirm a candidate's qualifications and, more important, help you, your parents, and other family members evaluate the person's character and personality. The answers to these questions should help all of you determine whether the candidate is capable of handling your parents' emotional and psychological needs. Having made it this far in the selection process, the candidate should have the necessary skills to perform their job; now it's just a matter of finding the person with whom your parents are most comfortable.

The CD features a checklist of questions to help you conduct interviews of Independent Home Care Providers and home care workers assigned by Home Care Agencies. The factors you need to evaluate are very much the same at this stage in the process. The checklist includes suggested questions to ask the candidate during the interview, and a list of post-interview questions that you, your parents, and other family members should answer. Feel free to add any additional questions that you feel are integral to determining whether any candidate has the right stuff to be your parents' home care provider.

The list of suggested questions is discussed in detail below. If an Independent Home Care Provider made your parents' short list, you'll notice that you asked some of these questions during your prescreening telephone survey. It's necessary to ask them again; given an opportunity to hear the candidate's responses in person, your parents and other family members can better evaluate the prospect's character and personality and confirm his or her qualifications and experience. If the candidate is a worker assigned by a Home Care Agency, then you'll be asking all of these questions for the first time.

Can you tell me a little bit about yourself? This seemingly harmless, open-ended question can be very intimidating for interviewees. It's a great opener because it not only allows you to get to know the candidate, but also allows you to assess poise, professionalism, and communication skills. Can a candidate communicate the unique personal traits and professional skills that she believes make her the right person to take on the responsibility of caring for your aging parents?

What specific things would you do to help promote and preserve my parents' independence and dignity? A candidate's response to this question could take many forms, but they should all express the same general theme: the way to promote and preserve the independence and dignity of our elder population is through contact, care, and nurturing; to offer a helping hand when needed, to listen intently to their concerns, to always respect their privacy and provide friendly conversation and companionship. Your parents' home is a place that makes them feel warm, comfortable, and secure; the caregiver's objective is to try to preserve this as long as possible, while helping your parents achieve a meaningful, dignified, and fulfilling lifestyle.

What made you choose this type of work? The candidate's response will also give you further indication of what this person is all about.

The person I'd want taking care of my mom or dad would be someone who absolutely loved his or her work. I'd look for someone who recognizes our seniors as strong, vibrant members of society, as people who live with purpose and make valued contributions to their families and communities; someone who genuinely cares and is passionate about helping others.

What prior experience do you have caring for and assisting aging adults? You asked this question during your telephone survey of Independent Home Care Providers, but hearing the response again in person will help your parents and other family members personally assess the candidate's qualifications and experience.

As to an interview of a home care worker assigned by a Home Care Agency, this will give your parents, you, and other family members an opportunity to confirm the qualifications and experience that the agency communicated to you.

Why do you believe you have the personality necessary to handle the psychological and emotional needs of an aging adult? The answer should offer some insight into what the candidate finds important, rewarding, and stimulating. You're looking to hire someone who chose this line of work because he or she finds it tremendously gratifying, and not just a means of earning a living.

Describe the finest person you've ever worked with. The answer should provide you and your parents some insight as to what qualities the candidate values and admires. Their description of the person they most admire is usually an indication of the type of person the candidate strives to be.

What type of person annoys you most? The characteristics of people who annoy a candidate will give you an indication of what the candidate strives not to be. It's also important to determine whether the traits the candidate mentions describe your parents; if they do, then the relationship is obviously unlikely to succeed.

What would you consider your weaknesses as a home care provider, and what are you doing to overcome them? This standard question is asked during interviews for many types of employment, and it's tough to answer. A candidate who says, "I have no weaknesses" might appear arrogant or untruthful, and if the response is humorous, he or she might come off as flippant. From an interviewer's point of view, this is a great question because it probes the candidate's skill set for soft spots. In some instances, citing a personality trait as a weakness could indicate that this prospect isn't right for your parents—something you want to expose before you hire someone.

A candidate familiar with the interview process should be able to cite a job-related weakness and frame it as an area for improvement. For example, the candidate might cite inexperience in handling people with Alzheimer's or other forms of dementia, and tell you how he or she plans to overcome it. Perhaps the candidate is taking a night course in the techniques of caring for and assisting people with Alzheimer's or other forms of dementia.

If my parents had a medical emergency, how would you handle it? The answer should make you feel comfortable about this person watching over your parents. The first correct answer is an immediate call to 9-1-1 to request an emergency medical response team. The next correct answer would be to reveal any medical training they candidate has, including CPR training, and how he or she would use this training under the pressured urgency of a medical emergency.

What's your attitude about smoking, alcohol, and drugs? People with alcohol and drug problems are less productive and likely to miss more days of work than those without substance-abuse problems. Your parents' attitude toward smokers will probably depend on whether they are or once were smokers. Whether a person smokes has nothing to do with how productive or caring he or she may be on the job.

Why did you leave your last job? This standard interview question can sometimes reveal some interesting responses. Most interviewees are trained not to respond with any kind of negativity or criticism of their former employer, however, sometimes things do slip out indicating the candidate does not have the patience or personality to deal with an aging adult.

If you could improve anything about your performance on your last

job, what would it be? The answer should be a good indication of what the candidate learned from prior home care experiences; it should reveal the prospect's creativity and provide a glimpse of his or her caring nature and sensitivity toward aging clients.

What do you like to do in your spare time? Do you have any hobbies? You might consider this question a bit personal, but it might offer some valuable insight into what this person is really all about. The candidate might even share an interest with your parents, which would create an immediate connection between them.

Having met my parents, do you believe this relationship will work for you personally and professionally? If so, why? Please be very honest—my parents' well-being depends on it.

Asking the candidate to respond honestly will increase your chances of getting a fully candid answer. Most people can relate to your situation: everyone has parents, and because of this, they'll likely put themselves in your shoes and offer the most honest information they can, even at the risk of not getting the job.

If we hire you, what specific things could we do to help you do your job better? This is another question designed to uncover soft spots in a candidate's skill set. Be wary of prospects who tell you they'll need a great deal of assistance caring for your parents; be equally wary of candidates who say they'll need no help at all.

One last question: Why should I hire you over the next candidate that walks through that door? This is a superb closing question because it gives candidates a final opportunity to sell themselves and convey why they deserve to be the one who gets to care for your parents. The question makes them communicate what distinguishes them from other candidates, usually by focusing on their true strengths, and will reveal their genuine enthusiasm for getting the job. It's important to announce that this is the last question so the candidate understands that this is his or her final chance to make an impression.

Do you have any questions? It's customary to end interviews by asking candidates whether they have any questions. Some human resource experts believe that not asking any questions might indicate a candidate's lack of interest or enthusiasm for the position. I'm not convinced that this so; I think it depends on how the candidate performed during the earlier stages of the interview. Make your own judgment here.

Closing the Interview

How you close an interview depends on how much you like the candidate. If you feel that he or she lacks the necessary skills to handle the job, or aren't sure, politely tell the prospect that you need time to talk with your family, and you'll contact him or her in the next few days; in the case of a home care worker assigned by a Home Care Agency, say you'll contact the agency with your decision in a few days. If you felt the candidate was great, say that you're very interested in retaining his or her services and will call within twenty-four-hours. Obviously, you want to talk with your parents and other family members prior to making a decision. Also, if the candidate is an Independent Home Care Provider, make it clear that hiring is contingent upon his or her references checking out and a positive result from your background investigation. (You'll do a background investigation only if a candidate becomes a finalist.)

If the candidate is a home care worker assigned by a Home Care Agency, the agency should have already conducted a background investigation. If you wish, you can ask to see the results of the investigation, which should be in the employee's personnel file. All the above steps are discussed in detail in "Step Five: Final Evaluation and Decision," the last step in choosing the best senior housing and care option for your parents. Read this section very carefully; these final steps are vital to making sure the candidate is the best person available to meet your parents' needs.

Conducting an In-Person Tour
of an Adult Day Program

If, after all your telephone surveys are completed, an adult day program makes your parents' short list, the next step is to take a tour. As with any senior housing and care option, never call to make an appointment; always make unannounced visits, so you can observe the program operating as it would on any other day. Sometimes, on days when visits are scheduled, program directors will have flowers brought in, have special meals prepared, and alert their professional staff that prospective participants are coming in. With unannounced visits, it's very difficult to try to hide any deficiencies in the program.

Be sure to use the "Checklist to Conduct a Tour of an Adult Day Program" on the CD. Make several copies of the checklist and use one at each program you visit, so you and your parents can easily compare all of them, which will help make the final decision easier.

As you tour each adult day program, be sure to write a comment for every area in the checklist, so you and your parents can have a clear record of the visit, including all your observations. If you don't take the time to note your observations while they're fresh in your mind, you won't remember them. The best way to fill out the checklist is to sit in one of the center's common areas immediately after the tour and write down everything you just observed. This way, if an additional question comes to mind while you're writing your thoughts, you can easily ask someone, and ask to see something again if you want to.

The checklist covers these important factors:

Exterior and Architectural Design – Arriving at the adult day center, what's your impression of the exterior and overall architectural design? Does it have a residential, home-like feel or does it feel more like an institution? Does the building appear to be in good physical condition? Is there adequate parking available for participants and guests?

While not as important as when your parents are considering moving into a senior housing and care community, you should still consider a building's appearance and design when evaluating an adult day program.

Interior Design and Décor – As you enter the building, what's your impression of the interior? Do you and your parents find it attractive? Does the décor give the center a residential, home-like feel?

As with senior housing and care communities, your parents will want an environment that's warm and inviting, not institutional. This isn't as important as when they're considering senior housing, but it's still significant.

Are the carpeting and flooring suitable for aging adults? Make a point of looking down now and then to take note of whether the floors and carpeting are in good shape, look nice, and are suitable for aging adults. What's suitable? Most state-of-the-art senior facilities install non-skid tile floors and carpeting, which are tight and firm to walk on, helping prevent falls and providing participants an easy walking environment. Make sure the center you're touring has this type of tile and carpeting.

Does the interior design have special features to make an aging adult's life easier? Look for any other senior friendly design features. Many senior facilities have handrails throughout the hallways and common areas for participants who need help walking.

Does the center have grab bars in the toilet and tub areas? Most programs provide a bath or shower service. Does the center use bathtubs or shower stalls? A shower stall with a molded or pull-down seat is much safer to get in and out of than a slippery bathtub. Raised toilet seats are also a popular feature, making it easier for aging adults to get on and off the toilet.

If your parents need an adult day center with an Alzheimer's/dementia care program, have the tour guide point out all architectural features designed to help memory-impaired individuals cope with everyday activities. Such features include continuous/circular hallways with certain patterns, colors, and distinct visual cues, enclosed outdoor patios, even lighting throughout the building or wing, and line-of-sight bathrooms, closets, and refrigerators. All of these features are discussed in detail in Chapter 3, Option 6, under "Advantages of an Alzheimer's/Dementia Care Wing or Community."

Lighting / Natural lighting

Does the center have good, even lighting? Is there enough natural light in the building? Research has shown that a lack of sunlight can negatively affect mood and health. It's been scientifically proven that our bodies need natural light just as they need clean air and water. Atriums and solariums have become more frequent additions to senior facilities. Does the center have either?

A center's interior design should include as much natural light as possible to help support and nurture aging participants. When choosing an adult day program, look for one with a building that allows adequate exposure to natural light, or choose one that provides your parents daily opportunities to spend time outside in the sunlight. Does the program have an outdoor courtyard?

Cleanliness is Next to Godliness

Is the building clean and free of unpleasant odors? Use your sense of smell continuously; it's unacceptable for anyone to live in an environment where the stench of urine is constant. Also, observe whether the carpeting and furniture are clean and free of stains.

Wheelchair Accessibility

Is the building designed for wheelchair accessibility? Are there ramps allowing easy wheelchair access to the building? Are all the bathrooms wheelchair accessible? Observe whether the hallways are wide enough for two wheelchairs to pass. If the building has more than one floor, be sure to note whether there's an elevator for participants who can't use the stairs.

Safety and Security

Are there emergency pull cords in the bathrooms if my parents were to suffer a medical emergency? If not, what other emergency response equipment does the program have to signal if your parents require emergency medical assistance? Does the program have the highly effective wireless system in which participants wears a call button? This system is safer and much more effective if a participant falls and is unable to get up.

Does the program offer a wireless wander prevention system to keep track of participants who tend to wander? If your parents have Alzheimer's or some other form of dementia, they'll be prone to wandering, which makes keeping track of them an ongoing safety and security issue. Some adult day programs that specialize in Alzheimer's/dementia care offer wireless wander prevention systems to help keep track of participants and prevent any harm due to wandering. If a participant were to wander away from a supervised area, the wireless monitoring device he or she wears would sound an alarm, alerting caregivers. If the program claims to have this system, ask them to demonstrate it for you; if they don't it, ask them what safeguards are in place to keep track of wandering participants.

While touring, did you notice a security guard in the complex? Are all exits clearly marked and do all doors have alarms? What type of security system does the center have? Many programs today have at least one security guard on site during business hours. Adult day programs usually hire outside security agencies that are experienced at securing multi-unit housing complexes and health care facilities.

Does the building have a sprinkler system? What about smoke detectors and carbon monoxide detectors? Are fire hoses and extinguishers easily accessible? Ask the director or administrator how often fire drills are conducted and whether you can review their emergency evacuation plan. Most programs will provide this on request.

Outdoor Courtyard

Does the center have an outdoor courtyard where participants can enjoy the outdoors?

Exposure to sunlight can help support and nurture the aging process, so an outdoor courtyard is a valuable asset. Most outdoor courtyards have walkways that are beautifully landscaped with trees, shrubs, and flower beds. Some have barbecue grills, picnic tables, chairs, benches, and gazebos, and some even have designated areas where participants can plant their own vegetable gardens.

While touring the outdoor courtyard, it's important to note:

► **Is the courtyard enclosed with a security fence?** The courtyard should have some type of enclosure to prevent participants from wandering off the grounds.

► **Is the walking area level and smooth to prevent unnecessary falls?** Uneven surfaces such as gravel or cobblestone aren't the best walking surfaces for seniors. A smooth, non-glare concrete or rubberized surface is ideal.

► **Is there an indoor/outdoor transition area?** Our eyes become more and more sensitive to the light as we get older, and it can take several minutes for an aging adult's eyes to adjust to bright sunlight. Some adult day programs have a shaded transition area such as a porch or an awning just before one enters the courtyard so residents' eyes have an opportunity to adjust.

Other Amenities and Activities

What other amenities does the center have?

Some programs offer swimming pools, spas, and exercise rooms for participants. Most have activity rooms where participants can enjoy a variety of activities including arts, crafts, billiards and cards.

The Nintendo Wii video game system has become a popular addition at many senior housing and care communities and adult day programs. These video games have revitalized seniors both mentally and physically. The Wii (pronounced "wee") allows residents to do something they may not have been able to do in years such as go bowling or play tennis. No bowling balls or tennis rackets are used; instead, the residents need only swing a small hand-held controller to simulate the rolling of the bowling ball or the swinging of the tennis racket. Physical therapists love the Wii because it motivates the residents to get on their feet, and swinging their arms puts more muscles to use and helps the residents regain and maintain their center of balance.

The quality of the amenities and activity programs is important because most activity programs take up at least half of the program's day.

The adult day program should meet your parents' needs for care and assistance and meet their intellectual and social needs by providing a place to have an interesting, enjoyable day of companionship and the chance to make new friends. The program should provide participants an opportunity to socialize and communicate with others that they wouldn't otherwise have if they stayed at home.

Professional Staff and Quality of Care

Is the staff friendly and courteous upon meeting you?

From the time you enter an adult day center until the time your leave, it'll be extremely important for you to observe the behavior of the program's staff. Make it a point to observe how they interact and communicate with the senior participants.

Is the staff friendly, courteous, and caring toward participants, showing them the respect they deserve? Observe whether they address participants by name. If they do, it might indicate that the staff cares enough to develop relationships with the participants.

Do the program participants look well cared for? While touring, carefully observe the participants' faces; their expressions are worth a thousand words. Do they look happy? Are they clean, well groomed, and adequately dressed? If you can, talk with some of the participants about how they like the program; especially, ask them what they think of the staff.

Does the program conduct periodic participant satisfaction surveys? Like many senior housing and care communities, some adult day programs conduct such surveys to help them continually improve their efforts to satisfy the wants and needs of their participants. The surveys are designed to get feedback on a program's accommodations, personnel, dining experience, social activities, and participants' satisfaction with the quality of care they're receiving. The surveys ask participants to grade the direct care staff's friendliness, attentiveness, and response time. If the program you're visiting conducts such surveys, ask the program director for copies of the results of the three most recent surveys. The feedback comes directly from the participants of the program, so the results will give you a valuable look into what your parents can expect should they decide to sign up for this adult day program.

Nutritionally Balanced Meals, Food Quality, and Dining Experience

Is the dining area attractive and suitable for everyday dining?

Is there a reasonably good selection of items on the menu? Take some time to review the daily menu. If the adult day program has a Dietitian, ask to speak with them about their nutrition program. Ask them to explain how the program meets the nutritional needs of its participants keeping in mind a senior's lower caloric intake. Make sure the Dietitian provides you with a clear, concise and logical response before accepting the menu as nutritionally balanced. Is the program capable of preparing special meals for your parents to accommodate a special diet if required?

Ask to tour the kitchen. Observe whether the kitchen is reasonably clean. Note whether there are separate areas for (i) food preparation, (ii) food storage, and (iii) dish washing and trash disposal. All quality kitchens will have separate areas for these functions.

Ask the person giving the tour whether you and your parents can have lunch at the center. By sampling the food, you and your parents can personally evaluate the quality of the food being prepared. If possible, have everyone order something different from the menu so several types of meals can be evaluated in one sitting. Is the food quality acceptable? Remember, your parents will be eating this food almost everyday.

Accommodations for Overnight Respite Stays

Does the program offer accommodations for overnight respite stays? Some adult day programs offer overnight respite services to the adult children or other caregivers to provide them with a much needed break from their evening or weekend caregiving duties. Adult day programs offering respite services will typically have furnished apartments available for participants to stay overnight, or over a period of days. The respite services allow the adult child caregiver a chance to get away for a special weekend or a weeknight by offering quality overnight care and supervision.

If the program offers overnight respite stays, ask to see the accommodations. Are they suitable and spacious enough for your parents' needs? Does the room have a kitchen or kitchenette? Does it have a TV? Does it have a private bathroom? Is an emergency response device available in case of a medical emergency?

Renewal and Replacement

Does the program look like it's kept up, renovating and replacing items such as carpeting, wall coverings, furniture, fixtures, and equipment? If everything looks like new, you'll know that management is putting money back into the program. During your telephone survey, you'll have learned the building's age, so you can determine whether management is doing its job renewing and replacing items. Does the building look its age or does it look better? Observe whether the carpeting and furniture are worn or outdated. Make sure all the TV sets are in proper working order, with good picture and sound.

Were You Given the Complete Tour?

Were you given a full tour of the entire center? Were you permitted access to everything you wanted to see in the building without violating the participants' privacy? Be wary of a tour guide who avoids a specific area of the building: he or she might be trying to hide something. You needn't be overly cynical or mistrustful, though; the person giving you the tour might have a good reason for not showing you something, but you should be aware of the possibility of their trying to hide a possible blemish in the program.

Overall Thoughts and Impressions of the Adult Day Program

Before you leave, be sure to write down any other observations you believe are relevant to your parents' decision. Also, write down your thoughts and impressions of the program as a whole. After observing the types of the participants, you should be able to answer the question "Will my parents fit in well with the rest of the participants in this program?"

The tour checklists are designed to have you grade the different areas of the program on a scale from one to ten, with one being the worst grade and ten the best. Complete the checklist while you're at the adult day center so you and your parents can have a clear record of your visit.

Conducting an In-Person Interview of a Hospice Care Program

If your parents have been diagnosed with a terminal illness and, having thoroughly prescreened all candidates using the telephone surveys, have narrowed their hospice care choices to a select few, the next step is to call the hospice care provider and schedule an in-person interview with one of their RNs. Some hospices will send one of their best-trained and skilled social workers for an interview and to assess your parents' needs; if you're given a choice, however, request an interview with the RN, who is, after all, the leader of the hospice care team and the one responsible for coordinating the care.

Due to the immediate need, you'll likely interview only one, but either the RN or the social worker will have a good idea which team members would be assigned to your parents and can probably tell you about their personalities and qualifications. The hospice team is commonly assigned based on geography: the hospice workers who live closest to your parents' place of residence will be assigned to their team. Remember that hospice team members can be replaced at your parents' request if they don't work out.

The Interview and How to Evaluate It

You need to evaluate specific things during the interview to make sure the hospice care team assigned to your parents is right for the job. The main objective of the interview is to learn whether the team leader (the RN) has the right chemistry and personality to handle the psychological and emotional needs of your dying loved one. If the hospice care program is a quality one, its employees already have the necessary skills to perform their jobs. You've already evaluated the recruitment, qualifications, and training of the program's staff during the telephone survey process; now it's just a matter of finding the people with whom your parents feel most comfortable.

> **Here are some questions to ask yourself while interviewing the leader of a hospice care team:**
>
> ► Will this person get along well with my parents?
> ► Would his or her demeanor and personality fit well with my parents'?
> ► Does he or she seem enthusiastic about caring for my dying loved one?
> ► Do I like and trust this person?
> ► Will the rest of the family like and trust him or her?
> ► Do I believe this is the right person to care for my parents in their final days?

Questions to Ask the Hospice Care Team Leader During the In-Person Interview

It's important to ask the types of questions that will not only confirm their qualifications, but also help you, your parents, and other family members evaluate the candidate's character and personality. The quality of a hospice care team is usually a direct reflection of its leader, so this interview will play a vital role in your final decision. How the team leader answers these questions should help you and your parents determine whether the team is capable of handling the physical, psychological, and emotional needs of the job.

On the CD you'll find a checklist of suggested questions to use in conducting interviews, as well as a list of post-interview evaluation questions that you, your parents, and other family members should answer. Feel free to add to the checklist any other questions you feel are necessary to determine whether this person and his or her team have the right stuff to be your parents' hospice care provider. After all, these are the last people your parents will be coming into contact with (besides yourself and your family) during their final days. The goal of hospice care is to allow your loved ones to spend their last days as pain-free and alert as possible, while surrounded by the people and things they love. Having a caring hospice staff with whom your parents feel comfortable could be considered your final act of love.

The questions on the checklist are discussed in detail below. Schedule the interview so other family members can interview the candidate and provide valuable support and feedback. It's important that all family actually hear the candidate's responses to these questions in person to better evaluate his or her character and personality as well as confirm their qualifications and experience.

Can you tell me a little bit about yourself? This seemingly harmless, open-ended question can be very intimidating for interviewees. It's a great opener because it allows you to get to know the candidate and assess his or her poise, professionalism, and communication skills. Can the candidate communicate the unique personal traits and professional skills that she believes make her the right person to lead the team of hospice care professionals responsible for comforting and caring for your dying loved one?

What specific things would you do to help make my parent's end-of-life experience as comfortable and pain-free as possible? Most everyone has a deep, dark fear that when their time comes, they'll die a slow, painful death alone and cut off from their loved ones in an unfamiliar surrounding such as a nursing home. The main objective of hospice care is to prevent this type of scenario from ever happening. Hospices accomplish this objective by providing their dying patients and their loved ones with comfort, compassion and dignity. Hospice care workers help make their patient's end-of-life experience bearable through human contact, care, and nurturing in a comfortable, familiar environment. Competent hospice care workers offer their dying patients a helping hand when needed, listen intently when they have concerns, always respect their privacy, and provide them with friendly conversation and companionship whenever possible.

What made you choose this type of work? The candidate's response to this question will also give you an indication of what this person is all about. When I was a sophomore in high school, I once asked my Dad for advice on what type of degree I should pursue. At the time, I was really confused about what I wanted to do with my life. My Dad, like he did many times in my life, offered me some very wise advice. He said "Mike, no matter what you choose to do with your life, make sure you love it and have a genuine passion for it. Living everyday of your life with passion is the best advice I could ever give you."

He was absolutely right. Having said this, I think the person I'd want taking care of my Mom or Dad would be someone that absolutely loved his or her work. I would look for someone that is genuinely passionate about caring for and helping others.

Tell us about your prior experience in caring for and assisting aging adults with a terminal illness. This will give you, your parents, and other family members the opportunity to confirm the worker's qualifications and experience communicated to you by the hospice.

What would you do if my parents were to suffer a medical emergency? How would you handle it? A hospice nurse I know told me she likes to answer this question with the question: What would you consider a medical emergency? She does this because she wants to make sure the family's focus has truly changed from curative to comfort-oriented care. In order to receive hospice care, your parent will be required to sign a consent form acknowledging they're changing their focus from curative to comfort care. It'll be extremely helpful if you, and the other members of your family, understand and respect your parent's final wishes.

Another option for hospice care patients is a DNRCC (do not

resuscitate comfort care) order. This is a written request not to have CPR (cardiopulmonary resuscitation) administered if your heart stops or if you stop breathing. Although it's not a requirement to enter a hospice care program, most hospice patients get the DNRCC order to reduce their suffering, increase their peace of mind, and give them more control over their own death.

Having met my parents, do you feel this relationship will work for you personally and professionally? If so, why? Please be very honest—my parents' well-being depends on it.

Asking the candidate to respond honestly will increase your chances of getting a fully candid answer. Most people can relate to your situation: everyone has parents, and can likely put themselves in your shoes and offer the most honest information they can, even at the risk of not getting the job.

If we hired you, what specific things could we do to help you do your job better? One hospice care nurse I interviewed replied, "All I ask is that you be honest, especially about your parents' symptom and pain management. Your family is going to play a huge role in your parents' end-of-life experience, so my team needs your honest and active cooperation in our effort to make their last days as comfortable as possible."

One last question: Why should I hire your hospice care team over the next one that walks through that door? This superb closing question gives the team leader a final opportunity to sell his or her team and convey why it deserves to be the one to care for your parents during their final days. The question makes her communicate what distinguishes her hospice care team from any other. The candidate will usually focus on her true strengths and will reveal her genuine enthusiasm for getting the job of comforting and caring for your dying loved one. It's important to tell the candidate this is the last question, so she understands this is the final opportunity to make an impression.

Do you have any questions? It's customary to end interviews by asking candidates whether they have any questions. Some human-resource experts believe that not asking any questions might indicate a candidate's lack of interest or enthusiasm for the position. I'm not convinced this is so; I think it depends on how the candidate performed during the earlier stages of the interview. Make your own judgment here.

Closing the Interview

How you close an interview depends on how much you like the person assigned to lead your parents' hospice care team. If at the close of the interview you're still unsure or feel the candidate isn't quite the right fit for your parents, politely tell the prospect that you'll contact him or her in the next few days with your decision. If you felt the candidate was great, say that you're very interested in retaining his or her services and will call within twenty-four-hours. Obviously, you want to talk with your parents and other family members prior to making a final decision.

Since the workers are employed by a hospice care agency, the agency will have already conducted background investigations on them. If you wish, request to see the results of these investigations, which should be in each employee's personnel file. All the above steps are discussed in detail in "Step Five: Final Evaluation and Decision," the last step in choosing the best senior housing and care option for your parents. Read this section very carefully; these last steps are vital to making sure the hospice care agency you're considering is the best available.

Step Five

Final Evaluation and Decision

Now it's time to help your parents make their final evaluation and decision. Before tackling this last step in your quest for the best senior housing and care option available, you and your parents should have completed the previous four:

Step One: Assessing Your Parents' Current and Future Care and Assistance Needs;

Step Two: Identifying All Senior Housing and Care Options Available in Your Parents' Desired Area of Residence;

Step Three: Conducting Telephone Surveys of All Senior Housing and Care Options;

Step Four: Conducting In-Person Tours and Interviews of All Senior Housing and Care Options That Make Your Parents' Short List.

The amount of time and effort you spent completing those four steps should make this final step very easy. All the information you need to make an informed decision is already at your fingertips. Based on your research, your parents should be able to narrow their choices to one or two candidates. There are, however, some important final steps you need to do before you can be sure the remaining candidates are the best possible option to meet your parents' needs.

Be Sure All Family Members are Involved

It's important to have the active involvement of all your parents' family members during the final evaluation and decision process. The ideal goal is family consensus, but the final decision rests with your parents, and everyone in the family should be informed of their final decision. Failure to keep everyone in the loop will only create problems down the line, making your parents' transition harder for everyone. If not handled correctly, old resentments, sibling rivalries, and control issues might resurface. This is tough for everyone, because all of you must adjust, accept your parents' new limitations, and come to grips with your own mortality.

Check References

Regardless of how good you feel about a finalist, it's important to ask for a list of references, which should include local physicians, geriatric care managers, hospital social workers and discharge planners, and current and former clients. If a former client is deceased, ask for the name and phone number of a surviving family member. Follow up with these references to confirm that the candidate's reputation for quality care is a good one.

To successfully check a candidate's references, you need perform certain steps. Here are some I picked up while checking references of potential candidates for a former employer:

▸ **Seek References Not Provided by the Candidate.** The references a candidate offers aren't always the most candid because of the references' close personal, professional, or contractual relationship with the candidate. To receive a more objective response, try calling local geriatric care managers, physicians specializing in gerontology, hospital social workers and discharge planners, and the local Area Agency on Aging. If you're checking the references of an Independent Home Care Provider, many of those referral sources might be irrelevant, since an individual is less well known than a senior housing and care community, Home Care Agency, or adult day program. In this instance, ask the reference offered by the candidate to give you the name and phone number of someone that knows the candidate either personally or professionally, and call this person as well. Continue this process until you have enough information and are satisfied with the results.

► **Ignore Written References Provided by the Candidate.** Some candidates have written references already prepared, and like to include them in the marketing packages they hand out to prospective residents or clients. It's best to ignore this "marketing copy" and call the reference yourself to confirm the praise in his or her written letter of recommendation. In many instances, it's been found that the candidates themselves wrote the letters of recommendation.

► **Check References by Telephone, Not by Mail.** Writing to companies or individuals to get references is an ineffective waste of time. Talking with a reference by phone is the best way to judge candor, sincerity, and enthusiasm for a candidate. Talking with the reference also gives you the opportunity to ask the spontaneous follow-up questions that inevitably arise during the conversation.

► **Be Friendly and Candid.** This might seem obvious, but it needs emphasis nonetheless. References are more likely to respond candidly if you're friendly and candid yourself. Speak to them with enthusiasm and let them know how grateful you are for their taking the time to answer your questions about the candidate. Let them know how concerned you are about hiring someone to take care of your parents, that you only want the best for your parents, and how grateful you'd be for any input—positive or negative—that they can offer. Everyone has parents, so most people will relate to your situation, put themselves in your shoes, and offer the most honest information they can.

Some Good Questions to Ask when Calling a Reference:

▶ How long have you known the candidate/caregiver/provider?

▶ Do you frequently refer clients to this caregiver?

▶ What type of feedback have you gotten from people you've previously referred to this caregiver?

▶ May I contact any of the people you've referred to this caregiver to get their feedback?

▶ Do you have or have you had any past association or contractual relationship with this candidate/caregiver? If so, please describe.

▶ What do you consider the caregiver's strengths?

▶ What are the caregiver's weaknesses?

▶ Are you aware of any acts of misconduct?

▶ Are you aware of any lawsuits pending against the caregiver?

▶ Would you, without reservation, place your parents' health and well-being in this caregiver's hands? Please be candid because my parents' welfare depends on it. If your answer is yes, please tell me why?

Conduct Background Checks

Caring for your parents is an important job, so you need to be very thorough when investigating a candidate's background and character. Use several third-party sources to verify the candidate has the responsibility and character to do the job. You can use any of the following resources to investigate a candidate's background.

Contact Nationally Recognized Accrediting Organizations

This is the best place to start your background check. Senior housing and care options can get accreditation by meeting the standards of quality and excellence set by an accrediting body. Accredited organizations are periodically surveyed to determine whether they meet, exceed, or fall short of those standards; you and your parents can access the survey results to verify the quality of care the candidate provides.

Remember that the accreditation process is voluntary, so not all organizations will have survey results or performance evaluations available for review. It's in your best interest to choose an accredited senior housing and care option, but if your finalist hasn't gotten accreditation, you can use other sources to complete the background check. For assisted living communities, accreditation is relatively new, and membership in these programs, while still small, is growing rapidly, so accreditation or lack of it needn't be the only deciding factor.

Here are some nationally recognized accrediting organizations to contact about a candidate's performance:

► **The Joint Commission on the Accreditation of Health Care Organizations (The Joint Commission)**

> **You can access a directory of all Joint Commission-accredited nursing care facilities, hospice care programs, and home care agencies at The Joint Commission's website: www.qualitycheck.org.**

Their online Quality Check™ lets you read the latest performance report of a nursing care facility, hospice, or home care agency to see how they rate compared to similar accredited organizations. If a facility, program, or agency is not in full compliance with the applicable standards, the requirements for improvement will be listed in the Quality Report as well as the summary page on Quality Check™.

It should be noted that Quality Check™ is a comprehensive directory that lists nearly all nursing care facilities, hospice care programs, and home care agencies available today. It lists both accredited organizations as well as non-accredited organizations. The Joint Commission added non-accredited health care organizations in order to provide a more complete inventory for its users. Nursing care facilities, hospice care programs, and home care agencies that are accredited by The Joint Commission will display a large Gold Seal of Approval™ under the Accreditation/Certification column on the website.

> If you don't have Internet access, you can request a specific organization's performance report by contacting The Joint Commission's customer service department in Washington, D.C.: 630-792-5800.

- ▸ The Commission on Accreditation of Rehabilitation Facilities (CARF)

> If an adult day program, assisted living community or nursing care facility make your parents' final cut, you can access a directory of all CARF-accredited organizations and the performance reports from their most recent evaluations by phoning CARF toll-free: 888 281-6531.

The information packet they send you will specify the areas in which the organization is exceeding CARF standards, any areas in which recommendations for improvement have been given, and the grounds for each accreditation awarded or denied. You'll also receive a comparison rating of conformance to standards with similar programs. Before CARF releases any information to you, they first send the packet to the organization, so it can respond to any of CARF's outcomes. This response, if there is one, will be included in the packet you receive. You can access more information on CARF at www.carf.org.

▶ **The Continuing Care Accreditation Committee (CARF-CCAC)**

If a Continuing Care Retirement Community is on your parents' final list, be sure to contact CARF-CCAC to find out whether the community meets all accreditation criteria.

> **For more information including a directory of all on CARF-CCAC-accredited communities nationwide, visit their website: www.carf.org/aging or phone them toll-free in Washington, D.C.: 866-888-1122.**

Contact the U.S. Department of Health and Human Services ("DHHS")

If your parents are considering a nursing care facility that is certified to participate in the Medicare or Medicaid program, then contacting the DHHS is a must. Federal laws govern this certification. Annual surveys are conducted to verify these services are being provided in compliance with Medicare or Medicaid standards. State survey agencies also conduct these annual surveys, and cite communities that fail to meet federal guidelines. Every nursing care facility certified to participate in the Medicare or Medicaid program is required to make the results of their last inspection available onsite for public review.

A new, five-star quality rating system was unveiled in December 2008 by the Centers for Medicare and Medicaid Services ("CMS"). This new system was designed to give consumers more useful information to compare nursing care facilities and help them make better, more informed long-term care decisions. In the new system, each nursing care facility is rated from a lowest rating of one star to a highest rating of five stars in three critical areas: (i) health inspection results; (ii) quality measures; and (iii) staffing levels.

> You can access the new five-star quality rating system and search the database of nearly 16,000 nursing care facilities by city, state, or zip code at www.medicare.gov/NHCompare.

The five-star quality rating system is a great place to begin your search for nursing care facilities that might meet your parents' needs. Be aware that a great deal of information on this website is provided directly by the nursing care facilities themselves and is not checked for accuracy; therefore, it's important you perform your own due diligence by visiting and touring the facilities as well as completing all five steps to selecting the best senior housing and care option before making your final decision.

Contact the Better Business Bureau (BBB)

Contact the BBB to find out whether a senior housing and care community, home care agency, or adult day program has any complaints filed against it. The BBB investigates each consumer complaint and acts as the liaison between the consumer and the businesses so disputes and problems can be quickly resolved.

> You can easily access an organization's reliability report by calling the local office of the BBB, or by conducting your own search at the user-friendly BBB website: www.bbb.org.

The reliability report will indicate how many complaints have been filed against a company in the past thirty-six months and whether any complaint has been successfully resolved. If not, the company receives an unsatisfactory rating.

Thinking of Hiring an Independent Home Care Provider?

If your parents are considering an Independent Home Care Provider, a professional investigation and background check is mandatory. Many professional investigative firms specialize in pre-employment background checks; their fees range from $100–$1,000 depending on how comprehensive a search you want. Here are some of the procedures they perform.

✓ **Name and Social Security Number Verification** – Is the candidate really who he says he is? Most investigative firms conduct fraud scans for aliases and false social security numbers.

✓ **Prior Employment Verification** – All previous employment is verified and confirmed, including hire and termination dates, job description, salary confirmation, and reasons for leaving.

✓ **Education/License/Certification Verification** – All educational degrees, professional licenses, and certifications are verified and confirmed. Does the candidate really have the achievements and qualifications she claims?

✓ **Chronological Review** – A chronological review from the time the candidate leaves high school to the present day is an important step to make sure that all employment and other activity is reported in his or her application or résumé. Any unreported gaps are identified and attempts are made to learn what the prospect was doing during these periods. Many candidates cover up bad employment experiences by omitting them from their résumés.

✓ **Credit History Review** – Review of a candidate's credit history can provide important information. A poor credit history with excessive balances and a high delinquency rate can indicate a lack of responsibility or character. Depending on the charges and where they're coming from, the investigator might even be able to determine whether the candidate has an alcohol or drug problem.

✓ **Court Record Search** – A thorough search of all local, county, and federal public records can uncover any criminal, civil, or bankruptcy activity. Does the candidate have a history of lawsuits either as a defendant or plaintiff? Has he or she ever been convicted of a crime?

✓ **Driving Record** – The candidate's driving record can be accessed by the Department of Motor Vehicles. Is the candidate a responsible driver? Will your parents' safety be jeopardized if the caregiver provides them transportation to and from appointments? Was the candidate ever convicted of driving under the influence of alcohol or drugs?

✓ **Workers' Compensation Claims Review** – Find out whether the candidate has ever filed a claim. This might help you determine whether he or she can handle the physical demands of the job (i.e., lifting your mom or dad from place to place). You can also judge susceptibility to on-the-job injuries. Access to this information is restricted under the Americans with Disabilities Act of 1990. Under the law, you must make a conditional job offer to the candidate prior to reviewing his or her Workers' Compensation records, and agree to hold the information in these records in the strictest confidence.

Under the Fair Credit Reporting Act and privacy laws, you must get the candidate's written consent to conduct a background investigation. Most professional investigative firms have consent forms to provide to your candidate, which will protect you if the candidate later disputes the investigation or claims you invaded his or her privacy. Don't hesitate to ask for a candidate's consent to conduct an investigation; this is standard operating procedure when hiring a caregiver. A prospect who refuses consent must be hiding something that would prevent you from giving him or her the job.

All Senior Housing and Care Organizations Should Conduct Background Checks on Prospective Employees

It's in their best interest to do so; after all, the organization's reputation is at stake. Organizations are frequently charged in court with "negligent hiring" because they don't bother conducting simple employee background checks. The checklists for conducting telephone surveys of the various senior housing and care options ask what steps the organization takes to recruit, screen, and select employees. For example, are background checks performed and references checked? If an organization says no, simply thank them for their time and hang up.

If the organization says they perform background checks on all prospective employees, you can go a step further to confirm that they're telling the truth by asking that they share some of their employee personnel files with you, including the results of their background investigations. Such investigations of employees are vital to organizations in the business of caring for our aging population.

Not an Accredited Organization?

Then conduct a professional investigation and background check. If the senior housing and care community, home care agency, or adult day program your parents are considering is not accredited, it's in your best interest to conduct a background investigation to make sure the organization is what it seems. Your parents' well-being is worth the small fee necessary to hire a professional investigation firm. When it comes to caring for your loved ones, peace of mind is a very good thing.

Background investigations of businesses are similar to investigations of individuals. The cost of such an investigation is similar to that of a pre-employment background check: fees range from $100–$1,000 depending on how comprehensive a search you want. Here are some of the procedures performed in background investigations of businesses:

- ✓ **Identification of All Owners and Principals** – It's important to know the identities of the owners and principals of the business so their individual backgrounds can be checked as well.

- ✓ **Background Checks of all Owners and Principals** – For each owner and principal identified above, an individual background investigation will be conducted, including a review of their credentials, credit history, and litigation activity.

- ✓ **Court Record Search** – A search of all local, county, and federal public records can uncover any criminal, civil, or bankruptcy activity involving the organization and its principals. Find out whether the organization has a history of lawsuits or judgments filed against it.

✓ **Credit and Financial History Review** – A review of the organization's credit and financial history can provide a wealth of information. A poor credit history with vendors and suppliers might indicate the organization is in financial trouble. Liens filed against the property also might indicate financial difficulties.

✓ **Credibility Assessment of the Company and its Principals** – This includes interviews with the organization's vendors, community leaders, and other references to corroborate the organization's reputation among the business community, and may include a search of all newspaper and magazine articles to search for any instances of bad publicity.

In most cases, there's no requirement for written consent to conduct a background investigation of a business. There may be instances where privacy laws apply and the business has to be notified to request consent. The professional investigation firm should be aware of all requirements and laws regarding privacy.

Review All Contracts and Agreements

It's imperative that you, your parents, and their attorney review and discuss the implications of all agreements and contracts your parents enter into with any senior housing and care provider. If they're considering a senior housing and care community, your parents will be required to sign a residency agreement which specifies the terms and conditions of their stay, including the fees they will be charged, refund provisions (if any), what services will be provided in exchange for these fees, and how much additional services will cost should your parents need them. The residency agreement will also state when the community has the right to terminate your parents' residency; depending on the agreement, they might have to move out of a community upon reaching a specified higher level of care or assistance that the community is unable to meet or if they can no longer pay the rent. These terms need to be understood prior to moving into a community. The residency agreement may also include a resident's bill of rights, which delineates your parents' individual rights. Home Care Agencies and adult day programs will also require them to sign a contract or agreement stating the required fees and the services to be provided. Review all contracts and agreements with your parents' attorney before signing anything. These agreements are fairly standard, but it's better to be safe than sorry.

Hiring an Independent Home Care Provider?

If your parents have decided to hire an Independent Home Care Provider, then you, your parents, and their attorney will need to draft an employment agreement. The agreement should detail the employee's salary, benefits, frequency of payment, hours of employment, and a list of the specific duties and services to be provided in exchange for their salary and benefits. The agreement should also include examples of unacceptable behaviors that would result in the termination of the employment contract. This helps avoid any confusion about why an employee was terminated, and helps you steer clear of termination disputes and lawsuits.

Review a Senior Housing and Care Community's Latest Audited Financial Statements

If a senior housing and care community is a finalist, it's crucial that you request a copy of its most recent audited financial statements from the executive director or administrator prior to making your final decision, because your parents will make a substantial investment in the community in the form of monthly fees and, in the case of a CCRC, a large initial entrance fee.

In addition to your parents' cash investment, their emotional welfare is at risk. If the community were to close due to financial difficulties, your parents would have to endure yet another move, and if the community had no insurance to cover their large initial deposit, they might have to move at the financial burden of their children or a government-funded program such as Medicaid. In bankruptcy proceedings, residents are usually the last in line when it comes to recouping their investment.

It's important that you, your parents, and their financial advisor or CPA review the community's current financial position. Regulations in some states require senior housing and care communities to carry a surety bond, which protects all residents' deposits and other community-held trust accounts. Be sure to inquire whether the community your parents are considering carries this insurance.

This sort of review isn't critical with home care agencies or adult day programs: if these go out of business, your parents don't have to move, and they can always contract with another agency or program. The closing could affect your parents emotionally, but their pain would be much greater if they had to pack up and move.

Trust Your Instincts and Let Go

If you've completed all five of the steps to choosing the best senior housing and care option for your parents, then their final decision should be easy. The last bit of advice I can offer you is to trust your instincts and feel comfortable with your parents' final decision. The due diligence you've performed to get this far should remove any uncertainty as to whether this option is the best for your parents. It's going to be difficult for you to fully trust their final decision; there'll always to be some degree of anxiety—after all, this is a major life change for your parents and it affects everyone who cares about them.

The time you've invested in helping your parents choose the best senior housing and care option is the most important thing you could ever do for them. I commend you for your dedication and your compassion. Your purchase of this book is an indication that family ranks high on your list of values. It's important to remember that the housing and care option your parents choose will never replace you. It's not easy to let go and entrust the responsibility for your parents' care to someone else, but, in time, you'll find that it provides the quality of life all of you deserve.

Chapter Seven

Helping Your Parents Cope with Their New Environment

Your parents' transition from their former home and independent lifestyle to their new home with supportive services won't be easy. The first month will be the hardest, and your involvement throughout this initial period will be crucial to its ultimate success. Here are some tips I've gotten from senior housing and care social workers and directors over the years.

Visit Your Parents' New Home Prior to Moving Day

If your parents have decided to move into a senior housing and care community, make a point of visiting there in the days prior to their scheduled move-in date; together, you should look at the apartment they'll be moving into and determine such things as:

- ► How would your parents like to arrange their furniture? Where will Dad put his favorite easy chair?

- ▶ Which personal belongings will they be bringing from home?

- ▶ What wallpaper or pictures would they like to hang, and where?

- ▶ Do your parents want to recreate the feel of their former home? If so, how can this be done? If not, what new look would they like to create?

The first step in a successful transition is your parents' active involvement in the planning and decorating of their own apartment. This will help provide them a comfortable and familiar living environment. Be sure to clear any improvements you and your parents have in mind with the community's executive director. Depending on the individual situation and on its budget, the community might repaint the apartment or replace the carpeting before renting the unit to a new resident. Ask the executive director if any such improvements will be made prior to your parents' moving in; if so, ask whether they can choose the color of the carpeting or paint.

In addition to visiting the apartment, walk through the halls and common areas and introduce yourself and your parents to the professional staff. Inform them that your parents will soon become new residents, and let them know when they'll be moving in. The sooner the staff gets to know all of you, the better they'll be able to meet your parents' needs and make them feel more at home. Familiarity with the staff before your parents move in will be very helpful on moving day: it's comforting to see familiar smiling faces amidst the strange new surroundings.

During your visit, stop and visit with some of the residents, too. Talk with the executive director to see if there are any activities or functions your parents might wish to attend while visiting. Some communities have daily cocktail hours or after-dinner gatherings where residents go to mingle. Your parents might want to attend one or more of these functions so they can meet some of the residents. Your parents might even make a friend or two before moving in.

Helping with the Move

The big day has arrived! Few things can be more difficult for your parents than leaving their private residence and moving to their new senior housing and care community. Make sure that all members of the family and extended family show up to help support your parents on this monumental day. Try to make it a festive one, with a party-like atmosphere. Family members should bring snacks and housewarming gifts, showing their love and support and how much your parents mean to all of you, and spend the day helping them get situated in their new apartment. If you go as a group, make sure to stagger your departures so the day's final goodbye isn't so distressingly sudden.

Visit Soon and Often

Be sure to visit your parents soon and often during their first month at the community. That's not to say you should visit less often after the initial thirty-day transition period, but that the first thirty days are the most critical. Your parents' lives will be going through a major change; in many cases, a final

transition, so they'll need your support to help them through this emotionally difficult time. Frequent visits by family and other loved ones help reduce feelings of isolation and loneliness, which can lead to depression and giving up on life.

If your parents need care or assistance, get involved in helping care for them. Learn about their care plan and help with their daily effort to get well or deal with their condition. Visit with the direct care staff as well; becoming a frequent presence and a familiar face can only make things better for your parents. Alert the staff about your parents' pet peeves, so they don't upset and discourage your parents early on. Maybe Dad dislikes being called by his first name and wants to be addressed only by his last name. Also, make the staff aware of your parents' regular routines so they're not changed. Maybe Mom enjoys reading the local paper first thing in the morning with black coffee, no cream, and no sugar. Make the staff aware of this so they can try to accommodate her. Whatever helps keep things the same for your parents will help tremendously in adjusting to their new environment.

Bring the grandchildren, young and old, to visit your parents whenever possible. Some might feel that the little ones' boisterous nature will disturb the peace of the senior community and could be too much for Grandma to handle. This couldn't be further from the truth. Most residents enjoy the change of pace that occurs when little ones visit. Next to the parent-child relationship, the grandparent-grandchild relationship is the most cherished; it allows your parents to continue in an important family role. They enjoy passing on their thoughts and views to the next generation. Encourage the older grandchildren to visit and talk with their grandparents about their family history. I regret not talking to my grandparents more often about what their early lives were like; it would have been fascinating to hear their thoughts on living through two world wars and the Great Depression.

You've Got Mail!

If you can't visit your parents as often as you'd like due to the location and distance from their place of residence, the next best thing you can do is write them as often as possible. A phone call is a great way to keep in touch, but nothing brightens a resident's day more than opening the mailbox and seeing a letter or package from a loved one. Having visited hundreds of communities over the years, I've witnessed this joy firsthand. Receiving regular mail, especially in the first month, will help your parents fight off any feelings of abandonment, loneliness, and depression. Try to coordinate your mailing with other family members so your parents can receive something nearly every day during the first thirty days. Mail is a great way to update them on what's going on with the family. Have the little ones draw a picture for Grandma that she can proudly display in her apartment for all to see. Send Grandpa your oldest child's latest term paper or a school project that made you proud—let your parents feel proud, too. Unlike a phone call, mail from loved ones is something your parents can touch and hold, something they can enjoy over and over again, proudly display in their apartment, and use as conversation pieces to brag about their grandchildren to the staff when they arrive to help Grandma with her bath. Never underestimate the power of love through the mail; it really will help your parents adapt to their new environment.

Dealing with Anger, Resentment, Guilt, and Self-Doubt

Your parents' adjustment to their new home and lifestyle will undoubtedly bring up a lot of strong feelings. As I've said all along, it' not going to be easy; it'll be an emotionally difficult time for everyone. After all, our aging parents' increasing frailty is a daily reminder of our own mortality.

Within the first few days, your parents are likely to express some dissatisfaction with their new living arrangements and may even demand to go home or come live with you or one of their other children. They might express anger and resentment toward you and other family members for putting them in this predicament. These feelings could result in a tremendous amount of guilt and self-doubt on your part. Please understand that this is perfectly normal.

Experiencing something new and different, and the element of the unknown, can often evoke fear and anxiety. Anyone who's gone through the experience of moving to a strange new town has experienced this to a lesser degree. Add to this the anxiety your parents are feeling about their increasing dependency on others and you can understand their initial reaction to this life-changing development. It's important to understand that these worries will pass with time, and so will their anger and resentment, and your guilt and self-doubt. If you've diligently followed the five-step process in this book, then your parents are in the best possible place they can be, an environment that will help preserve and promote their independence and dignity, which is all you could ask for.

The most important advice I can give to help you get through the first few days is to be a good listener. Don't ignore your parents' concerns or get defensive; this can only make matters worse. Encourage them to air all their concerns about their new accommodations. All they want is to know that you still care. Show this by listening to them; opening your ears and your heart to them will help them through this tough transition. Communication is the key to resolving any problem—and this situation is no exception.

Chapter Eight

Plan Ahead and Gather the Essential Information Now!

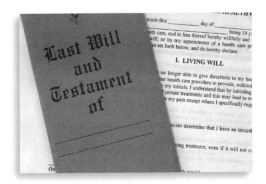

Once your parents decide to address their future housing and care needs, specific items need to be gathered and kept safely in a file for when it's time to carry out their requests. The CD includes a checklist you can use to gather all the necessary information. Having this information handy will make things much easier on you and your family should your parents experience a medical emergency or become incapacitated.

Here are some of the important documents and information you should gather:

Your Parents' Personal Information

► Dates of birth

► Places of birth

► Location of their birth certificates

▸ Social Security numbers

▸ Place(s) of employment

▸ Education

▸ Religious affiliation

▸ Location of their church, synagogue, other

▸ Name of their clergy

▸ Military service, and

▸ Pets — include the animals' names and their veterinarian's phone number

Copy of Last Will and Testament

Have your parents made a last will and testament? A will is a legal document that instructs how a person's property should be distributed after death. If your parents don't have a will, state law will determine how their property is distributed. If one of your parents passes away intestate (without a will) any property will be distributed among the surviving spouse and children. If at the time of his or her passing, your parent has no spouse or children, then all property will be distributed among any other relatives according to a statutory formula.

Choosing an Executor

One of the more important decisions your parents will make when setting up their will is choosing an executor. The executor is the person your parents will appoint in their will to handle their property and distribute it as their will directs. The most important thing your parents must consider in selecting an executor is whether they can trust the person. If some of the beneficiaries in your parents' will don't trust the executor, it can lead to hostility among family members.

Your parents should also choose a person who is willing to take responsibility for performing the duties of the job. To make sure, your parents should discuss it with the person ahead of time and receive his or her consent. Additionally, they should choose at least one alternate executor to serve if the primary executor cannot.

Where Should Your Parents Keep Their Last Will and Testament?

A last will and testament does not need to be on record or filed with any government agency. All your parents need to do is keep it in a safe place. If they should pass away, their executor will need to locate their will. You can help by knowing where it is so it can be easily found if something happens to your parents. Most people keep their wills in a safe deposit box; others keep them at home in a fireproof metal box.

Copy of the Durable Power of Attorney

One of the most important legal documents your parents will need is a "durable power of attorney," which is a contractual agreement between your parents and whoever they decide should make the financial decisions for them if they become unable to make those decisions for themselves. Usually given to a spouse or an adult child, the durable power of attorney allows this person access to your parents' bank accounts to pay for such expenditures as health care or any other debts they might incur.

A durable power of attorney must be signed by your parents and witnessed and/or notarized for the document to be legally binding. Consult your parents' attorney to make sure all the necessary steps are taken to ensure its legal effectiveness.

Copy of the Durable Power of Attorney for Health Care

Another contractual agreement your parents should consider if they don't have one already is a "durable power of attorney for health care," which allows them to appoint another person, called an agent, to make health care decisions for them if they become temporarily or permanently unable to make those decisions for themselves.

Your parents can select any adult to be their agent. Since this person will be making important medical decisions for them, they should choose someone they trust and have confidence in, and who's familiar with their wishes, values, and religious beliefs. Once your parents have chosen someone, they should discuss the matter with that person to make sure he or she understands the duties and agrees to accept the responsibility.

Some examples of the powers that can be given (or denied) to the agent under the durable power of attorney for health care are the power to: terminate extreme measures for life support; donate your parents' organs; authorize an autopsy; and direct the disposition of your parents' remains. Under the durable power of attorney for health care, the agent must exercise power according to you parents' wishes, which they have communicated to him or her in any manner, including orally.

Like a durable power of attorney, a durable power of attorney for health care must be signed by your parents and witnessed or notarized to be legally binding. Consult your parents' attorney to make sure all the necessary steps are taken to ensure its legal effectiveness.

A Copy of Your Parents' Living Will

Do your parents have a living will? This is a document instructing your parents' personal physician and other health care providers whether they want life-support procedures or treatments given to them if they are terminally ill or in a permanent unconscious state. The living will becomes a part of your parents' medical file when given to their physician; it is binding unless the physician notifies your parents upon receipt of the document that he or she will not honor it. The living will is probably unnecessary if you have a durable power of attorney for health care with a life-support provision, as this usually takes precedence over a living will.

A Copy of Your Parents' Do Not Resuscitate Order (DNR)

A DNR order is a written request not to have CPR (cardiopulmonary resuscitation) performed should a person's heart stop or breathing stop. People with terminal illnesses or other grave health conditions are usually the ones who write DNR orders, which can reduce suffering and increase a person's peace of mind and control over his or her own death.

List of Names and Phone Numbers of all Professionals Familiar with Your Parents

It's important to have a list of your parents' professional contacts in case of emergency. The list should include their primary care physician, any medical specialists, attorneys, accountants, eldercare consultant, trust officer, and the primary and alternate executors of their last will and testament.

Names and Phone Numbers of All Your Parents' Close Relatives, Friends, and Neighbors

In case of emergency, it's helpful to have a list of the names and phone numbers of your parents' closest family and friends handy so you can contact them for help and support.

A Copy of Your Parents' Medical History, Listing all Medications and Dosages

Compile a list of all medical conditions your parents have seen a physician about in the past five years. What health problems are they experiencing? Also, list all prescription medications your parents are taking, including the dosage for each, and note whether they're taking any over-the-counter medications. This information will be invaluable if your parents become incapacitated and unable to communicate with their new caregivers.

Information on All Types of Insurance

Gather information on all your parents' insurance policies, including health and medical insurance, long-term care insurance, life insurance, homeowner's or renter's insurance, and car insurance. For each policy, record the name of the insurance company, its address and phone number, the policy number, and a copy of the policy. If you don't want to deal with getting copies of these lengthy documents, note where the policy is stored for safekeeping (e.g., your parents' safe deposit box). Make sure these important documents are in a safe place and not in danger of being destroyed by fire, flood, or some other cause.

Life Settlements

I'd like to mention a fairly new financial service called life settlements. Life settlements allow your aging parents to sell an existing life insurance policy to a financial institution in exchange for an immediate lump sum cash payment. This could be another option for your parents to fund their long-term care costs.

Copies of all Income Tax Returns and Tax Records

Be sure to get copies of all your parents' income tax returns and tax records. At the very least, get the location of their tax documents. Often, your parents' CPA will keep office copies of their returns and other records.

A List of All Checking and Savings Accounts

Get the name of the bank, the bank's address, contact name, and a copy of your parent's latest bank statements. Obtain this information for all checking and saving accounts.

Information on Safe Deposit Boxes

Get the name, address, and phone number of the bank or banks where your parents have safe deposit boxes; also note the location of the keys as well as the names and phone numbers of the people with access to the safe deposit boxes.

List of All Assets

Get a list of all pension plans, profit-sharing plans, trust funds, individual retirement accounts (IRAs), 401(k) plans, investment or brokerage firm accounts, online trade accounts, stocks, bonds, and all other investments. Note the account numbers of all trust and investment or broker accounts, including the names and phone numbers of all trust officers, brokers, and investment officers.

For pension and profit-sharing plans, be sure to get the name of the company sponsoring the plan as well as the name and phone number of the administrator or personnel director in charge of it.

For all assets held in trust funds, IRAs, 401(k) plans, and investment/ brokerage firm accounts, list the account numbers of all the accounts, including the names and phone numbers of all trust officers, brokers, and investment officers. Get a copy of the latest statement for each account, which usually lists the types of securities held, the number of shares or units held, and their current market value. Statements relating to IRAs and 401(k) plans are usually sent out quarterly, while trust account and investment/brokerage firm accounts are sent out monthly. For stocks, bonds, and other investment securities not held in trust funds or at investment or brokerage houses, compile a list of all securities, including the certificate numbers if possible.

For online trade accounts, make sure to list the account numbers, used IDs, and passwords for all accounts. Account balances and activity for any time frame can easily be accessed through these online accounts.

Real Property

Get a list of all real property your parents own, including their primary residence. If there's a mortgage on any of these properties, get the name of the mortgage holder as well as his or her address and phone number.

Personal Property

Sit down with your parents and compile a list of all major personal property they own; include cars, boats, household furnishings, jewelry, and coin or art collections, etc.

List of all Debts

Compile a list of all debts, including mortgages, loans, lines of credit, and credit cards. Get the account number for each debt instrument, along with the names, addresses, and phone numbers of all lenders.

Information on Funeral Arrangements

Compile all information on your parents' last wishes regarding their funeral and burial arrangements; include any cemetery lots owned, their location, and the location of the deed. Are there any further funeral instructions? If so, to whom were they given? Note which funeral home your parents chose, and its director's name and phone number. Also list any organizations to be contacted and the name and phone number of the clergy selected to perform the memorial service.

Chapter Nine

Long-Term Care Insurance —
Is it worth it?

The affordability of long-term care is an issue for most Americans: few have money to burn, and, unfortunately, few are willing to think about how they're going to pay for long-term care until they actually need it. To get the care they need, most seniors have no option but to spend down their hard-earned retirement savings to near zero (generally less than $2,000 in countable assets) and turn to the state and federally funded Medicaid program, which helps pay their long-term care costs once they meet the low income and asset criteria.

The problem is, once you start depending on the government to pay for your housing and care needs, you lose the freedom to decide where you'll be housed and cared for. For example, many assisted living communities don't accept residents who qualify for Medicaid; many still accept only private-pay residents. Most nursing homes accept Medicaid patients, but economic concerns limit the number of Medicaid patients they can allow. The reason is simple: generally, the amount of money the Medicaid program pays a nursing home per day for a patient's stay is the lowest of the four main forms of reimbursement (private-pay, Medicare, Medicaid, and private long-term care insurance). Because a nursing home's operating budget and cost structure are typically very tight, to remain in business most can accept only a limited number of Medicaid patients. Some nursing homes accept only Medicaid patients, but to operate a facility that depends on Medicaid funds alone, the cost structure must be at bare minimum levels. When visiting a nursing facility that accepts only Medicaid patients, be sure the quality of care is adequate to your parents' needs.

This is not to say a Medicaid-only nursing care facility is incapable of providing quality care. I've visited several that are providing some of the best care in their market areas. To accomplish this, these nursing homes are operated by some of the best professionals in the business. They run their facilities so efficiently that they can somehow make it work. Most of these facilities are not-for-profit organizations or have not-for-profit sponsors that supplement their Medicaid-reimbursement revenue streams with charitable contributions from benevolent sources. The problem is, these facilities are so few and far between that they have extensive waiting lists; your parents might have to wait months or even years before they can move in.

Medicaid Estate Planning

Medicaid estate planning remains the foundation of the elder law and estate planning business. Medicaid estate planning is the manipulation of income and assets to qualify otherwise ineligible clients for the Medicaid program. Estate planning lawyers have found ways to protect their clients' assets, preventing the spouse of an aging senior needing care from becoming impoverished and the adult children from being left with nothing when their parents pass away.

To protect these assets, however, the Medicaid program has imposed some very restrictive requirements, including a sixty month look-back period. For example, if your parents needed long-term care today, and transferred all their assets to you fifty-nine months ago, they would not qualify for Medicaid, would be barred from the program, and would have to pay for their care. Qualifying for the Medicaid program is very complex. I've heard of many cases in which an estate planning attorney thought he was complying with all the rules but made one small mistake resulting in the elderly client being banned from the program.

Here's my take on using Medicaid estate planning to protect your assets: if you have the financial means, buy private long-term care insurance to protect your assets. Leave the Medicaid program to those for whom it was intended: low-income individuals who can't afford to pay the high cost of long-term care or long-term care insurance.

One survey suggests that nearly a quarter of all Americans don't have a clue as to how they're going to pay for the cost of their long-term care. Many think a government program such as Medicare already covers them. In fact, some even believe that their regular health insurance covers these types of costs.

Market research has shown that the single greatest fear among seniors is being sent to a nursing home. The research also reveals that the fear is heightened by the anxiety of leaving a surviving spouse impoverished because of their stay in a nursing home. A friend's grandmother experienced this "spending-down" phenomenon firsthand and found it extremely unpleasant. Her grandmother had been very careful with her money all her life, saving for her retirement years only to have her savings disappear upon her admittance to a local nursing home. If you're an adult child, I advise you to consider buying long-term care insurance. Don't rely on government and public funds to bail you out in the end. The graying of America is not to be taken lightly. The exponential growth of seniors will put a tremendous amount of pressure on these public programs, and in order for them to survive, all Americans need to do their part.

Old age is a gamble, which is why you should consider protecting yourself. Private long-term care insurance can provide our aging population many more options than the restrictive Medicaid program can. Nearly all such insurance policies underwritten today cover assisted living, Alzheimer's care, home health care, adult day services, and nursing care.

How Much Money Should You Have to Consider Long-Term Care Insurance?

Obviously, it's not worth paying the premiums for long-term care insurance if your only source of retirement income will come from Social Security. How much money should a person have before considering long-term care insurance?

The answer depends on which financial advisor you talk to. Some advisors and consumer publications recommend buying long-term care insurance only if you have more than $50,000 in assets (excluding your home and car) per person in the household ($100,000 per couple), have an expected annual retirement income of $30,000 per person in the household ($60,000 per couple), and can comfortably afford the policy premiums at a level of 20 to 30 percent over what they are today. Keep in mind that your retirement income will be fixed and might not keep pace with inflation, so your ability to pay the premiums may decrease in the future. (The section on premium increases below provides more information on how and when insurance companies are allowed to raise their premiums.)

I suggest an easier and more conventional benchmark of affordability: as a general rule, no one should spend more than five to eight percent of his or her income on long-term care insurance premiums. If you currently earn $70,000 per year, you should spend no more than $3,500–$5,600 on premiums.

Before you buy long-term care insurance, consult your attorney, CPA, financial advisor, or eldercare consultant; these professionals can help you determine whether your financial position makes it a sensible purchase.

Buy Long-Term Care Insurance
While You're Healthy, Wealthy, and Wise

The best time to consider buying long-term care insurance is when you're in good health. Insurance underwriters will consider your health when determining whether to qualify you for a policy. Certain preexisting health conditions may disqualify you from coverage: a heart condition, emphysema, Alzheimer's disease, Parkinson's disease, and other chronic ailments. If you wait until your health deteriorates, you run the risk of becoming uninsurable; or your premiums might jump to an unaffordable level, so you end up right where most elderly Americans do — spending down your hard-earned retirement savings to zero.

What Types of Long-Term Care
Insurance Policies Are There?

With today's growing demand for private long-term care insurance, there are several types in the marketplace. Buying a long-term care policy is like buying a car: the more options you want, the more it costs.

First, let's examine the components of a policy, and then, what options are available in each component. The options you choose will determine how much the policy will cost you annually.

Here are the ten basic components and options of a long-term care insurance policy:

▸ Types of care covered

▸ Benefit amount

▸ Benefit period

▸ Benefit triggers

▸ Elimination or waiting period

▸ Inflation protection

▸ Waiver of premium

▸ Non-forfeiture benefits

▸ Guaranteed renewable and lapse protection, and

▸ Spousal discounts

Types of Care Covered

Each policy is different. You can choose as many options as you feel you need to cover your risk and protect your assets. The more services you want included in your coverage, the higher the premium.

Most policies allow you coverage on all these services:

▸ Adult day service

▸ Home health care, including part-time intermittent skilled nursing services, home-support services, and physical therapy

▸ Assisted living services

▸ Alzheimer's/dementia care services

▸ Skilled and intermediate care nursing care services, and

▸ Respite care services

Benefit Amount

A long-term care insurance policy will pay you a daily benefit amount covering all, or a portion of, the cost of adult day services, home health care, assisted living, Alzheimer's/dementia care, nursing care, or respite care services. It's up to you to determine what daily benefit amount provides the best coverage. For example, let's assume you bought a policy that pays a daily benefit of $180. Let's say the average cost of a nursing home stay in your area is $210 per day. Choosing the $180 benefit, you'd receive benefits totaling $65,700 per year ($180 × 365 days), while the annual cost of your stay would total $76,650 per year. You'd have to pay the difference ($30 per day) between the private-pay rate ($210 per day) and your policy benefit ($180 per day)—$10,950 per year. Is this sufficient coverage based on your financial position?

One way to decide what daily benefit amount is best for you is to estimate what your total projected monthly income will be upon retirement in today's dollars. Be sure to include any future income earned on your assets, as well as your projected social security and pension income. Subtract your projected monthly living expenses from your projected retirement income and then subtract the monthly cost of skilled nursing care in your area. If this calculation results in a monthly shortfall, then annualize this figure and divide it by 365. This yields the estimated minimum daily benefit amount you'll need to prevent a depletion of your assets. You can do further analysis to figure out how much of your retirement savings you're willing to dip into to pay for part of your long-term care costs.

Here's an example illustrating how to estimate your daily benefit amount.

Total Projected Monthly Income at Retirement	$5,000
Less: Projected Monthly Living Expenses	(4,000)
Less: Projected Monthly Cost of Skilled Nursing Care	(6,300)
Projected Monthly Shortfall	(5,300)
Times 12 Months	× 12 mo.
Projected Annual Shortfall	$(63,600)
Divided by 365 Days	/ 365
Projected Daily Benefit Amount Required	**$174**

Based on those numbers, you should buy a policy with at least a $174 daily benefit amount to preserve your retirement savings. In fact, I would recommend buffering this amount upward to protect yourself from overestimating your future income or underestimating your future costs. Faced with this choice, I would get a policy with a daily benefit amount of $180.

Remember the general rule: don't spend more than five to eight percent of your current income on insurance premiums. The higher the daily benefit amount you choose, the higher the annual premium. For most people, it makes more sense to buy a policy that will cover the lion's share of your long-term care costs rather than one that pays every cent; this way you'd pay a lower premium and still be protected from a financial catastrophe. It's wise to consult your attorney, CPA or elder-care consultant when estimating your daily benefit amount.

Benefit Period

The benefit period is the length of time a long-term care insurance policy will pay for your care. Most insurance companies offer benefit periods of two to five years as well as a lifetime benefit period option. A five-year benefit period will cost more than the same policy with a two-year benefit period. The benefit period commences when the policyholder begins receiving benefits under the policy, not when the policy is bought.

Instead of specifying a benefit period, some policies include a maximum benefit limit, which specifies a maximum dollar amount of benefits paid during the policy's duration. This is sometimes referred to as the "Lifetime Maximum Benefit." If your policy includes such a benefit, do a little math to determine whether this is adequate. Let's say you chose a daily benefit of $150 per day and have determined that five years of coverage is suitable; then the maximum lifetime benefit amount based on your requirements should be $273,250 ($150 daily benefit × 365 days per year × 5 years).

Benefit Triggers

Long-term care insurance policies contain benefit triggers, which require the policyholder to exhibit certain "qualifying impairments" before the policy begins paying benefits. In a typical policy, the benefit trigger requires the policyholder be unable to perform at least two activities of daily living (ADLs) for at least sixty to ninety days.

These ADLs are:

- Bathing
- Dressing and grooming
- Toileting
- Transferring or moving from place to place (e.g., from bed to chair)
- Walking, and
- Eating

Other benefit triggers include cognitive impairments such as Alzheimer's disease or other forms of dementia, which may render the policyholder unable to perform certain activities such as properly managing medications. Before purchasing a policy, make sure you fully understand the benefit triggers.

Who decides when a policyholder has a qualifying impairment? After all, this is what triggers the payment of your daily benefits. The insurance company decides! The insurance company will have its own physicians examine the policyholder to determine whether there's a qualifying impairment. Most policies include language requiring the insurance company to consult with the policyholder's personal physician and caregivers.

Elimination or Waiting Period

The structure of a long-term care insurance policy includes another component called an elimination or waiting period, sometimes referred to as the "deductible period." The elimination period is simply how long a policyholder must wait before the policy starts paying benefits for care. Most policies allow you to choose an elimination period ranging from 20–100 days. The length of elimination period you choose depends on how much money you have available to pay for services during the elimination period, and how much you can afford in premiums. The longer the elimination period, the lower the premium. Some insurance companies offer policies with elimination periods of more than 100 days; however, I do not recommend purchasing one. Let me explain why below.

Suppose you chose a policy with a ninety-day elimination period. Under the policy requirements, once you've satisfied the benefit trigger with a qualifying impairment, you must then pay for the first ninety days of care out of your own pocket. This can be quite costly, depending on your initial care needs. Let's say you needed to be admitted to a nursing home with a daily rate of $210. Under this policy, you'd have to pay $18,900 during the elimination period before you got any benefits.

Remember: if your parents qualify, Medicare will pay a portion of their home health care costs or their stay in a nursing home (the most costly of all the housing and care options). Medicare will pay 100 percent of the charges for the first twenty days. For days twenty-one through one hundred, your parents are required to pay $128 per day (the 2008 co-pay amount, which increases annually), while Medicare pays the difference. After the hundredth day, your parents pay for everything out of their own funds. Therefore, if your parents qualify for Medicare, they would only have to pay $8,960 (70 days × $128 co-pay per day) out of their own pocket during the ninety-day elimination period as the first twenty days are covered.

Inflation Protection

The most valuable option you can add to your policy is inflation protection, which makes an upward adjustment to the daily benefit you'll receive to account for the escalation in long-term care costs. Obviously, including this feature will raise the amount of the premium, but it's well worth it. As we've all seen in the past several years, escalation of long-term care costs is something we should expect.

Let's say you buy a policy today with a $180 daily benefit amount, and you choose not to include the inflation protection option. The average nursing home rate is $210 per day. Based on past increases in long-term care costs, assuming an annual escalation rate of 5 percent, ten years from now nursing home rates could be $342 per day. Without inflation protection, you'd pay $162 per day ($342 minus $180) or $59,130 per year out of your own pocket. Frightening, isn't it? I strongly recommend including the inflation protection option in your policy, with a daily benefit amount that increases at a compound annual rate of 4 or 5 percent. Inflation protection will increase your premium, but, as you can see from that example, the policy is worthless without it. If you can't afford the inflation protection feature, I suggest not buying long-term care insurance at all.

Some insurance companies offer a choice of two inflation protection options: one called "simple interest inflation protection" and the other "compound annual interest inflation protection." Be sure you choose the compound annual interest inflation protection. Why? Let's compare the effects that the simple and compound annual increases would have on your daily benefit amount assuming you chose a $180 daily benefit amount.

	Daily Benefit Amount With		Dollar Difference in Daily Benefit
	Simple Interest Inflation Protection of 5%	Compound Interest Inflation Protection of 5%	
Today	$180	$180	$0
Five Years from Now	$225	$230	$5
Ten Years from Now	$270	$293	$23
Twenty Years from Now	$360	$478	$118
Thirty Years from Now	$450	$778	$328

As you can see, the longer you hold a policy, the more significant the difference in daily benefits paid. Just imagine what would happen if you bought a policy with no inflation protection at all! If you plan to hold a policy for any considerable time, it's extremely important to buy one with compound annual interest inflation protection. Otherwise, the policy will become worthless after a certain period.

If the policy contains a lifetime maximum benefit amount, be sure the inflation protection is applied to this amount as well as to the daily benefit amount. Inflation protection will not benefit you if it applies only to the daily benefit amount.

Most policies do not limit the number of years an inflation adjustment can increase your benefit amount; however, be aware that some do. I've seen some policies limiting the inflation adjustment to twenty years; others will adjust the benefit amount until the policyholder reaches a specified age. Be sure to ask your insurance agent whether the policy you're considering has any such limits—if you buy your policy while you're relatively young, they could have a huge effect on your daily benefit amount.

Let's look at a quick example that highlights this point. Let's say you obtained a policy with the $180 daily benefit option when you were 50

years old. The policy also contains a 5 percent compound annual interest inflation protection; however, the inflation adjustment is limited
to a maximum of twenty years. Twenty years from now, the maximum
benefit would be $478 per day and would be capped at that amount for-
ever. Now, suppose that thirty-three years from now you'll need twenty-four-hour nursing care in a nursing home. Say that today's nursing
home rate in your area is $210 per day; after assuming an estimated av-
erage annual increase of 5 percent, it would cost approximately $1,051
per day thirty-three years from now. The maximum benefit you could
receive would be $174,470 per year, while the annual cost of your care
in the nursing home would be $383,615. You would be paying approx-
imately $209,145 out of your own pocket in the first year of coverage
alone. As you can see, if you buy your policy while you're still relatively young, getting one with no limit on the number of years you can receive annual inflation adjustments is extremely important. In fact, one
can make a good argument for waiting until you're at least sixty-five or
seventy before you consider buying a long-term care insurance policy
with an inflation protection limit of twenty years.

Waiver of Premium

Most policies waive the annual premium due on a policy once the
policyholder has moved into a long-term care facility, but this usually
won't become effective until after a stay of twenty to one hundred con-
secutive days in the facility. So, upon initially moving into a long-term
care facility, you might be paying for premiums on your policy in addition to your care during the elimination period. Be sure you're aware
how many days' stay is required before the waiver of the policy premium becomes effective.

Non-forfeiture Benefit

Some policies offer a non-forfeiture benefit, which provides for con-
tinued coverage at a reduced benefit amount if the policyholder stops
paying the premium after some period of time. Some non-forfeiture
benefits may also provide the return of a portion of the premiums paid.

Guaranteed Renewable with Lapse Protection

Most policies are guaranteed renewable for life as long as the premiums are paid on time. This means the insurance company cannot cancel your policy for any reason other than your failing to pay the premiums.

Most policies also provide lapse protection for policyholders who, as a result of some form of dementia, forget to pay their premiums. This would prevent cancellation of your parents' coverage if they forgot their payments. Most lapse protection coverage provides third-party notification: a family member or loved one is notified of the delinquency and the pending cancellation if the payment obligation isn't met.

Spousal Discounts

Nearly all insurance companies offer a spousal discount if both you and your spouse apply for long-term care insurance. Discounts are usually in the range of 10–20 percent.

Thirty-Day Free Look Period

Every insurance carrier is required by law to give you a thirty-day free look period to review its policies. Should you be unhappy with it for any reason during this period, the free look allows you to cancel the policy and get a full refund, no questions asked.

Premium Increases

Most long-term care insurance premiums remain level, not increasing over time. This doesn't mean your premiums will never increase, but it does mean that the insurance company can't raise your premiums due to your advancing age or failing health. The only way an insurance company can raise your premiums is if they raise them for an entire class of people in the state, and only after approval by the State Insurance Commission.

There are some policies with a feature called attained-age pricing, which has premiums that start low and increase with the policyholder's age. Be sure to avoid such policies, as they may become unaffordable by the time care is needed.

Review the Insurance Company's Financial Position

When considering a long-term care insurance policy, it's important to review the financial position of the insurance company you're thinking of buying it from. You might be holding this policy for a long time, and it would be unfortunate if you diligently paid your premiums for years only to have the company go bankrupt. Your best bet is to stick with large, well-known insurance companies and review their ratings in current publications from Standard & Poors or Moody's, which you can usually find at your local library. Consult your attorney, CPA, or eldercare consultant if you need additional help.

Group Long-Term Care Insurance Plans Offered by Employers

The growing popularity of long-term care insurance has led many employers to include it in the benefit packages they offer to attract and retain employees. Typically, employees must pay all the costs of the insurance without an employer contribution, but, because it's a group plan, the premiums are usually 15–30 percent lower than for an individual policy with the very same coverage. Also, depending on the size of the enrollment, group plans may offer a specific level of coverage without evidence of good health.

Before buying into your employer's group plan, you should be aware of the distinct disadvantages of such plans. Your flexibility regarding the amount of coverage and available options could be limited to only the coverage and options offered to the group. Employer group plans commonly use attained-age pricing, which entails premiums that start low and increase as the policyholder ages. Group plans usually don't offer policies with level premiums. Under employer group plans, insurance companies are more focused on the highest enrollment rather than on providing a well-designed and effective plan. The low initial premiums may be attractive to some, but the plans usually fail to meet the employees' needs over time. Be sure to consult your attorney, CPA, or eldercare consultant before enrolling in an employer group long-term care insurance plan—many aren't worth the paper they're printed on!

Switching Policies

Not long ago, I reviewed a long-term care insurance policy that one of my family members bought more than fifteen years ago. Frankly, the policy is outdated and worthless, primarily because the buyer didn't get the inflation protection option. Because of this, his benefit is stuck at eighty dollars per day, which is entirely inadequate considering his current financial position. Also, I've met with many people who bought group long-term care insurance through their employers. Several discovered that the plans their employers negotiated with their insurance companies had severe coverage limitations. In such cases as these, it's best just to cancel the existing policy and buy a new and improved policy with better coverage and options. Use the information I've provided to evaluate your existing policy and determine whether it can stand the test of time.

Insurance companies are constantly changing and often improving the coverage options available to people seeking long-term care insurance. If you have a policy and are dissatisfied with the coverage, contact your insurance agent to inquire about an upgrade. Some insurance companies automatically upgrade existing policies to new and improved coverage, while others only notify the policyholder of new and improved policy options and offer to upgrade at a higher premium.

A Comparison of Premiums Based on Age

To research the current cost of private long-term care insurance, I called a friend who works for an agency of a large insurance company to see how affordable it really is. I also wanted to see how a policyholder's age when he or she bought the coverage affected the premiums. I asked my friend to get quotes for both females and males in good health, with the following coverage options and riders:

▸ **Benefit Amount** – $150 per day, $180 per day, and $210 per day covering adult day care, home health care, and facility care such as the care provided in an assisted living, Alzheimer's/dementia care, and nursing care facility;

- **Benefit Period** – Five years (1,825 days)

- **Benefit Triggers** – Policyholder must require care due to a cognitive impairment or the inability to perform two or more activities of daily living for a period of at least ninety days

- **Elimination Period** – Ninety days

- **Inflation Protection** – Compound annual increases in the benefit amount of 5 percent with no limit

- **Guaranteed Renewable with Lapse Protection**, and a

- **Non-forfeiture Benefit**

To see the effect of age on the cost of annual premiums, I asked my friend for quotes for men and women aged 50, 55, 60, 65, 70, and 75. Additionally, I had him run quotes with benefit amounts of $150, $180, and $210 per day to get an idea of the effect of the daily benefit amount on the annual premium levels. It was interesting to learn that the rates didn't differ because of gender; therefore the table will show only one column of rates, which are applicable for both sexes. The results are summarized in the table below. Remember, the coverage options are identical as listed above.

Male or Female	Annual Premium (in 2008 dollars)		
Age	$150 Daily Benefit	$180 Daily Benefit	$210 Daily Benefit
50	$2,186	$2,623	$3,060
55	$2,595	$3,114	$3,633
60	$3,080	$3,696	$4,312
65	$4,104	$4,925	$5,746
70	$6,176	$7,411	$8,646
75	$9,984	$11,981	$13,977

Obviously, the older you get, the more expensive the annual premiums become, but the younger you are, the longer you'll likely be paying premiums. You have to decide for yourself when it's time to buy long-term care insurance. Remember: you must be healthy to get a policy. People in poor health, with certain preexisting ailments such as a heart condition, will not be considered for coverage.

At first glance, long-term care insurance might not seem worth the price, but if you break it down, it's really quite affordable and a wise investment. Based on the table above, let's say that at age fifty you buy a policy with the $180 daily benefit option and all the other options listed previously, and let's suppose you'll need to live in an assisted living community at age eighty-three. You'll have paid annual premiums of $2,623 for thirty-three years, totaling $86,559 ($2,623 × thirty-three years). Today's average assisted living community rate for a person requiring assistance with two activities of daily living is $100 per day; using an estimated escalation rate of 5 percent per year, this would equate to a rate of $500 per day when you reach age eighty-three. The cost of your stay for one year would total $182,500 ($500 per day × 365 days). Pause to absorb this for a moment. Your thirty-three years of premium payments are paid for in less than half a year at the assisted living community. Is long-term care insurance worth it? If your goal is to preserve your assets, you bet it is!

Getting the right amount of long-term care insurance can be very complex. Have your attorney, financial advisor, CPA, or eldercare consultant help you analyze your projected financial position to determine how much coverage and which options and riders are the best fit for you.

Can You Take A Tax Deduction for Your Insurance Premiums?

In an effort to persuade more Americans to take responsibility for their long-term care, Congress passed the Health Insurance Portability and Accountability Act of 1996, under which premiums for tax-qualified long-term care insurance policies were deemed tax deductible. Before you get too excited about this great tax break, let me offer you some advice: when shopping for long-term care insurance, don't base your choice on whether it's a tax-qualified policy. The tax benefits you'll derive are far too small to have any significant impact.

Those who itemize their deductions and whose medical expenses exceed 7.5 percent of their adjusted gross income are the only ones who'll get any tax relief by deducting their premiums. Also, there's an age-based limit on the amount of premiums a taxpayer can deduct. For example, in 2008, if you were between fifty-one and sixty, you could only deduct $1,150; between sixty-one and seventy, you could deduct only $3,080; and if you were over seventy-one, you could deduct a maximum of $3,850. You can only take the deduction if your total medical expenses exceed 7.5 percent of your adjusted gross income.

Based on these tax laws, only a small percentage of taxpayers will qualify for the deduction, and even if they do qualify, the tax benefits are insignificant, so don't worry about whether the policy you buy is tax-qualified; focus instead on whether the policy meets your family's needs.

Final Thoughts on Long-Term Care Insurance

With the current economic crisis and the enormous growth of our senior population on the horizon, our government's public programs alone will undoubtedly be unable to handle the huge cost of caring for all senior citizens. Private long-term care insurance is going to have to play a vital role in filling the gap created by the lack of funds available from publicly funded programs such as Medicaid and Medicare.

If you have the financial means, I would highly recommend you buy private long-term care insurance. Long-term care insurance gives you the financial freedom to choose from a lot more housing and care options that you would otherwise not be able to afford without it. It's a valuable investment that brings long-term prosperity by preserving your assets and protecting you and your spouse from impoverishment should one or both of you require long-term care. If you can afford it, do your part, and leave the dollars allocated to the state and federally funded Medicaid program to the lower-income Americans who really need it.

Once you decide that long-term care insurance is right for you and have determined that you can afford it, carefully calculate how much coverage and which options you need. Shop around. Talk with several insurance companies, but remember to stick with the larger, more reputable ones. Talk to an insurance agent that you or a friend know and trust. Have the agent provide you with an outline of the coverage for each policy so you can easily compare the policies that various carriers offer. Make sure you get the inflation-protection option and remember that you have a thirty-day free look period. If you feel you've made a mistake in buying a policy, you have the legal right to cancel the policy for a full refund within thirty days.

I've given you all the information you'll need to make an informed decision. Your awareness and knowledge about the different components and options available in long-term care insurance will tell an insurance agent that you're an educated buyer. Remember: consult your attorney, financial advisor, CPA, or eldercare consultant before signing a policy.

Chapter Ten

CPA ElderCare Services Are Available to Help

When your parents need help and you need advice about what to do, whom do you call? Let me tell you about a widely unknown resource that's available to you and your parents in your area: CPA ElderCare Services.

CPA ElderCare Services

Often, adult children or other family members don't live near their parents or loved ones, and many find it troubling that they can't be there to watch over their parents as often as they'd like to be. They wish they lived closer so they could take care of all their parents' immediate needs. Recognizing this, the American Institute of Certified Public Accountants (AICPA) developed a new service area for CPAs in 1999 called CPA ElderCare Services.

CPA ElderCare Services uses CPAs as trusted family advisors and professionals who can assist their senior clients (such as your parents) and their families in dealing with eldercare issues. If you're concerned about your parents' well-being and live a considerable distance away, or if other commitments prevent you from allocating enough time to meet their everyday needs, engaging a CPA to provide eldercare services just might be the answer.

CPA ElderCare professionals can provide your parents a variety of direct, consulting, and assurance services. The CPA ElderCare professional will form a team of professionals: geriatric care managers, your parents' personal physician and other healthcare professionals, their attorney and other elder law attorneys, their financial advisor, insurance agent, and many others to help meet all their needs.

The CPA ElderCare professional will act as the team's "quarterback," coordinating all the services provided to you and your parents. Here are some of the services a CPA eldercare professional might provide:

► Arranging for a qualified geriatric care manager to visit your parents' home for an in-home needs assessment

► Helping set care and assistance goals for your parents and developing a customized care plan designed to promote their independence and improve the quality of their lives (compiled by the geriatric care manager)

► Arranging for the appropriate level of care (home support services, assisted living, etc.) and payment for such care, and periodically visiting your parents to ensure they're receiving care that meets the standards set by the family at the outset

► Gathering and sorting mail periodically, making sure legal documents, bills, and other outstanding matters aren't neglected

► Paying outstanding bills and handling ongoing financial transactions for your parent

- ▶ Depositing and accounting for all your parents' income, and making sure that the expected income is received and deposited in the appropriate accounts

- ▶ Supervising your parents' investments, making sure they're being handled by their investment advisor or officer in accordance with your parents' investment goals

- ▶ Handling your parents' income tax preparation

- ▶ Making transportation arrangements for your parents when needed

- ▶ Communicating unusual or unexpected situations to family members when they arise (e.g., while visiting, the CPA may have noticed that your parents' roof is leaking and needs repair), and

- ▶ Periodic reporting to family members on your parents' current state of affairs

The periodic reports would provide you and your parents a report on their current position from both a financial and care standpoint. The financial portion might include something as simple as a list of deposits and withdrawals, or could include something more detailed, such as a compilation of your parents' current financial statements. The care portion of the report might include an assessment of whether the care and assistance goals that you and your parents initially set up and approved are being met and whether the level of care and the setting in which it's being provided are still appropriate. Of course, the CPA Eldercare professional would use the input of all members of the team, such as the geriatric care manager, to compose the health care portion of the periodic report.

Since CPA ElderCare services are fairly new, their cost may vary. The CPA will usually charge by the hour, or might arrange for a fixed monthly fee regardless of the number of hours spent providing services. CPAs typically charge anywhere from $50 to $300 per hour, depending on the type of engagement and the experience levels of the staff working on it.

No More Fear...Only Hope

In most fiction novels, the epilogue is the final chapter of the story where the author reveals the ultimate fate of the characters. What is the ultimate fate of the characters in this story? My goal was to write a book that could help families breathe a little easier during a difficult and emotional time. In order to accomplish this, I needed to write a book that would help alleviate the fear people were feeling and replace it with hope.

Much of the anxiety is created by fear of the unknown. My book helps to eliminate this fear by educating my readers. I believe that knowing what to expect is half the battle. No one should be left in the dark about what options are available or be forced to make some life-changing decision without having all the pertinent information at hand.

I then tried to replace the fear with hope by providing my readers with a plan. With multiple options to choose from and the various complexities associated with each, it was obvious to me that families were desperately looking for an easy-to-follow roadmap to help them find the housing and care option that is the perfect fit for their aging parent. ***When there is hope, there is always reason to believe our lives can get better!***

I wish you all the best in your journey to find the best senior housing and care option for your parent. Please visit my author website at www .iffenwen.com for new and upcoming developments in the senior housing and care industry. My website and blog will offer more information and advice on how to deal with issues that arise when your loved ones can no longer care for themselves. There is also a link to contact me. Please do so! I would love to hear how things are going. Please share your success stories as well as some of the challenges you faced so I can address them in the future!

Index

About the Author

An advisor and consultant to the senior housing and care-industry for over eighteen years, Mike Campbell has visited hundreds of senior housing and care communities across the country and, in his travels, has witnessed both the best and worst of senior housing and care.

Mike is a CPA with a degree in Business Administration from Ohio University. He is a member of several professional organizations, including the American Institute of Certified Public Accountants.

Mike began his career at Ernst & Young, LLP in Cleveland in 1988 providing accounting and auditing services to health care clients. In 1991, he joined Ernst & Young's National Post Acute Care Consulting Practice, with responsibility for coordinating all aspects of financial feasibility studies with more than half a billion dollars in obtained tax-exempt bond financing for senior housing and care projects across the country. Mike also assessed operations, sales, and marketing for various long-term care providers.

In 1996, Mike joined Karrington Health, one of the largest assisted living developers and operators in the United States. While at Karrington, he developed new and innovative market area assessment methodologies for assisted living and Alzheimer's/dementia care settings that were adopted and implemented by the parent company.

In 1999, Mike formed Campbell Consulting Services, LLC, where he continues to serve clients in the senior housing and care industry. In *When Mom and Dad Need Help*, Mike shares his knowledge as a dedicated consumer advocate, helping families find quality long-term care for their loved ones through education and planning. He hopes the byproduct of his efforts will result in an improved long-term care system nationwide.

Mike currently resides in Concord, Ohio, with his wife Diane and his three beautiful daughters —Danielle, Nicole and Christy.